*Housing Action in an
Industrial Suburb*

LAW, STATE AND SOCIETY SERIES

Editors

Z. BANKOWSKI, *Department of Public Law, University of Edinburgh, U.K.*
M. CAIN, *Department of Law, London School of Economics and Political Science, U.K.*
W. CHAMBLISS, *Department of Sociology and Anthropology, University of Delaware, Newark, U.S.A.*
M. McINTOSH, *Department of Sociology, University of Essex, Colchester, U.K.*

Housing Action in an Industrial Suburb

ANN STEWART

School of Law, Warwick University,
Coventry, England

1981

ACADEMIC PRESS

A Subsidiary of Harcourt Brace Jovanovich, Publishers
London   New York   Toronto   Sydney   San Francisco

ACADEMIC PRESS INC. (LONDON) LTD.
24/28 Oval Road
London NW1

United States Edition published by
ACADEMIC PRESS INC.
111 Fifth Avenue
New York, New York 10003

British Library Cataloguing in Publication Data

Stewart, Ann
    Housing action in an industrial suburb.
    1. Housing - Saltley, Eng. (Warwickshire)
    I. Title
    333.5′ 3′ 0942496   HD7334.B/   80-41464
    ISBN 0-12-669250-5

Test set in 12/13pt. Bembo by Permanent Typesetting & Printing Co. Ltd. Hong Kong.
Printed in Great Britain by St Edmundsbury Press, Bury St Edmunds, Suffolk

Preface

I would like to clarify two points which affect the content of this book. The first is the use of the term owner-occupier to describe a lessee of a building lease. Although I make it clear in the text that strictly this is a legal misnomer, I would like to avoid any confusion at the outset. Long leaseholders pay a premium to obtain ownership of their homes. The only difference between a freeholding owner-occupier and themselves is the renting of the land. Leaseholders think of themselves as owner-occupiers and are treated as such by everybody with the possible exception of the freeholder. The use of the term is, therefore, more appropriate than the strictly correct term of tenant.

Secondly, the masculine form of pronoun is always used. Although this is the convention it is particularly inappropriate in this context. Many of the most active residents in Norton Residents Association are women and most of my contact has been with them. It is unfortunate that the particular influence of women does not appear in the text.

I would like to thank a number of people: all the members of the Birmingham Community Development Project who were always generous with their time, thoughts and material; Lee Bridges who gave his critical support over a number of years; the Law and Social Science Committee of the Social Science Research Council for granting the studentship which gave me the opportunity to carry out much of this study; Rita Smart who typed the manuscript, often far into the night; finally, and most important, to Geoff Green without whose unswerving comradeship this book would never have been completed.

December, 1980

Ann Stewart
Coventry

Contents

Introduction: the Saltley context

This book is about a housing struggle. This struggle takes place in Saltley which is a middle ring district of east Birmingham. This area, like many other similar areas of industrial cities, was classified in the 1970s as a problem. It contains a rapidly deteriorating housing stock, a very poor environment and the main type of industry has changed from manufacturing cars, buses and railway carriages to warehousing. The last change has brought a steady fall in the number of jobs available over the last fifteen years. It is a picture of decline in a century from a once salubrious suburb catering for the prosperous workers employed in industries located on green field sites to an inner city problem area. This decline, like so many other areas, attracted national attention in the 1970s when various forms of state projects were set up to investigate the causes for the decline and to attempt to stop it. Saltley obtained a Community Development Project (C.D.P.). There were 12 of these established in various parts of the country funded 75% by central government through the Home Office and 25% by the particular local authority concerned. Their action-research brief was to investigate the reasons for multiple deprivation, to recommend changes and to act on their proposals.

The concern of this book arose out of the C.D.P.'s preliminary research which found that the majority of the houses in Saltley were held on leasehold tenure. This system reached the height of its popularity in the late nineteenth century. The land-owner, known as the freeholder, leased out a parcel of land to a builder in exchange for a rent. The builder built a house on the land and sold it to a landlord who took over the lease. The present residents have obtained their houses through subsequent sales, so they own the house but still lease the ground underneath it from the descendants of the freeholder. As the leases in Saltley were created mainly between 1880 and 1910 for a term of 99 years, in 1972 they were running out. When they expire the houses, as

1

well as the land, revert back to the freeholder and the owner-occupiers become tenants. Houses in Saltley were consequently very difficult to sell and residents were not willing to engage in extensive repairs to their houses although they were deteriorating rapidly. Therefore the effect of the leasehold system was to hasten the decline of the area.

The Leasehold Reform Act had been passed in 1967 to help residents in areas like Saltley. Its main provision enabled the residents, known as long leaseholders, to purchase their freeholds, that is to buy the land from the freeholder. If they qualified under the Act a resident could force the freeholder to sell. The Act was designed, therefore, to upgrade leasehold areas to freehold status thereby stemming the decline by stimulating residents to improve their secure homes and creating a sound market in sales.

One would have expected residents in Saltley to have used the rights given by the Act to purchase freeholds, but the C.D.P. research in 1972 revealed that residents were not buying their freeholds although they were eager to purchase and had tried to do so. This book tackles the question as to why the Act was not working and what action could be taken to make it work. It was soon clear that there were no simple answers such as improper or inadequate use of procedures, inadequate use of professional legal advice, or ignorance of rights. All of these factors were present but only as manifestations of much wider issues such as the distribution of property and power, the relationship of professional advisers both with their working-class clients and with large property owners and the operation of the housing market in an inner city area.

From the beginning residents organized themselves into groups and, with C.D.P. help, fought to obtain their freeholds. It was a continuous battle to overcome diverse difficulties. Residents attempted to enforce their legal right to enfranchise by painstakingly following the procedures laid down in the Act, battling through each stage, by marshalling their economic strength through collective action and by combating professional hostility by employing professional advisers who were accountable to the residents collectively. They fought an uphill battle, obstructed all the way by the other interested parties: the freeholders, middlemen, solicitors, valuers and estate agents. They had not been successful prior to C.D.P.'s arrival and despite all the injection of enthusiasm, cash and expertise, they were still no better off in 1974. Yet by the end of 1975 something had changed. Freeholds could be bought. In 1979 although the area was still predominantly leasehold, enfranchisement had become a relatively routine practice and hundreds of people had bought their freehold.

This break was crucial to the evolution of our analysis of housing struggles in Saltley and the part played by law in them. The analysis which we developed in the early unsuccessful years considered the Leasehold Reform Act as unworkable in the face of opposition from powerful landowners since these propertied groups could obstruct legal rights through their economic strength. These freehold sales might have suggested that our analysis was wrong and that there could be a remedy to specific housing problems as long as legal rights were enforced. Indeed by 1975 we were changing our minds but not to extol the successful enforcement of these legal rights but to question the nature of success defined in this manner. Rather we were evolving a materialist analysis which defined enfranchisement, not as a solution, but merely as the consequence of the historical transformation of this industrial suburb. During 1974 and 1975 Birmingham C.D.P. workers joined others working from sister C.D.P.s and developed collectively a materialist analysis of their inner-city areas primarily out of their work on industry and employment. Our understanding of inner-city housing was closely related. Saltley showed in acute form the deep problems facing British capitalism in the 1970s. Not only had it become an industrial wasteland, but a dumping ground for marginal or reserve labour in a housing stock which was old and in desperate need of repair. Therefore the struggle was not only against the capitalist process of production (the way in which commodities and surplus value are produced), but also against the process of reproduction (the way in which the labour necessary for this production is maintained and replaced both physically and socially). Crudely, the workforce has to be accommodated in an environment best suited to the changing needs of capital.

Houses form part of the cost of the reproduction of labour power; that is they are necessary to provide shelter. Briefly, the important relations of capitalist housing production are as follows. Workers pay for them out of wages. There is, therefore, a conflict of interest between the industrial and financial sectors of capital. Industrial capital wants wages to be as low as possible so as to reap greater surplus. Finance capital, although it creates no surplus itself, uses it up providing the capital to purchase housing in the form of loans to all parties, producers and consumers. The higher the cost of this finance, the more workers must pay for their accommodation, so the greater their demand for wages to cover their housing costs as well as other necessities of life. Like all other commodities, houses are created as a use value through the capitalist process of production and circulated via the market for an exchange value. But there are some differences between houses and other commodities. First, they remain fixed to a parcel of land which itself is not a factor of production. Land is not a commodity; it cannot be produced by labour. Yet producers of commodities are obliged to pay land-owners a tribute called rent. Secondly, they are consumed through different tenures, the main forms of which are public and private renting and owner-occupation.

Leasehold tenure in Saltley forms a crucial link in understanding the nature of housing since it is a device which joins land to the other elements of housing production. The relations of production were orchestrated through the building lease. Lord Norton who was the land-owner, the builders, landlords and residents were linked together in the late nineteenth century by the leasehold system. Subsequently, the houses have been exchanged and consumed using the same legal device, but the presence of this form has materially affected the evolution of the social relations of housing and has highlighted the significance of leasehold as a tenure form.

Did the C.D.P. workers' understanding of class relations lead to better campaigning and ultimately to victory? Undoubtedly it had an effect. A clearer analysis of housing and a more acute perception of the market forces led to more apposite action. It shifted the strategy from the traditional pressure group activity now ingrained in the ideology of social democracy, but it alone did not explain why freeholds, long-denied residents, were being offered by land-owners after 1975. It became clear that the forces operating in the housing market had changed. By the 1970s owner-occupation had become the dominant tenure form both economically and ideologically. Ideologically all other forms are compared unfavourably with it. Materially it is supported and encouraged with such government incentives as tax relief to borrowers and a whole structure of measures to encourage people to move into the sector, such as loans for deposits, preferential tax rates for building societies and local authority mortgages. Home ownership has now spread its net out to catch working-class people on relatively low incomes living in older property. Leasehold reform is inextricably bound up with the growth of owner-occupation.

The 1967 Leasehold Reform Act allowed long leaseholders to become complete owner-occupiers. A leasehold house, although bought at a premium through a process almost identical to a freehold house, represents to the resident a declining economic asset. At the end of the lease the house is not the resident's capital asset, but the property of the freeholder and the resident becomes a tenant paying a weekly rent. This had become, it was argued in Parliament in 1966, unfair and anachronistic. It also denied the essence of ownership which lies at the ideological heart of owner-occupation.

A further change in the market had also occurred by 1975. The state policy of wholesale redevelopment had been replaced by renewal. Whole areas of poor quality housing were to be renovated with grant aid rather than knocked down and rebuilt. The redevelopment stopped for a number of reasons but surely it is not merely coincidence that the bulldozers stopped at the edge of the byelaw artisan dwellings which were, by the early 1970s, predominantly owner-occupied. Redevelopment entails the construction of council dwellings to house displaced owner-occupiers and private tenants. Renewal consolidates owner-occupation by allowing the occupant to "do up" his own house.

The two policies of owner-occupation and rehabilitation stopped the bulldozer at the edge of Saltley in 1972. By 1974 the area had been divided into Housing Action Areas and General Improvement Areas. Both are the mechanisms through which renewal takes place. It could then be argued that the Leasehold Reform Act was designed for these conditions and therefore worked as a result. But this statement makes vast assumptions. What is meant by "to work"? To what end? For whom? If to work means that an individual legal right to enfranchise is now available and enforceable then, in the main, this has been achieved. Yet nobody looking at the houses in Saltley or talking to the residents would see or hear of success. The problems which led the C.D.P. workers to isolate leasehold reform as a contributing factor are still present in different forms. The cost of leasehold enfranchisement has become as much a problem as the earlier denial of the right to buy. The major issues remain, the poor environment, the decaying physical fabric of the houses and economic decline.

Thus this book does not chart a belated success story. It describes change and, for Saltley, decline. It describes the class relations involved in the provision of housing in Saltley since it is here that the answer lies to the conundrum: the Act works but the problem deepens. Why was Saltley a leasehold area? What part has leasehold tenure played in the transformation of the area? Did it give the original land-owner power to arrange the forces of production in a manner which laid the basis for future exploitation? Has it subsequently played an independent part in the class relations of Saltley so that professionals, freeholders and middlemen can make a business out of its reform? I attempt to discover the historical forms of class relations in Saltley and to place leasehold tenure in this context. This has meant broadening the study to look at the history of the building lease to discover why it developed and specifically how it has been used in Saltley. It has also meant charting the conflicts in which it has played a part and the reasons for the many attempts at reform. Ultimately it has led me to consider the nature of legal form and its connection which economic relations. I believe that my study of leasehold tenure shows that law merits attention on both political and theoretical grounds.

Politically, without careful analysis of law, housing and other struggles involving legal rights campaigns will fail. Even if it succeeds, a dedicated time-consuming struggle to enforce legal rights runs the risk of harming the material position of residents. It is necessary to travel beyond the interpretation of a "big baddy" property company refusing to sell freeholds to poor inarticulate people. It is necessary to travel even beyond, knowing that the problem lies in owner-occupation by working-class people who are owners not because they choose it but because they have no alternative. Ultimately the legal form which the problem takes obscures, but is both a reflection of and a contributor to, the social relations of housing production and consumption. When the houses were built a wealthy land-owner gained out of industrial capital, which required workers to be housed decently near their factories, and out of landlords who profited from their own rentier activities. Now it is a company, based abroad for tax reasons, which gains out of the need for shelter which is provided in the exploitative form of owner-occupation. The social relations of leasehold tenure now involve the local state which has stepped in to alleviate the obvious crisis in housing provision for this section of the working class in Birmingham by buying up freeholds and subsequently selling off again. The problem lies with housing provision itself. This analysis sees comparisons of the relative advantages of different tenures as secondary to the need for good housing which is provided for its use value and not for the market. Campaigning with this understanding is far from a demand for the enforcement of rights. It allows residents to see more clearly who are and who are not likely to be their friends.

At a theoretical level a study of the building lease can provide a basis for a discussion on the nature of legal relations. Does law act as a mere tool of economic power or can it create or at least transform social relations? There is now a considerable body of Marxist literature on the rule of law but the debate takes place at a highly abstract level. Any substantial empirical work, perhaps predictably, has been directed at either the present operation of the criminal law and its social history, or the work relation (Hall *et al.*, 1978; Thompson, 1977; Hay *et al.*, 1978). Some have been made to chart the evolution of legal form in the transition to capitalist production. The best known works are those of Renner (1949) and Pashukanis (1978 and 1980). All of these have been of a general nature and have not concentrated in depth on any particular form. Although analysis is important it should address itself to the crucial political questions. Is struggle with and around law worthwhile? If so, when and under what circumstances? What can be achieved and how? Thus "a far reaching theoretical criticism of law ... is essential if a properly materialist approach is to distinguish itself from a radicalism that unconsciously remains imprisoned within a bourgeois frame of reference" (Editor's Introduction in Pashukanis, 1978, p. 9). There is, therefore, a need to look at common law forms of private rights in the context of political struggle. The legal form of building lease which was originally an expression of the economic relations of housing production survives today although it has outlived its original purpose. Is it now a redundant inert form or does it contribute independently to the processes of consumption? I want to show that the building lease was developed to promote a process of production; that it welded together a landed relation but that by the late nineteenth century it reflected the prevailing balance of forces between aristocratic land-owner, builder, financier, landlord and tenant. Subsequently in the process of consumption it has contributed independently to the market processes. The relation is not landed but financial between a property company, sundry speculative dealers and an "owner-occupying" resident. I want to show that its function has altered dramatically since it no longer promotes the market process but constrains the extension of owner-occupation. Yet it not only constrains but also provides large payments for a particular unproductive sector. My modest aim, therefore, is to try to examine this debate in the leasehold context and to attempt some sort of fusion which I believe is vital if political as well as theoretical objectives are important.

Since I believe it is important to place leasehold tenure in a class analysis, I first introduce Saltley and its problems and then in Chapter 2 I spend some time looking at the history of the building lease, in particular its use in the mass production of houses. Because leasehold tenure ties together the forces of production and circulation, which in themselves reflect a balance of class relations, historically it has appeared as the cause of slums, an important means of preventing slums and even as a means of land nationalization. Our primary concern is with the first of these roles. In the 1890s and in the 1960s long leasehold tenure has been singled out as a prime factor in the decline of old residential areas. Its history as an ideological device is recorded in Chapter 3 particularly in the debates leading up to the Leasehold Reform Act 1967. Chapter 4 introduces the struggle in Saltley, the Act and its procedures. The cost of enfranchisement has been a very important element in the campaign and I attempt to show how the Act itself creates a particular market through its valuation practices. Chapter 5 and Chapter 6 deal with Saltley, the campaigns and how the analysis and action have developed. Lastly I try to pick out some conclusions.

1   A Study of Saltley

Saltley is located on the eastern side of the city of Birmingham. It has a population of 13 900 contained within relatively well defined physical boundaries which include the railway and canal systems on two sides of its triangular boundaries. It is also ringed by an industrial belt. Saltley is a middle ring district situated between the redeveloped inner core and the newer, more prosperous suburbs. It is classified now as an inner-city area: in other words it is experiencing a process of decline. It can be summed up as follows:

> Saltley's already inadequate housing has grown old, and can no longer be adequately maintained by those who live here. Maintenance and other costs have become prohibitive for ordinary workers.
>
> Those who could afford to have moved out, while immigrants needing cheap housing have begun to move in. Local industry has declined. The number of jobs available has gone down consistently since the early 1960s. Unemployment has gone up and relative wage levels have gone down. Unemployment levels have been about one and a half per cent higher than Birmingham levels for several years, and these have increasingly been above the national average. Unemployment levels for young workers have been even higher, at 13 per cent for 16-19 year-olds (excluding school leavers) in summer 1976. The skill levels of Saltley's workers have gone down even since 1966 as have the number of economically active males. Some local workers have been forced to take worse jobs, while others have been forced out of work, or forced to leave the area to find it. (C.D.P. 1977a, p. 6)

Ten thousand jobs have been lost over the last ten years. They have been replaced by a few unskilled warehousing jobs, 100 acres of derelict or vacant land, unemployment and uncertainty.

Saltley has envolved and declined in only 150 years. The C.D.P. report

"The Cost of Industrial Change" summarizes this process as a direct product of a capitalist mode of production: "the existence of areas like these is shown to be useful and even necessary to the normal operations of the economy" (C.D.P., 1977b). The new industries which came to Saltley in the nineteenth century boomed before they bust. A similar process happened in the residential area which was built for the skilled workers in the great engineering and railway works.

> Until the first war the terraced houses ... in then ... suburban Saltley were seen as the solution to the problem of housing the working class — profitable to builders and landlords and a great improvement on the slums which crowded most labourers and their families into the central areas ... of Birmingham. Today the solution has become a problem....
>
> Behind all the changes which have taken place on the surface lies the central contradiction between wages and housing costs. It is as true now as when these areas were built that a substantial section of the working class cannot afford to pay for decent accommodation out of their wages. Industry needs their labour: it requires a healthy workforce and an end to unhealthy slums. Yet the wages they pay for labour are so low and unequally distributed that the poorest families cannot afford improved living conditions. The collapse of the system of building for private renting can be traced back to this. So can the imposition of rent control from 1915, the expansion of subsidised council housing between the wars, and the shift out of private renting into subsidised owner-occupation even in the poorest areas of our cities. (C.D.P., 1978, p. 5)

This chapter describes the historical forces which shaped the local housing market in Saltley. The development went through four overlapping stages.[1] First came the railways, then the factories which depended on them. Thirdly, the state intervened to organize the basic infrastructure of the area, its sewerage and drainage, its electricity and gas and its roads. Finally, houses were built for labourers and artisans employed in the local works and on the railways.

Before the middle of the last century Saltley centred on a small hamlet east of the River Rea (now Saltley Gate, the most dilapidated sector of the area). In 1851 the village had only 34 houses, all of which were large, and a total population of 695. The London Road (renamed the Alum Rock Road) ran through the village to Duddeston on the other side of the river. There was a toll bridge by the river, a few corn mills nearby but there was little industry. The land was owned by Charles Bowyer

Adderley, later Lord Norton, and William Hutton.

> The railways forced their way into Saltley by Acts of Parliament. In 1838 the first London-Birmingham Railway cut Adderley's 415 acre estate in half and defined Saltley's southern boundary. Four years later the Midland Railway Companies line from Birmingham to Derby circled the northern and western fringes of Saltley along the Tame Valley. But it is clear that from 1840 onwards the Norton family orchestrated the next three stages in Saltley's development, first disentailing their Saltley estate by Private Act of Parliament, then selling off their land for industry and services in the lowland areas for the railways, and finally leasing the rest for house-building. In 1845, Wright set up a railway carriage works in Saltley. By 1890, 3 of the 5 independent railway carriage manu-facturers in Britain had their factories in Saltley and most of Birmingham's gas was made there. In the next twenty years Saltley's population increased 10 fold to 40,000. (C.D.P., 1978, pp. 37-38)

James Adderley wrote in 1910:

> The great reason why Saltley should commend itself to those who are not necessarily residents there is that so many things are made here which all England and the world use. Railway carriages, motor cars, taxi-cabs, aeroplanes, ammunition, oxygen gas and a hundred other manufacturers are to be found in Saltley. More-over we team with railway men, especially London and North Western and Midland men. What should we be and where should we go without these splendid fellows. (Adderley, 1910, p. 39)

The residential development took place between 1860 and 1906 but the peak period occurred between 1889 and 1906. Three hundred houses were built in the 1860s and 1870s, many of them on a small freehold estate which Henry Wright had bought from Norton in 1850, but 4000 were built in the later period. Both Hutton and Norton generally leased their land to builders rather than sold, and thereby controlled the layout of their estates and the standard of each house. James Adderley wrote of Lord Norton:

> To the late Lord Norton is due the foresight of building wide and healthy streets. With the help of the late Lord Norton and the agent of the great Sir Robert Peel he laid out Saltley so that it should never become a slum. (Adderley, 1910, p. 35)

By 1915 Saltley was considered a middle ring district. It and other areas like it enclosed the city's central slums. As Chapter 2 will show this "housing problem" worried the politicians. There were 43 366 back-to-back houses, which were privately rented and in appalling condition. They were forcibly patched by the city's housing committee between 1900 and 1914 but then remained largely untouched until 1935 when there were still 38 773 back-to-backs. The drive to clear these areas did not occur until the mid-fifties. The problem was that the unskilled workers living in the slums could not support a rent which would have covered the cost of building new houses to a minimum standard without subsidy. Before 1900 a more substantial group could have afforded such a rent but after this their economic position was progressively undermined and the state intervened with subsidies.

Outside the privately built, by-law controlled districts like Saltley came a ring of publicly provided council housing. Birmingham built only 300 before 1914 but this figure had increased to 13 008 by 1926. Between 1924 and 1931, 32 829 council houses were built in comparison to 14 869 private enterprise houses. After 1931 the number built by private enterprise increased rapidly with the fall in the cost of production. By 1959 there were 50 268 municipal houses and 54 536 private houses which had been built since the First World War. The council houses were occupied by the same respectable working class as were catered for by private enterprise in Saltley. The problem came when slum dwellers were rehoused in the 1930s because they could not afford the rent levels without some subsidy to their wages.

Saltley lay in the middle. It provided houses for the skilled workers in the new industries. These workers could afford the higher rents which the higher by-law standards imposed. All the slums and 90% of the by-law areas were rented. The problem of wages not meeting rental costs had led to the collapse of the private building sector and, in 1915, the introduction of rent control. In Saltley the internal rent structure became complex because of the succession of Rent Acts, beginning with the 1915 Increase of Rent and Mortgage Interest Act and moving through the 1920 Act which allowed a 40% rent increase on 1914 prices, then the 1923 Act which allowed decontrol with a change of occupier and the 1935 Act which reversed this for lower rated property in the area. All rents were controlled until 1923, thereafter for ten years they could be increased when the tenant left. In 1935 decontrol stopped for all houses under £13 rateable value. This covered nearly all the houses in Saltley. By 1939 rent levels were between 42½p and 62p inclusive of rates. This was not significantly different from council levels. Small non-parlour houses

were between 48½p and 62p, parlour houses were between 57p and
81½p. Letting remained a viable proposition for landlords throughout
the interwar period in Saltley because prices and wages fell continuously
from their immediate post war peak. Rent covered the increase in the
cost of repairs and, although rates increased, the rents were inclusive.
Management and insurance rose but not significantly. The interest on the
original capital cost of purchase remained constant and, therefore, became
relatively and absolutely cheaper.

But despite the profitability of renting the shift to owner-occupation
started to occur during the 1920s. It was not a result of 'gentrification'
since most of the sales were to sitting tenants.[2] The population was made
up of skilled men working in the big local factories or on the railways.
Some of the better off independent traders moved out to the newer
suburbs but wage levels of those remaining were relatively stable.
Owner-occupation developed as an alternative to renting because it
provided a way around rent control and gave landlords a greater return
on investment. For in the 1930s even an average industrial worker could
afford to pay more than a controlled rent. The pattern of the property
transactions was fairly constant until the 1950s. The first landlords were
dying off during the 1920s and 1930s. But their properties remained in
the family since most set up trusts in their wills appointing trustees to
manage the property for beneficiaries. The entrepreneurial flair
disappeared with the death of the original landlords and trusteeship
imposed an inertia on property dealings. The trustees seemed to have
little feel for the market and no ability to arrange mortgages and
generally preferred to rid themselves of the complexities of selling to
individual owner-occupiers by selling to entrepreneurs in block.

The shift to owner-occupation was spear-headed by this new wave of
entrepreneurs in touch with the market and with sources of finance.
They made their major impact after 1931 when owner-occupation was
expanding rapidly in the newly built areas. Their method was to buy
these blocks of houses then split them up by way of underlease and sell to
the sitting tenants or new owner-occupiers when the tenant died or left.
They absorbed the occupier's capacity to pay increased housing costs by
pushing up the price of each house. Often they made a substantial gain.
For example, S.J.J. Ltd, having bought a block of six houses in Arden
Road from the trustee of the original landlord, sold five of them to
Blossomfield Developments for £1750 in 1962. Gradually as the houses
became vacant Blossomfield sold them off to owner-occupiers. One of

them was sold for £1575 to the present occupier in 1966. A.H. Bolus, estate agent, paid £1725 for ten houses in 1947 to the former landlady Elizabeth Whitthall, who had bought them in 1918 for £965 with a mortgage to the Birmingham Incorporated Building Society which she had only paid off in 1945. Within two years Bolus sold off a number of these houses, including one in 1949 for £650. The average capital gain on each house dealt with this way before the war seemed to be between 25% and 35% and between 40% and 45% in the 1950s and 1960s.

The choice between owner-occupation and renting was finely balanced in Saltley so long as residents' jobs were secure. These remained so, on the whole, until the 1950s unlike some other older areas. As the "Costs of Industrial Change" points out, Saltley's industries, gas, railways and railway carriage construction were linked to stable markets for a longer time.

Rail technology was relatively advanced by the turn of the century and was to remain broadly unchanged for another fifty years. The Empire had expanded into new countries and opened them up for British investors to exploit. These now provided a continuing market for railways and railway carriages. But the most striking difference was that a second phase of growth began alongside these earlier industries.

Towards the end of the century many of Birmingham's old, small-scale engineering trades were transformed into the new metal and machine-tool trades which produced first bicycles and then motor cars . . . .

Early competition in the motor industry was acute . . . . Still the industry did survive and it took root in Saltley with a wide number of manufacturers . . . .

Saltley offered the advantages of a location close to the mass market of the South of England. This advantage was consolidated when in 1926 the national grid brought, for the first time, unrestricted sources of power to areas outside the coalfields. Here again, progress for some areas meant decline for others. The northern coalfield area saw the national grid further undermine their central role in the economy just at a period when their investments were running into deep trouble.

But for Saltley these developments meant that, although it was hit by the post-war slump, it was still based on an expanding economy when . . . local economies . . . were thrown into deep depression. The Second World War and the expansion of working-class

consumption after 1945 extended its development for another
decade to reach a peak in the fifties. (C.D.P., 1977b, pp. 19-20)

The building societies reinforced the ideology of owner-occupation,
and its rapid spread in the new suburbs after the depression showed the
residents of Saltley that owner-occupation was possible. Residents could
afford the purchase price which translated into little more than the
average rent payment. One house in St Saviours Road was bought in
1934 by Pearl Estates for £225. It was resold a year later to a property
dealer for £285. He sold it within a month to an owner-occupier for
£395. This involved a capital gain of 40%. The occupier obtained a
mortgage with a building society at 4½%. His weekly repayments were
40p, less than the average weekly rent. The problem is that the cost of
repairs, insurance and legal costs are not offset. The capital gain and
service charges start to eat into that proportion of wages set aside for
housing and thereby exclude systematic repairs. This problem became
acute after the Second World War when use value, which reflects the
state of repair, and exchange value increasingly diverged.

The war damaged Saltley considerably. Over 300 houses were
completely destroyed. After the war, damaged houses were repaired with
compensation from the Government. Between 1950 and 1954 the
Council built new houses and maisonettes as replacements. During the
next 20 years most houses were fitted with the basic amenities of an
inside W.C. and bathroom. Owner-occupiers have tended to patch and
paint but the basic physical structure of Saltley has remained the same.

The problem of Birmingham's inner slum area was finally tackled in
1955 when the first phase of comprehensive redevelopment started. The
areas were gradually pulled down and the population, in the mian,
rehoused in council houses. The programme rolled on to the early 1970s.
It included the building of two massive council estates on the outer
boundary of the city, Chelmsley Wood and Castle Bromwich.

Until ten years ago it was likely that the Council would pull Saltley
down too and rebuild it under a later phase. ''It is the view of the Public
Works Committee,'' said its Chairman in 1963, ''that at some time in
the future the area will need to be comprehensively redeveloped''
(Evening Mail, 25/5/62). By 1975 the first row of substantial by-law
houses was finally cleared. But policies changed. Opposition to the
process of redevelopment and to its outcome became widespread. Years
of waiting in derelict conditions for a high-rise flat were no longer

acceptable. By the late 1960s and early 1970s the national economic crisis was deepening and public expenditure cuts were thought necessary. In 1969 the Housing Act introduced General Improvement Areas (G.I.A.s). These are areas designated by the local authority as capable of benefiting from large scale improvement. Grants are made available. In 1974 the Housing Act introduced Housing Action Areas (H.A.A.s). These are areas which are designated to be worthy of retention but in need of even more improvements to give them a thirty-year life. Higher grants are available. Saltley was divided up between a H.A.A. and several G.I.A.s. By 1974, therefore, redevelopment had been replaced by an improvement policy.

Saltley's physical appearance, although ageing, remained the same. Its financial structure had changed drastically. The increase in owner-occupation had accelerated after the war. From 15% in 1940 it increased to 22% in 1950, to 40% in 1960 and to 53% in 1973. With the reimposition of blanket rent control in 1939 landlords increasingly found it more profitable to take their capital out of houses and reinvest it elsewhere. Rents were frozen and repair costs increased. But wages were rising and there were no price controls in the owner-occupied sector. The pattern which had developed in the interwar years continued. Dealers dominated the process, to give examples from after the war:

> John Peutherer, a director of Cornwall Estates, bought 7 houses in Ash Road in 1946 for £1030, with the help of a mortgage from Birmingham Incorporated Building Society, from the wife of a rentier who had owned them for 20 years. Peutherer sold them for 30% profit two years later to Harold Shakeshaft who sold them for another 25% profit 3 years later to Macdor Builders who were lent £1,000 of the purchase price by Birmingham Citizens Building Society. Each house cost them £291 and they immediately began to sell to sitting tenants for between £400 and £450, a profit of at least 30%. Similarly in 1964, various Dennis Fell companies bought 9 houses in Hams Road from the trustees of the original landlord — a Conservative Councillor and brassfounder, Arthur Ellaway. They paid £4600, an average price of £510 a house, and were helped with a mortgage from the Hastings & Thanet Building Society. Within 6 months they sold the first house for £1300, a profit of 150% and more sales followed at even higher prices as houses became vacant. (C.D.P., 1978, p. 87)

Most of the owner-occupiers buying between 1945 and 1960 were tenants, either sitting tenants or from slum areas. Wages had risen in the post war economic boom which sustained jobs in Saltley. They could afford to pay more for their housing needs than their current controlled rent. Rising house prices absorbed this capacity. Fixed rents did not. Until 1957 landlords could not relet vacant houses at the higher rents and, even in the seven years after the 1957 Rent Act, decontrol never became universal. In 1964 control was reintroduced and has remained ever since although the system of fixing the rent has changed.

Even decontrolled rents could not adequately cover the cost of maintaining and repairing old by-law housing and remain within the financial limits imposed by the relatively low wages of the unskilled workers who were moving into Saltley. Ironically, owner-occupation in Saltley provided a solution for those who could not afford economic rents and who were denied council houses. The solution was temporary. House prices rise in line with increased wage levels but necessary repair costs were not taken into account.

Until 1950 it was easy to obtain a building society mortgage. Eighty-five per cent of the new owner-occupiers did. But building societies became increasingly reluctant to lend as leases shortened and the discrepancy between use and exchange value increased. Between 1950 and 1959 they granted nearly 70% of all mortgages, this dropped to 45% between 1960 and 1969 and down to 8% between 1972 and 1974. In the 1950s those owners who were also dealers would stand as sureties for the purchaser to the building society. But this did not last, so by the 1960s the dealers were lending money through their own companies. The Dennis Fell Group used the Saltley and District Permanent Money Lending Society because Neville Bosworth, Birmingham Council's Conservative leader, was a director of a number of their companies. Melluish used Constant Finance, Richardsons used JKL finances.

In the 1960s and 1970s Saltley has been declining more rapidly.

> The motor industry, whose arrival seemed to be the saving of Saltley, turned out to provide only a temporary reprieve. In the event, it too is now declining and only slightly after the decline of the earlier generation of industry. Saltley's early industries were railway carriages, gas and the railways. Amalgamation in the railway carriage industry brought Wright's works and four others together in 1905 and by reorganising, the companies succeeded in holding on to their overseas markets. By 1919 the north-east firm of Vickers had bought into the company, and then in 1928, at the height of the slump, it reorganised to produce Metro-Cammell out of the rolling stock interests of Vickers and Cammall Laird shipbuilders.

Although the company can point to its mark on London's tube trains, most of Metro-Cammell's profits came from selling goods abroad which it succeeded in doing until the market finally faltered, bringing severe and rapid rationalisation in the late fifties. It tried unsuccessfully to raise productivity but there was little scope for significant productivity increases in this craft industry. As a result, there have been many redundancies, especially in the years 1959-1964. The Saltley site of Metro-Cammell, which in 1958 employed 1,800 workers, was sold off in 1962. The company has diversified production at the later, adjacent Washwood Heath site which now produces railway carriages and buses.

The four gas works which had been taken over by Birmingham Corporation in the 1850s, and then by the Gas Board, survived successfully until the late 1960s, when the search for cheap fuel rapidly eliminated them. In the railways too there was a similar rapid decline as major technical change in signals and maintenance brought rationalisation. Other light industries like Hughes Biscuits, a subsidiary of Rowntrees, closed down, and Southalls only survived without more losses by closing other factories elsewhere.

While all this was happening, things were still going relatively well for the motor industry. But decline, rationalisation and reorganisation was to begin there too, soon after. Between 1966 and 1974, employment in the local plants of Leyland Motors (itself a product of several mergers since it first moved into the area as Forward Radiators in the 1920s) fell from over 14,000 by nearly 5,000. Reorganisation had already brought about the closure of the old Morris Commercial site in Adderley Park which had figured so significantly in the area's early growth. Production was concentrated in the later and larger works at Common Lane, removing 4,000 jobs in the overall reorganisation.

Between 1966 and 1974, 8,400 jobs were lost in Saltley. Three quarters of those were cut by two firms — British Leyland and Metro-Cammell. Vehicle manufacture fell by 31%, gas making was eliminated and jobs halved. The workers of Saltley did not lose their jobs because firms actually relocated. There is only one example of this. The jobs were eliminated as the companies reinvested and directed their capital towards concentrating production somewhere else.

So far the changes in the older parts of Saltley's industry like gas are less important in terms of employment than in terms of land use. Over the last decade one third of the land once occupied by thriving traditional industries had fallen empty. And the process is still only in its early stages. Although many jobs have been lost, Saltley has

probably not yet suffered the full effects of the decline of the motor
industry. The area still contains a major British Leyland works at
Washwood Heath. (C.D.P., 1977b, p. 31)

Just as jobs were declining so was the environment. Intrusive industry
increased and the volume of traffic grew. The houses have grown older,
leases are shorter and repairs are needed urgently. Ownership of land also
changed in the 1960s. Saltley reflected the national position. Property
companies and institutions were becoming significant in the city land
ownership system. The ownership pattern is shown in Fig. 1. There
were now three major landowners in Saltley: Huttons descendants
retained most of their estate; Norton's descendants sold off most of theirs
in the early 1960s to two property companies. The eastern half of the
estate was bought in 1961 by C. & P. Estates for £150 000. In 1962
London City & Westcliff (L.C.&W.) bought the western half, the freehold of 850 houses, for £80 000. They were "cock a hoop", delighted to
have bought a piece of land ripe for redevelopment for such a pittance.
The Council had sent a representative to the auction but he was not
empowered to bid more then £60 000. The Conservatives opposed the
idea anyway, calling it "creeping nationalization". Alderman H.E.
Tyler, a Conservative member of the Public Works Committee, said:

> This is another example of socialist determination to press on with
> the extension of municipalisation.
>
> It is a socialist land grab and nothing more. This is not a "twilight
> area" and there are some very good properties. The occupiers
> should be given the opportunity to buy their own freehold.
>
> The corporation has no right whatever to acquire land unless that
> land is wanted for a specific purpose. (Evening Mail, 25/5/62)

L.C. & W. told the press that they could build three times as many
houses on the land as then existed. The pattern was clear. The traditional
owners were being superseded by property companies whose aim was to
profit not from estate management but from the redevelopment of
valuable inner-city sites.

L.C. & W. put in repeated proposals for redevelopment, industrial and
residential, right up until 9th April 1973. They were, however, turned
down consistently because the area was zoned as residential and their
mixed use plans "would consolidate existing non-conforming uses in
[the] area". Nevertheless the company consolidated its holding by
buying in as many leases as possible. This involved buying out the

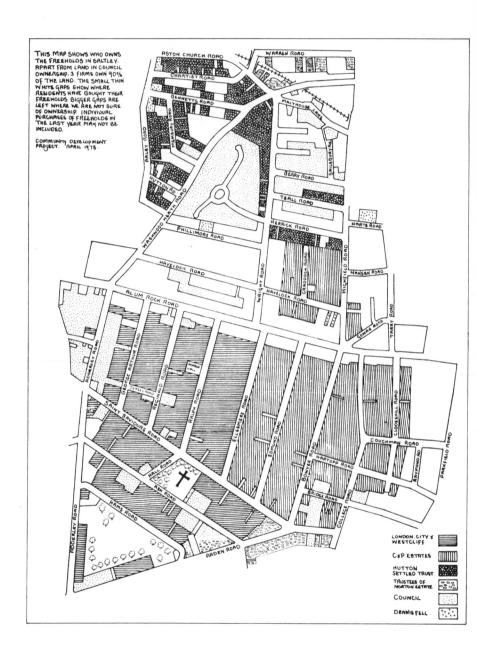

Fig. 1. Who owns Saltley? — this land ownership map was produced for a public meeting with local M.P. Dennis Howell in April 1975.

landlords of weekly tenants as well as holders of superior interests to long leaseholding owner-occupiers. When the Leasehold Reform bill was being discussed in 1966 they tried (through their agents) a policy of intimidation by serving dilapidation orders on the leaseholders. These were schedules of repairs required under the leasehold covenants. Schedules had never before been served on such a large scale on long lease property. Usually schedules are served on property just prior to the expiry of the leases whereas these leases usually had between 15 and 30 years to run.

This action worried the majority of leaseholding occupiers and also their landlords since the schedules required extensive repairs to be carried out. The situation was made more confused by the chains of interests involved on each individual lease. Each lessee passed the dilapidation order down to the lessee below until it reached the occupier or, if the occupier was a tenant, his immediate landlord. Generally residents did not known who was responsible for these orders or how to combat them. They were resisted by the newly formed Norton Residents Association (N.R.A.) with the help of local M.P. Dennis Howell and they managed to have the schedules suspended but not removed. The policy of intimidation was, however, effective. Landlords particularly were persuaded to sell out to L.C. & W. in exchange merely for the non-pursuance of the dilapidation orders.

The 1967 Leasehold Reform Act was a bitter blow to L.C. & W. Residents now had the ability to block comprehensive redevelopment of the estate by buying their individual freeholds before their leases fell in. The company decided to obstruct and they were very successful as later chapters describe.

The leasehold system was thought by C.D.P. to be an important independent element in Saltley's decline. Only later, as Chapter 6 will show, was the importance of leasehold enfranchisement integrated into an understanding of the local housing market. Initially it was thought that the leasehold system had an effect in two ways, first on the individual residents, and secondly on the area as a whole. It affected both residents and prospective buyers. On an individual level many owner-occupiers were very distressed by the dilapidation orders in 1967. Even then many houses were occupied by elderly people who could not afford the outlay. The effect had been to create insecurity, uncertainty and frustration. The knowledge that at any time the freeholder could serve an order which the owner-occupier might not be able to meet creates insecurity. The knowledge that the freeholder could apply for planning permission to redevelop the land and uncertainty of how the planning authorities would respond reinforced these feelings. No access to or control over these external agencies had led to frustration, so had the inability to secure the legal right to enfranchise. The greatest problem of all for the individual was the process on expiry of the lease. The resident becomes subject to the dilapidations on a property which is no longer their economic asset. Anybody who was able to tended to move away before this event occurred, leaving behind the 'fag end' with its problems for the incoming and probably unsuspecting leaseholder.

But C.D.P. thought that the leasehold position was important, not so much as it affected present owner-occupiers, but for its deterrent effect on prospective buyers. The dilapidation orders remained still on the majority of London City & Westcliff's property and, since their existence must be disclosed to a prospective purchaser, the houses were very difficult to sell. Those who might otherwise be able to move, could not. These included elderly people with houses far too big for their needs.

The critical factor, as we saw it then, was the reluctance of building societies to lend money on houses with less than 40 years lease remaining (in addition to their general reluctance to lend on old property). The alternative sources of finance open to buyers were bankers, finance houses, and the corporation. Banks and finance houses insist on relatively short repayment periods thus by implication high monthly repayments which make it hard for a prospective buyer to repay such loans. The problem is compounded because finance houses such as Julian Hodge and Cedar Holdings and the clearing banks lent at interest rates which varied, even in the early 1970s between 18 and 25%. Clearly the fringe bank mortgages, which required payments of up to £20 a week in interest alone, contributed to the economic decline of the area.

A corporation loan seemed to be the best prospect. But there were problems. Some estate agents argued that Birmingham Corporation undervalued property and gave a disproportionately low mortgage advance, although the Housing Department denied this. Other agents were reluctant to wait for the corporation to advance money because it took longer than the banks.[3] Instead, they were often prepared to deal with a prospective landlord who had the money available.

These difficulties applied to freehold property too, but a third factor related specifically to leasehold houses. Section 43 of the Housing Act

1958 requires a local authority mortgage to be paid off at least ten years before the termination of the lease. Consequently the shorter the lease the shorter the repayment period and the higher the monthly repayment figure. The department's general guide is that the mortgagor's monthly outgoings on the house, which include mortgage repayments plus rates, should not be greater than the husband's weekly gross income. Taking an example typical of Saltley in 1973, a mortgage of 90% on a £3 500 house, of £3 150 at 11% over 25 years, requires £34.50 a month repayments. Add on £6 per month for rates and the month's outgoings come to £40.50. A successful applicant must have had a weekly gross income exceeding this. If the lease had less than 35 years remaining, then an applicant will have had to repay the mortgage over less than 25 years which increases his monthly repayment. For example, in George Arthur Road, with leases even in 1973 of less than 20 years to run, repayment would have had to have been squashed into a very few years and might not have been accepted by the corporation.

Potential house purchasers balanced these possibilities against buying a house in the suburbs. In the first year the outgoings do not amount to much more. Given the uncertainty in the area and the popular feelings that it is deteriorating fast, many prospective residents could buy elsewhere for only marginally greater sacrifice. Agents and solicitors advised this course, not only for these immediate economic reasons, but because of the general troubles with leasehold in the area.

The primary effect had been to reinforce the change away from an economically and racially mixed area towards one which was predominantly immigrant and poor since the constraints had a different effect upon different ethnic groups. Many prospective Asian buyers had been able to avoid these difficulties by internal finance or by establishing themselves in the area, first of all as part of an extended family. Most vacant houses in the area went to Asian families who were young and economically self-sufficient. This was not true of the whites. The residents were old and, on the whole, economically less viable. The few newcomers formed, on the whole, an exploited group. They had perhaps accepted a fringe bank mortgage with vast interest rates or they had fallen foul of some dubious practice such as rental purchase or drip mortgages. The latter is a form of hire purchase for houses were the legal title does not pass to the buyer until all the instalments have been paid off. In Saltley the period over which payment is made usually corresponds roughly to the length of lease left. The outcome is that the occupier has no chance of buying the freehold since he has no legal right to enfranchise. Similarly he cannot raise money on the security of his property. This makes improvement policy unworkable.

It was already clear to us in 1973 that short leases would effectively hold up the Council's new improvement policy for Saltley. Leaseholder owner-occupiers would not spend money improving houses when they knew that they would be obliged to give the houses to the freeholder in the near future. Nobody improves another's house. In addition many occupiers were not only unwilling but financially incapable since the only asset they could use as security, the house, was declining and worth very little. Enfranchisement is an essential prerequisite of the renewal programme but it entails a double economic burden, first to purchase the freehold and then to finance the improvements.

We thought that as the leases became shorter the area would inevitably decline since it was faced with dilapidations and the prospect of becoming private rented. The houses were declining assets and these increasing burdens would mean that the residents would become more and more reluctant to maintain and improve them. Residents would face increasing insecurity and anxiety about the future and many would have little chance of escaping since a short lease, besides depressing the value of the house, in itself makes the house more difficult to sell.

The answer to the problem was leasehold enfranchisement. As we saw it then this would set the local housing market in motion again and help prevent Saltley's further decline and even facilitate its development. Despite an evolving policy of renewal the owners of the land were obstructing. The aim was to break the obstruction by whatever means possible and then all would be well.

Notes

1. The information used in the following pages is taken from "Private Housing and the Working Class" (C.D.P., 1978) which was gathered by a group of us in Birmingham and Benwell.
2. Gentrification is a term used to describe the process whereby the middle class moves into an area and displaces its working-class residents.
3. C.D.P. and the Centre for Urban and Regional Studies carried out a survey in 1974 which shed light on the mortgage activity in Saltley. This is dealt with later.

2   The Making of Saltley

Chapter 1 introduced Saltley as a product of the capitalist processes of production and reproduction. It was a declining inner-city area with a housing problem which had been analysed in part as a problem of the leasehold tenure structure. Why was Saltley a leasehold area? What is the significance of this form theoretically and politically? The next two chapters arise out of a need to understand the history of class relations in the Saltley housing market. This does not involve a monolithic description of the physical fabric nor a demographic account of its occupants. Nor is it a history of a few acres of land which Lord Norton's biographer described as developed by one man's foresight and philanthropy.

It is rather an attempt to provide a materialist analysis of the capitalist processes of production and consumption. The Saltley estate was laid out by the land-owners, Hutton and Norton, between 1860 and 1910. Why did they use leasehold tenure to organize the production process? Was this form particularly apposite for the nineteenth century building process which involved numerous small builders, speculators, rentiers and financiers as well as land-owners? What was the nature of the class relations between all these parties? In order to understand these specific relations it is necessary to disentangle the forces at a theoretical level. The process in the late nineteenth century in Saltley concerned the production of a particular commodity using a specific legal form. This chapter will attempt to point out the theoretical and political significance of this process using Lord Norton's estate development as the main example but drawing out similarities and comparisons with other estates.

The next chapter will concentrate on the process of realization and consumption, distinguished here from production for the purpose of analytical clarity. Houses in Saltley have been exchanged in the market for a 100 years. Leasehold tenure has continued to play a significant part

25

even though the balance of class relations is now very different.

Much debate rages over the nature and relative importance of the different processes involved in the provision of housing. Is the key to the problem of housing the production process or the consumption of this costly item? (See Ball, 1978, pp. 78-79.) At a theoretical level the validity of any distinction must be questioned. The fact that capitalist rent represents a relation of distribution does not mean that it is unrelated to the process of production.

> The structure of distribution is completely determined by the structure of production. Distribution is itself a product of production, not only in its object, in that only the results of production can be distributed, but also in its form, in that the specific kind of participation in production determines the specific forms of distribution, i.e. the pattern of participation. (Grundrisse, p. 95, quoted in Massey and Catalano, 1978, pp. 32-33)

> Surplus value produced by labour under capitalism is distributed in accordance with the structure of ownership of the necessities of production.... Landowners share in the distribution of surplus value. [Thus] ... ground rent is a payment made as a result of a social relation rather than as a return to the productivity of land itself ... [it is] a result simply of the prior distribution of ownership as a condition of production. It is not land which commands a rent but land ownership. (Massey and Catalano, 1978, p. 33)

Some elements of house building in 1860 were very different to those prevailing now. Technically the process was primitive, the builders were men of small capital, not Bryants or Wimpeys. The land-owner usually owned a hereditary estate and had large resources; today land is held by pension funds, the state and developers and construction companies. Financiers in 1860 were solicitors, doctors, gentlemen and women generally not institutions like building societies, banks and pension funds. Purchasers were landlord rentiers not owner-occupiers or the local state. But in essence the capitalist process remains the same despite the very different class relations. At its simplest a land-owner provides land on which a builder builds a house which he sells to a consumer who borrows money off a financier to pay for the purchase. Houses are commodities produced by the industrial sector. This is not immediately clear for a number of reasons. First, unlike most other commodities they are not generally produced in factories but on a parcel of land which they will occupy for the rest of their useful life. Secondly, their value is high; that is, much more labour time is expended in the production of each unit than for most, if not all, items necessary for the subsistence of labour. Thirdly, unlike most other commodities, a house has a long useful life: official estimates place it as sixty years. Thus a house is "consumed" over a longer period than most other commodities, which like cars or televisions become obsolete in a few years.

The builder like other industrial capitalists obtains surplus value from the production of commodities. But builders must obtain land on which to build from land-owners and they must pass on this cost to the occupier when he buys or rents the house. The relationship between these parties does not create surplus value as Engels stresses when he contrasts the sale of labour power with the sale of housing:

> The capitalist causes the purchased labour power firstly to produce its own value which remains in his hands for the time being, subject to its distribution among the capitalist class. In this case therefore an extra value is produced, the total sum of the existing value is increased. In the rent transaction the situation is quite different. No matter how much the landlord may over-reach the tenant it is still only a transfer of already *existing*, previously *produced* value, and the total sum of values possessed by the landlord and the tenant *together* remains the same after as it was before. (Engels, 1935, p. 24)

> we are dealing here with a quite ordinary commodity transaction between two citizens, and this transaction proceeds according to the economic laws which govern the sale of commodities in general, and in particular the sale of the commodity land property. (Engels, 1935, p. 25)

He goes on to point out that the cost includes building and maintenance costs of the house, the land value and the state of the relation between supply and demand. Thus the payment to the land-owner constitutes a transfer of surplus value: a sum which arises because capital requires land on which to operate and that requirement cannot itself be manufactured. As Marx states it is a non-reproducible condition of production which is "the monopoly of certain persons over definite portions of the globe" (Capital, Vol. 3, p. 615).

The relationship between industrial and landed sector is competitive because it involves a conflict over the distribution of surplus value. This is because housing is a necessary part of the cost of reproducing the labour force and the level of housing costs will affect the level of wages. "Demands by landlords for rents in excess of those relating to the costs of producing a dwelling could be met by a transfer of surplus value from capitalists via workers' wages and subsequent payments of rent'' (Ball, 1976, p. 39). Tenure does not alter this potential. Land-owners, housing landlords, workers and capitalists are involved in antagonist relations over the cost of housing. It is a social relation which is expressed in concrete terms as rent:

> If land [which is not the product of exchange] appears in exchange, then production relations in this case do not connect commodity producers with commodity producers, but with a landowner; if the price fluctuations of plots of land have a different influence on the course and distribution of the production process from the price fluctuations of the products of labour, then we are dealing with a different social relation, a different production relation, behind the same material form of exchange and value. This social relation is subject to special analysis, namely in the context of the theory of rent. (Rubin, 1972, p. 45)

Thus in Saltley between 1860 and 1910 Lord Norton acquired a proportion of the surplus value extracted by builders from building workers because all the building lessees were obliged to pay him a ground rent. This did not make Norton an industrial capitalist but, as we will see later, led him into potential conflict with the builders. This conflict was not limited to the rent relation since the surplus also had to be shared out with financiers. Because houses are costly commodities builders required finance to support the building process and so finance capital is an important element in the relationship between builder and land-owner. Both loan and land costs distribute surplus value away from the industrial sector of capital to unproductive capitals. In the building process in Saltley land-owners appropriated a disproportionate share of the surplus compared to financiers because leasehold tenure spreads ground rent over 99 years and thereby reduces the initial capital costs.

The class relations in Saltley were bonded together by a legal form: the building lease. Lord Norton granted a large number of leases primarily to builders. He was not alone in using this form rather than selling land freehold, since by the end of the nineteenth century a third of the urban population of England and Wales was accommodated in houses built under the long leasehold system. In 1889 the Select Committee on Town Holdings, whose brief included a study of the various tenures upon which houses were built in England and Wales, considered the building lease and its distribution in some detail. A similar study was carried out in 1913 by the Liberal Party and published in its report ''The Land''

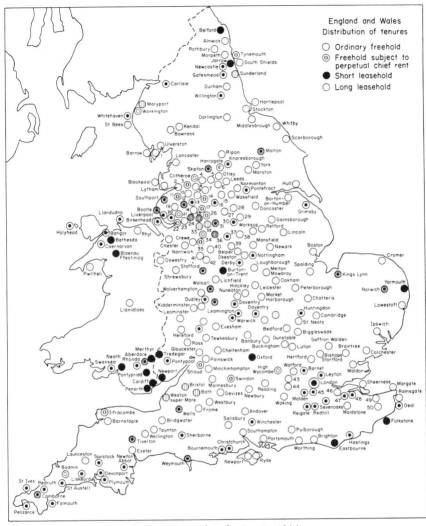

Fig. 2. Tenure distribution in 1914.

Key to numbers : 1, Dalton; 2, Preston; 3, Blackburn; 4, Burley; 5, Shipley; 6, Bradford; 7, Todmorden; 8, Accrington: 9, Rawtenstall; 10, Darwen; 11, Chorley; 12, Bolton; 13, Bury; 14, Rochdale; 15, Dewsbury; 16, Huddersfield; 17, Oldham; 18, Middleton; 19, Wigan; 20, Prescot; 21, St Helens; 22, Widnes; 23, Warrington; 24, Salford; 25, Manchester; 26, Ashton; 27, Derby; 28, Barnsley; 29, Rotherham; 30, Sheffield; 31, Glossop; 32, Staly bridge; 33, Stockport; 34, Macclesfield; 35, Congleton; 36, Buxton; 37, Bakewell; 38, Chesterfield; 39, Matlock; 40, Leek; 41, Newcastle-under-Lyme; 42, Stoke-on-Trent; 43, Uxbridge; 44, Staines; 45, Croydon; 46, Gravesend; 47, Rochester; 48, Chatham; 49, Whitstable; 50, Canterbury. Taken from G. Green

(1914) which included the map in Fig. 2 showing the distribution of tenures. These are almost identical to those found in the earlier 1889 report. The Select Committee summed up the distribution as follows. The freehold purchase system was adopted in by far the largest number of towns in the Northern, Midland and Eastern counties although there were a few towns where the system of grants in fee form was in vogue and the long lease system was in use in many towns principally situated in Lancashire and Cheshire. There were also some notable cases where the 99 year system prevailed, such as Jarrow, Sheffield, Southport in the North, Birmingham, Oxford in the Midlands and Great Grimsby in the Eastern counties. The leasehold system was by far the most usual in the Metropolis and suburbs and in many of the towns in the south and west of England, such as Eastbourne, Folkestone, Falmouth and Bournemouth. Life leases were found principally in Devon and Cornwall. Towns in South Wales were almost universally built on the leasehold system which also existed in a large number of places in North Wales. The committee considered the terms of occupation of the differing types of tenure and suggested that the working and artisan classes did not, on the whole, own the houses they occupied except in the case of ''better class of houses'' such as on the Bedford Estate in Blooms-bury or the suburb of Beckenham. They also noted the influence of localized industries in small towns or in the suburbs of large towns. This tended to show that more workmen owned their houses in these areas. In Jarrow, for instance, between a third and a quarter of lessees occupied their houses; in Festiniog 700 out of 2050 occupied; at Bethseda near the Penrtyn slate quarries there were 803 leasehold and 216 freehold houses, largely occupied by their owners. In places which were larger or not so dependent on one local industry the proportion of occupying owners seem to be smaller, for instance, on the Scaresbrick estate in Southport where 20% of occupiers were owners.

What was the origin of this form and why was it used by some land-owners and not others? In order to answer these questions it is necessary to look back at the feudal system of production (since the legal form and its use had evolved out of the feudal shackles) and describe briefly the nature of land ownership under feudalism, the origins of leases and the particular form of the building lease. Property mainly in the form of land was the basis of production in feudalism:

> It was this property relationship [between lords and serfs] on which was based the right to extract the surplus from the class of serfs.

The latter performed labour in order to provide their means of existence directly.... They also performed, however, 'surplus labour' for the lord; labour which might be appropriated in produce, in labour hours or in cash .... In a capitalist mode of production, all these relationships are transformed. The production of the surplus now occurs through the manufacture of commodities. Surplus labour is no longer extracted as rent, perhaps as labour itself, but in value form, as commodities. ... Under a feudal mode of production, the serfs possessed their own means of production; the surplus labour they performed was *defined juridically* as the right of the landowner, as the rent. Under a capitalist mode of production, the means of production are owned, not by those who *perform* the surplus labour, but by those who appropriate it, who control the process of production.... Thus... the private ownership of land was fundamental to the feudal mode of production; it is in a sense 'technically unnecessary', to the capitalist mode of production. (Massey and Catalano, 1978, pp. 23-25)

Legal forms were thus central to feudal society.

The system of land ownership involved two basic concepts, tenure and estates. The doctrine of tenure stipulated that all land was held of the crown either directly or indirectly in one or other of the various tenures. Each form of tenure involved a type of service in return for the occupation of the land, but gradually these services were standardized. There were three types of tenure: free, unfree and a third, miscellaneous group, and each type had its own subdivisions. The main tenures were the free tenure in socage which, after 1645, became known as freehold and the unfree tenure of villeinage which later became known as copyhold and lost its unfree status. In 1925, when copyhold was converted into freehold, the doctrine of tenure ceased to have any practical significance. Freehold tenure, which remains as a historical oddity, means that theoretically no land can be held by a 'subject' but only from the crown. The common use of the terms freehold and leasehold tenure, which is used in this book, embodies a legal confusion. To be precise these should be called freehold and leasehold estates.

Under the doctrine of estates land could be held for different periods of time. There were three estates in land within the feudal system, the fee simple (by which land was granted to a tenant and passed to any of his heirs), the fee tail (by which land was granted to a tenant and any of his descendants) and a life estate (by which land was granted to a tenant for his life). These were known as freehold estates. At first the three estates of freehold were the sole estates recognized by law. The only other lawful right to the possession of land was known as a tenancy at will, under which a tenant could be ejected at any time, and which gave him no estate at all (Megarry and Wade, 1975, p. 43). The other class of estate, that of leaseholds, grew up outside this system. The familiar type of lease, the term of years, was known by the middle of the thirteenth century and was relatively common by the fifteenth. It was not regarded originally as property (the object of ownership) and did not attract a 'real' remedy. If a tenant of a leasehold estate were wrongfully ejected, he would not necessarily be restored to his property by a court, he might simply be compensated. Therefore leases were foreign to the feudal system of landholding by tenure. They were individual personal arrangements under which one party allowed the other the use of land in return for a rental payment. Thus they were contractual and were enforceable only by the parties to the arrangement.

The development of the lease came with its legal protection. The tenant became fully protected against other persons by the use of the writ of ejectment which evolved at the end of the fifteenth century. The common law courts allowed the leaseholder to recover the land specifically from any wrongful claimant. Once the leaseholder was able to recover land for all comers, it could no longer be denied that he had an estate in land or that he held on tenure. Thus the action of ejectment shifted the basis of title from a feudal to a capitalist concept. It became a proprietal interest and the relationship between landlord and tenant, which had had no place in feudal land law, came to be based on tenure.

Leasehold was not the only form evolving. As McPherson (1975) has shown the whole concept of property needed transformation as the capitalist system developed. The feudal system recognized both common and customary rights. Individuals had the right not to be excluded from uses on or related to land and property in land was generally limited to certain uses. Different people had different rights in the same piece of land and many of these rights, often established by custom, were not fully disposable by the current owner either by sale or by bequest. As Thompson (1976) has shown with his research on inheritance in the eighteenth century, common land gradually became the object of private property rights which were themselves becoming more absolute. As the capitalist market economy developed, limited rights were replaced by the unlimited rights of private property holders to exclude others from some use or benefit. As these rights became unconditional on the performance of social functions and freely transferable, land itself could become a capital asset rather than a means of acquiring regular tributes.

These changes can be seen more specifically in the evolution of freehold and leasehold tenure. Both were evolving to facilitate the new market economy but leasehold held early advantages. As it developed outside the feudal system of production, its personal property status meant that it was immune from feudal burdens and the intricacies of the freehold legal procedures and unlike other land, it could be bequeathed by will (Megarry and Wade, 1975, p. 11). It allowed a greater flexibility and potential for capital development at a time when the freehold tenures were still heavily bound up with feudal shackles.

As Aspinall (1978) has pointed out, the origins of the building lease derive from the use of the lease for a term of years for agricultural or investment purposes. Terms of 50 and 80 years are found in the reigns of Richard II and Edward IV. The practice of developing land for building using this tenure appears to have gained popularity during the fourteenth and fifteenth centuries and from the middle of the sixteenth century onwards building leases were widely used by corporate owners on urban estates in both London and provincial towns. The antecedent of the building lease for urban estate development was the burgage. This was a strip of land held in towns by the burgesses of the medieval boroughs. A fixed annual rent was charged for the use of these plots as a contribution to the borough farm. Prior to the mid fifteenth century the use of the building lease was confined to a few isolated devises for life or short term of years. In the seventeenth century the character of leasehold tenure changed dramatically and was linked to the expansion of cities. Aspinall (1978) points to two feudal constraints on freehold building. The first was the laws of inheritance which involved the custom and practice of primogeniture. This directed that the landed possessions of a person dying intestate should be exclusively the property of the eldest son or the eldest male heir. The second related constraint was the practice of strict settlement. Settlement involves the practice of giving property to particular persons in succession. A series of interests are created by a single gift, whether by deed or will. The object of a strict settlement is to preserve a family estate intact through succeeding generations. Land would be inalienable except through the eldest son who would resettle the estate on his majority. The effect is to give each person a life interest. It protected the accumulation of estates and assured their descent as a whole to a single proprietor. It was not until the mid nineteenth century that the restrictions on alienation were reduced by statute. Corporate owners were similarly restricted by the terms of charitable endowments and foundation charters. These would prohibit alienation through the sale of the fee simple or demise on long leases. Thus both types of owners were obliged to use short leases for development.

The pressures to develop increased during the eighteenth century when the inadequate powers to facilitate building proved more restrictive. Leasing under strict settlements was limited to short terms, 21 years or less, which would not give the lessee adequate security of tenure to induce substantial building. Also the doctrine of waste[1] prohibited limited owners from pulling down and rebuilding houses. So both private and corporate owners resorted to Parliament to obtain legal sanctions to extend terms and avoid waste doctrines. Between 1727 and 1812 there were 2100 Private Acts of Parliament involving settled, entailed and otherwise shackled estates, over 210 of which secured leasing powers. The first 99 year term in London was granted to the Pulteney Estate in 1783. After this 99 years became the standard term in London as well as the provinces.

The use of the building lease boomed in the nineteenth century. But Private Acts of Parliament were cumbersome and above all costly and there was a need for a flexible land policy to facilitate development. Constraints on corporations to grant leases for 99 years were removed by a number of Public and General Acts between 1835 and 1858, so that they were no longer obliged to go through the Local and Private Bill procedure. Private settlements were dealt with under the Settled Estates Acts of 1856 and 1877 which were consolidated into the Settled Land Act 1882, called Lord Cairns Act, which gave the person who controlled the estate for the time being, the tenant for life, wide powers of dealing with the land. These powers included powers of sale, exchange, lease and mortgage. The 99 year lease for building was incorporated into the powers under the Act. Thus the outcome of all this legislation was a great increase in the number of land-owners who could legally grant building leases and a considerable lengthening of terms on many corporate estates. However, by itself this legal history provides an inadequate explanation for the use of the building lease. Freehold tenure was also being freed from its shackles by the same Acts so that by 1882 both corporate bodies and settled estates could have sold outright. The holder of the life interest was given the right to sell subject only to the supervisory powers granted to the trustees of the settlement. Aspinall

(1978, pp. 33-34) considers that the rigidity of the English land ownership system was balanced by a customary practice which was amended to incorporate economic rationality. Profit maximization was not always the immediate rationale. However, he stresses that economic considerations were strong. The absence of short term building leases from most northern towns is probably because land was cheap and thus undermined the cost advantage which leaseholders enjoyed in London and a few towns in the provinces. The northern towns which used the 99 year system all experienced rapid growth in the second half of the nineteenth century. Again this cost advantage depended on the scale of land ownership. The larger the owner, the greater the monopoly, the stronger the incentive to defy or overcome customary practice and maximize profit. So in London and in some provincial towns the structure of ownership allowed direct exploitation of the market. These explanations are not wholly satisfactory. As Daunton (1979) suggests, although concentrated ownership permitted some owners to opt for 99 year leases, it alone does not explain why they took the opportunity. Was it more profitable? Was it a preference for a long term income over the short term gains of outright sale and, if so, why was the choice made? If freehold sales were dominant where land was cheap, does this suggest that the critical factor was the availability of finance for land purchase by builders? I intend to explore these questions more fully by looking at the development of the building lease in Saltley.

The development of suburban areas like Saltley was seen in part as a solution to the late nineteenth century housing crisis which had produced cramped unhealthy slum areas in the city centres and very little purpose built working-class houses. Attempts were made in the major cities to overcome these problems. The way they were tackled and the methods adopted was predicated on the particular social and economic relations of each area.

Like many English cities Birmingham was expanding in the latter part of the nineteenth century. It avoided the worst urban poverty since it was endowed with early drainage and plentiful water, trade success and a population of skilled artisans. Builders could make reasonable profits out of speculative building and were able to exploit the success of building societies for working people at least until the 1870s. Birmingham had slums but not a housing problem to match that of the other industrial cities.

'Small Masters' ran the city's old industries from small workshops often at the back of their houses. Guns, jewellery, leather, buttons and brass products dominated their output, but Birmingham was famous for its 1001 trades, packed tightly with houses in the old city. (C.D.P., 1978, p. 37)

The land in the city was in the hands of a small number of large owners (See Fig. 3).

Vance (1967) maintains that the availability of land in the central area was crucial in the siting of Birmingham's industries since rigid control over the use to which land could be put was available through the leasehold system. The method implies a contractual relationsip between one or a few owners and many tenants, so that the attitudes of the owner towards use could affect the manner of occupation of many. Owners often sought middle-class tenants through the careful exclusion of industrial or commercial activity. Few owners built for the labourer so only downgraded property fell into the occupation of the working class.

It was only when an owner made the decision to develop his land for industrial working class could the gun-smith or brazier hope to move out of the old, often medieval buildings, at the very heart of the city. (Vance, 1967, p. 107)

Land-owners continued to resist conversion of great blocks of urban land for housing of the workers and their industries. Thus, when the gun trade found a site on St Mary's estate in the mid eighteenth century, it became fixed as to location. The jewellery trade also suffered the same restriction on location, first on the Newhall estate and later on the adjacent Vyse estate. Vance (1967, p. 107) argues that

although there is little doubt that process-ties need to be near selling agents (factors), access to raw materials and other manufacturing links provide an explanation of the creation of workshop districts, immuring of the working class by leasehold restrictions tended to give those areas a specific scale.

In the late nineteenth century the physical layout of Birmingham was transformed by the second industrial revolution in two different ways. First, the central areas became even more crowded. Although it was claimed in 1886 that there were gardens right in the centre and that doctors and lawyers lived close in Newall Street and Bennetts Hill (Briggs, 1952), there was much infilling and a proliferation of tiny courts of blind back houses to accommodate the greatly expanded population: it doubled once before 1866 and again between 1866 and 1914. The pattern was of workshop courts: typically, one or two front houses, with "shopping" and up to six tenements in the court behind. These developments probably represented investment by people with small capitals. When the inner suburbs of Newtown, Ladywood, Duddeston, Nechells, Lozells and Highgate were built in the 1860s and 1870s this traditional layout of workshop courts was preserved. Conditions were cramped and squalid. Like other cities, the slum areas were physically isolated. In Birmingham the Western side was inhabited by the middle class. Industrialists lived in Edgbaston, just one mile from the centre. The working-class areas on the East caused the authorities to worry but, unlike London, the social problem never took on a central political significance (see Stedman Jones 1976, pp. 150-230). Secondly, many new industries were built on the outskirts of Birmingham serviced by the railways.

> Late 19th century expansion was not a proliferation of this same pattern. Instead great works were built in the suburbs, on the greenfield sites near railways, and each employed hundreds, even thousands of workers. 'Small Masters' were gradually displaced by the factory system. (C.D.P. 1978, 37)

So the old trades were losing their predominance but they were also mechanizing their production in line with the large factory production which was taking their place. Conglomerates like G.K.N. and B.S.A. were established next to the new purpose-built houses for the working classes on greenfield sites outside the city centre. The economic transformation was reflected in the social structure. The old trades had linked small owners to their employees. Many tradespeople had been skilled artisans themselves. The large combines developed a different set of social relations. The working class was divided into two groupings: the skilled workers engaged in making and adjusting tools and the semi-skilled machines operatives. The Birmingham Trades Council, established in 1886, represented the skilled groups like the Cordwainers and Mill Sawyers. These artisans, because they earned good wages, were likely to own their own houses. The City Council, on the other hand, was controlled by the new business men: Chamberlain, himself a prominent local business man, and his Liberals took control of the Council in the late 1870s. By then big business men were a significant proportion of the Council.

> Big business continued to make up a fifth of the Council in the 1880s and 1890s while the group of small business men contracted

to 15% in 1896. At the same time, the professional group grew steadily larger until it was almost as large as the big business group in 1896. Hennock (1969 : 197) states that "it is plain that the years since the late 1870s to the creation of Greater Birmingham in 1911 formed a single period as far as the social composition of the Council is concerned." The Council during this period was dominated by a combination of big businessmen and professional men. (Morris and Newton, 1970, 113)

On the eve of the First World War the Council consisted of 42 manufacturers, 5 merchants, 14 lawyers, 13 other professional men, 15 retailers, 10 working men, 5 builders, 2 farmers and 12 others of miscellaneous occupations. (Briggs, 1952, p. 129)

The housing problem existed in Birmingham as elsewhere and pressure on the overcrowded inner area was increased by demolition. The railway companies carved their way through when building the two stations of Snow Hill and New Street. Warehousing and commercial development had their toll as well. When the Colmore leases in the city centre fell in the area was redeveloped for commercial use. The greatest source of displacement was the City Council itself. Under Chamberlain's Improvement Scheme (which was made possible by the passing of the Artisan's Dwelling Act 1875) 93 acres of central land were purchased to create the new city centre. This involved leasing the plots to private enterprise to develop. Not surprisingly, since houses were not a profitable proposition, the development was of a commercial nature.

The activities of the Council in developing the centre were criticized because it did not provide accommodation. In response, the Council tried a number of experimental schemes. They built 22 two storey cottages in Ryder Street in 1890 and 82 similar houses in Lawrence Street in 1891. They cost £182 and £172 respectively to build and were let at 27½p and 25p each. This rent was far too high for those displaced by improvement. In 1884, 27 000 houses were let at 17½p per week or less. No further attempts were made at this type of solution. But the housing problem remained. The Milk Street development was the next attempt by the Improvement Committee to find a solution. The development here was carried out by private enterprise under lease from the Council. Rents again were high.

Birmingham had its own "Bitter Cry of Outcast London" in the form of two pamphlets, "The Housing of the Poor" published by J.A. Fallows, a local socialist councillor from Bordesley, in 1899, and "Scenes in Slumland'' by J.C. Walters (see Mearns, 1883; Stedman Jones, 1976). Their effect was to act as a catalyst to the Council.

In 1901 the Housing Committee was set up under the chairmanship of Nettlefold. Its policy was always to refuse to recommend a large-scale programme of municipal building because this would cramp private enterprise. This remained its policy until 1914 when a Special Housing Committee reported with a similar line that council building was not as cheap as private. Hopes were pinned instead on private building in the suburbs backed up by cheap transport and repairs to the central area. By 1913, 28 265 houses had been repaired but the housing problem remained. In 1914 there were over 200 000 people living in 43 366 back-to-back houses (Briggs, 1952).

The second type of scheme to improve working-class conditions was the plan to erect model dwellings. A company was formed in 1848 with a capital of £6000 to erect model lodging houses. Nothing happened. A further attempt was made in 1883 with the setting up of the Artisans Dwelling Company. Like all new buildings they were obliged to comply with the by-laws introduced in 1876 which fixed minimum standards of construction and appointed a building surveyor to approve plans and give permission to build. Their aim was:

> to purchase plots of land in healthy localities... easily accessible from the centre of the town and to build thirteen cottages and dwellings suitable for working men, which can be let at rentals varying from 15p to 25p per week, and upwards. (Prospectus, 1883)

and to provide a cottage with a small garden and a pigstye [sic] for 25p. The model dwellings movement, however, did not become a significant factor in alleviating the problem.

More significant was the Freehold Land Society set up by James Taylor. The movement developed in the 1860s and was backed by leading Liberal M.P.s. The aim was to buy up land and to sell off plots for development. The problem, caused by the earliest owners who built in an irregular reckless manner, was checked by regulations on the building line. The conditions included various stipulations: that the minimum price for each site should be not less than £130; that no trade or business was carried on and that front gardens be provided. The society claimed in 1871 to ''have created a great love for freeholds'', and Chapman and Bartlett claim that: (1971, p. 243)

> It is impossible to resist the conclusion that the Birmingham

Freehold Land Society which was born and grew rapidly as a radical democratic organisation in the early 1850's, was quickly taken over by an artisan elite and small manufacturers.

and that by 1867 it was a sedate middle-class movement. The type of housing, however, was not dissimilar to that provided by land-owners under their leasehold developments on the greenfield sites for the employees of the new factories. Because the conditions for building were similar and the controls as strong, the houses in Saltley provided by Lord Norton are barely distinguishable from these houses.

Most of the virgin suburban lands in late nineteenth century Birmingham were owned by big land-owners (as the map in Fig. 3 shows) who gained substantially from the huge expansion of industry. Saltley was owned by two families — the Huttons, descendants of William Hutton the Birmingham historian who had moved there in the late eighteenth century, and the Nortons who, by marriage, had owned the land since the Norman conquest. Charles Bowyer Adderley later to become Lord Norton (1814-1905) was described by his biographer William Childe-Pemberton as a statesman and philanthropist: "Always a conservative he was at heart a Reformer in the literal and best sense of the word — an 'improver'" (Pemberton, 1909, p. 1). He sat in Parliament for 64 years, 37 of those in the House of Commons. He was keen on colonial matters, particularly New Zealand, penal legislation and juvenile offences. He was also made president of the Board of Trade in 1874. Norton describes his property, which he inherited at 23 from his uncle, as follows:

> Hams a charming country house in central England, (15 miles from Birmingham) Saltley a suburban town property, adjoining such a busy place as Birmingham; Norton, a colliery and mining district; with another sort of manufacturing town near at Uppingham; then Peterborough (a small property near), a fen district, requiring much draining and engineering. (quoted in Pemberton, 1909, pp. 27-28)

He also continued:

> I formed not to seek to enlarge the property but to get all I had into good order, that when I died it might show good stewardship, materially as well as morally, and that I might leave my vineyard better than I found it. (quoted in Pemberton, 1909, p. 28)

His biographer considered that:

> he found himself in possession of an ample income of which,

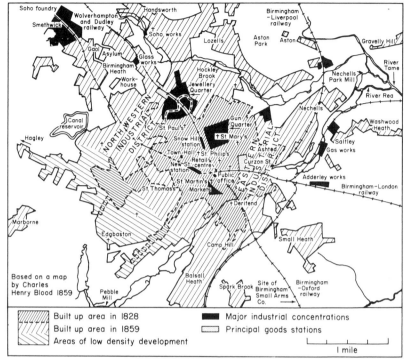

Taken from Wise and Thorpe (1970).

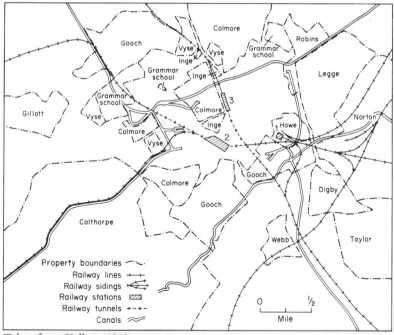

Taken from Kellett (1969).

Fig. 3. Urbanization of nineteenth century Birmingham.

however, he felt he was but the steward to spend in accordance with his sense of duty and for the public good. (Pemberton, 1909, p. 4)

He started his good stewardship early. In 1837 Sir Robert Peel, the Prime Minister, told Sir Charles that the part of his estate in Saltley "ought to be worth all the rest so near a town, most certain of sustained prosperity as central and depending on a variety of trades". Peel also "wrote to Lord Lincoln Commissioner of Woods and Forests to send the best men down to lay out Saltley for building". The residential part of the estate, which was laid out according to this plan so that "it should never become a slum", was not developed substantially until 1880

> The development of Saltley went through four overlapping stages. First came the railways, then the factories which depended on them. Third, the State intervened to organise the basic infrastructure of the area, its sewerage and drainage, its electricity and gas and its roads.

> Finally, houses were built for labourers and artisans employed in the local works and on the railways. The railways forced their way into Saltley by Acts of Parliament. In 1838 the first London-Birmingham Railway cut Adderley's 415 acre estate in half and defined Saltey's southern boundary. Four years later the Midland Railway Company's line from Birmingham to Derby circled the northern and western fringes of Saltley along the Tame Valley. (C.D.P., 1978, p. 37)

But it is clear that from 1840 onwards that Norton orchestrated the next stages in Saltley's development. By a Private Act of Parliament in 1840 he organized the family settlement to facilitate the sale of land for industry and services in the lowland areas to the railways and the leasing of the rest for house building.

Wright set up a railway carriage works in Saltley in 1845. By 1890, three of the five independent railway carriage manufacturers in Britiain had their factories in Saltley and most of Birmingham's gas was made there. In the next 20 years, Saltley's population increased ten-fold to 40 000. Norton sold the freehold of roughly half the Saltley Estate.

> The railway companies bought land for sidings: the London and North Western Railway paid £1687 for two acres in 1864, £1200 for another acre in 1873, and £2973 for 1.5 acres in 1878; the Midland Railway company bought 10 acres in 1876 for £5271.17.6d. Then local firms expanded — for example Wright's old firm, now the Metropolitan Carriage and Wagon company,

paid £16,300 for 62 acres of poor, sloping land which constitute the firm's present site. Finally the State bought in, paying for example £2314 in 1873 for seven acres of land on which to construct drainage works, and £6000 in 1906 for four acres on which to construct a postal depot. (C.D.P., 1978, p. 40)

Suburban development of this kind transformed not just the industrial but also the residential structure of great British cities. In the second half of the nineteenth century a clear division developed between the production of middle-class housing and purpose-built houses for the new industrial working classes. Then there was a further division between the earlier working-class houses of minimal standards built in and around the existing central city areas, and the later by-law houses built in the suburbs. By the 1870s builders began to concentrate on this second, more substantial house type, to provide accommodation for skilled artisans and clerks whose regular employment, high wages and shorter hours of work allowed them to live on cheaper land outside the town centres.

Saltley was one of these new working-class suburbs. Few houses were built before 1870, and most of the workers on its railways and in its factories lived nearer the city in the wretched houses in Vauxhall, Nechells and Duddeston. But 4000 houses

> were built in the great boom period from 1889-1906. The peak in the area, 1897-1899, coincided with the peak in the national building cycle, and the tail-off in Saltley ward reflected both the national trend and the completion of Norton's development plans. 90 per cent of the houses were three up, three down, with substantial back gardens. The earlier ones, before 1880, fronted on to the streets, the latter ones built before 1900, were more substantial, with bigger rooms and small front gardens. In the final phase, the houses were the most substantial of all. (C.D.P., 1978, p. 40)

Stedman Jones (1970) describes how in central London, middle-class houses were gradually transformed into tenements or rookeries for the working classes. Overcrowding went hand in hand with a deteriorating physical fabric. The pattern was similar in central Birmingham. Then new by-law suburban areas in both cities (for example Camberwell as described by Dyos (1961), Aston, Small Heath, Sparkhill and Saltley in Birmingham) constituted a break with this process of filtering down. The industrialists of Birmingham City Council saw their development as part of a concept of filtering up. Better houses were built on the outskirts so allowing the 'better' workers to move out of the central districts so alleviating their overcrowding and squalor.

The production of houses in the eighteenth and nineteenth centuries was carried out almost entirely by speculative building. The options available to the land-owner when he uses the lease system are: first, he can turn builder and employ his own labour to work under his orders; secondly, he can engage a builder under a contract to perform the whole of the task for him; thirdly, he can decide, while keeping as tight a control as he wishes over the nature of development, to lease land to the individual firm or building association who could either do all the work or sub-contract to others, or do part of it and then assign all the interests in the property to someone else (Dyos, 1961). The last option involved contracts based upon a building agreement between the land-owner and contractor for the granting of leases for completed houses at a certain house rent or for an overall ground rent. This method allowed the builder to create a leasehold (or improved) ground rent which he or the assigns received from the occupiers of the house. In the Georgian era the landlord and speculative builder usually chose the second option whereby the land-owner agreed a lump sum with the master builder for the whole structure. It involved subcontracting but seemed to work satisfactorily for the large houses built for wealthy individuals. Most nineteenth century land-owners used the third option which involved the use of the building agreement. There, although the contractor was legally responsible for building all the houses in the building lease agreement, he usually disposed of some of the plots to smaller builders who worked under his supervision:

> One builder takes three properties and lays out his main roads. He cuts the land up. Although the land is ready for building, if he were to build upon it all at once he would create such a supply that it would be beyond the demand, therefore, he, having eventually got the profit rent to look to, waits and gets a smaller builder, a man of his own class, but a smaller man to take a portion of this land of which he has got the whole. Then that man in his turn lets to some one else, or perhaps to a number of small builders, who are able to build two, three or four houses and who could not be trusted with the land to build more. They would come to grief before they had finished and so in that way four or five interests are carried out before you get to the actual occupier. (Town Holdings, 1888, p. 304)

These interests quickly become complex, especially when, in addition, mortgagees became property holders by default. This method involved the possibility of obtaining an improved ground rent which is the difference between the rent stipulated in the building agreement and the rent which the rent contractor could obtain for the site.

> General mode of dealing with building land... is for the freeholder to let in a large block to a well-to-do builder... and to let it at such a rent as will give the builder about one third of the ground rents as profit to himself.... . That may be done, and is done in various ways. For instance, a builder himself may take up a lease to £60 a year ground rent for a large house, or any number of houses you like and may grant an under lease to some one else at £90 ground rent. (Town Holdings, 1886, pp. 303-304)

The improved ground rent was a way of bailing out a builder if he was in trouble, for they were bought up by the land-owner. Thus, the land-owner was giving a loan whose principal would never be rapaid; instead a percentage was added to ground rent which he was to receive.

The class relations of housing production in Saltley involve the land-owner, who is the lessor, the lessee, who is the person responsible for building, the financier, the rentier and the occupant (See Fig. 4).

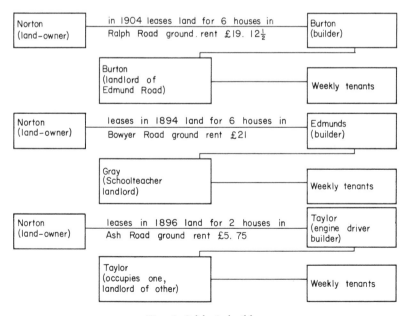

Fig. 4. Saltley's builders.

Virtually all Norton's leases were of blocks big enough to build from 2 to 12 houses. The lessees were not all builders; they fell into the three categories identified by Aspinall (1978, p. 33). First the biggest category was the speculative builders who actually built the houses either for sale to landlords or to become landlords themselves. The sale would either be by means of underlease creating a ground rent improvement or by assignment which transferred the whole interest. The latter was more common in Saltley. Second were speculative developers who were specialists in the entrepreneurial side of housing creation and not necessarily house builders. Herrick and Teall in the northern part of Saltley are examples. They took on the head leases of substantial blocks, 10 000 acres, and parcelled out smaller blocks to builders taking an improved ground rent in the process. The third category which the lessees fell into is the small-scale investor whose contribution to the building process was isolated and short lived. Unlike the specialist these people would limit their activities to one enterprise. Norton did not seem concerned about the type of lessee as long as the terms of the contract were carried out.

The leases were for 99 years and contained a number of conditions; first an obligation to pay a ground rent. Usually this was fixed at a peppercorn for the building period. After this it worked out at between £1.00 for the poorer houses and £3.00 for the biggest, the equivalent of £37.50 and £75 per plot if capitalized at 4%. The lease then stipulated the amount to be expended on building each house, which ranged between £175 and £200 per house, and the time allowed for their construction which was usually not more than 2 years for the larger blocks. The lease also included covenants which prevented the building of back houses with less than £12 rental yearly. Although none were built on the Norton estate many were built in courts on Henry Wright's neighbouring estate. The repairing covenants were also numerous and strict, extracts from these are given below:

> On 29 September 1894 Lord Norton granted a building lease to T.E. Edmunds on a plot of land in Bowyer Road. The lease included the following terms:
>
> to have and to hold the said piece of land with the appurtenances and assigns from the day of the date hereof for the term of 99 years to be computed from the 29th day of September 1894.
>
> *yielding and paying* therefor until the 24th day of June 1895 the rent of a peppercorn if demanded and thereafter

yielding and paying yearly and every year during the said term the rent or sum of £16.10s. [£16.50]

And also that the lessee, his executors, administers or assigns shall and will at his and their own costs and charges within the space of 12 calendar months now next ensuing erect and build upon the said piece of land hereby demised six and not more than 6 good and substantial messuages or dwelling houses fronting to Bowyer Road aforesaid according to a plan, elevation and specification to be approved of in writing by the surveyor for the time being of the lessor .... And shall and will pay out and expend in the erection of each of such dwelling houses the sum of £180 at the least.

At all times during this demise at his own expense as often as need shall require to effectively repair and keep in good substantial order and repair the property hereby demised and all fences there to belonging and cleanse all the sinks, gutters, culverts, drains, sewers and privies belonging to the said premises and the said messuage or dwelling-house and all other buildings erected on the said land in such good repair and condition and the sinks, gutters, culverts, drains, sewers and privies so cleansed and in such good repair shall and will at the expiration or other sooner determination of this demise peaceably leave and yield up unto the vendors or their assigns.

Not to use the premises hereby demised or any part thereof for the making of brass or as a tavern, public house or alehouse or otherwise for the sale of beer or other intoxicating drinks either under the Grocers license or otherwise or for a manufactory for the making of oil or vitriol or aquafortis or for the purpose of carrying on the trade of a soap boiler, catgul, spinner, tallow, chandler or tallow melter nor use exercise or carry on or permit to be used, exercised or carried on thereupon any trade or business which may be noxious, offensive, noisy or a nuisance to the tenants or occupiers of any messages lands or tenements adjoining or near to the said demised premises.

Though builders formally leased parcels of land large enough to build only a few houses, many were next to each other, so some builders built whole streets. For example, James Young built all of Hams Road in 1906 and much of nearby Ash Road. John Dowse built Reginald Road and nearby Jersey Road all to a standard pattern. Other builders erected only a few houses. In all, around forty different firms were involved, the majority locally based in Saltley itself or nearby Washwood Heath and Small Heath. This local connection had advantages: it was easier to organize a building site if it was close to the builders' yard and near his other jobs. The bricks came from local works, the Adderley Park Brick Company, the Globe Brick and Tile Company and the Parkfield Brick Company. All were controlled by Lord Norton and he extracted royalties on their brick production. Such was the advantage of a big land-owner. Transport costs for bringing in bricks from other works made the local product competitive even with royalties. For instance Norton leased land for brickmaking to the Adderley Park Brick Company Ltd in 1881 for 16 years for a ground rent of £92.15 for about 29 acres. He also levied a royalty of 12½p for every 1000 bricks made with a minimum of £93.75 per quarter annum. The other conditions were also strict. The company was obliged to fence the areas, not remove plant and machinery without consent, not remove clay and sand, keep the plant in good repair, make 3 million bricks a year, keep accounts open for inspection, give quarterly accounts to Norton and so on. In fact all the local companies paid more than the minimum royalty. In 1905 as a result of a total valuation of the estate for death duty purposes the average royalties between 1900 and 1905 were as follows: Adderley £360 per annum (300 minimum); Globe £273 per annum (250 minimum); Parkfield £148 per annum (125 minimum). Their capital value was estimated to be £12 160.10.

> The building business was extremely precarious.
> Houses were built speculatively on money borrowed through solicitors. John Dowse, for example borrowed from a solicitor, Henry Huggins and from Birmingham Incorporated Building Society. William Hougham built some of St. Saviours Road using money from the Birmingham Incorporated Building Society and from individuals: Edward Stringer JP who lived in wealthy Edgbaston lent £350 at five per cent in 1890. Charles Burton who built in Edmund Road borrowed £900 at four per cent in 1904 from a syndicate consisting of a Birmingham spinster, a gentleman and a solicitor. This money was to be tied up in labour and materials until the terrace of houses was ready for sale. It is clear that the builders did not keep the covenants of the lease and spent only as much as they could on the erection of the house, since the sale price to the first landlord was invariably lower than the amount specified by the landowner. (C.D.P., 1978, p. 40)

Sometimes the lessees did not succeed in building at all. For instance the Midland Land and Investment Corporation Ltd took two leases from Norton in Arden Road on 7th and 8th November 1877. The first involved 2576 sq. yds and a ground rent of £20, and the second involved 2637 sq. yds and a ground rent of £20.58. Both contained convenants to spend £3600 on the construction of 24 houses with an annual value of £15 each. The work was to be completed in 2 years. On 20th June 1883 the liquidators of the company assigned the leases to John Jelf described as a gentleman but in fact a solicitor. On the same day he made an agreement with Norton to reduce the number of houses from 24 to 12 on each lease and to extend the time limit to 9 years. In July 1888 Jelf himself was declared bankrupt. On the 17th July his trustee in bankruptcy, Walter Norton Fisher, and his mortgagee Annie Wilson Taylor, a spinster from Penzance, surrendered the land to Norton.

Another saga concerns the fate of Saltley Hall and its surrounding acres. The Hall stood near Park Road overlooking the new Adderley Park which was donated to the City of Birmingham in 1856. (Park Road was later renamed Ash Road.) On the 14th September 1861, C.B. Adderley agreed a lease for 99 years at a ground rent of £40.33 with Philip Fabian Briody described as a foreign merchant. The lease involved 4840 sq.yds. and the agreement was to build several good and substantial dwelling houses within 3 years expending £1000 at least on the venture. The covenants were of the usual strict nature and added further details about the type and elevation required for the houses. Four years later Briody needed money so he mortgaged the land to the Birmingham Benefit Building Society No. 4 on the 6th September for £400.50. The five trustees in 1865 consisted of a boot maker, a brush maker, a jeweller, a builder and a gentleman. A grocer and a house agent replaced two earlier trustees a little later. In February of the following year he further charged the land for £65.25 to the same building society. On the 28th August 1866 he assigned the equity of redemption (his portion left after the mortgagees had been satisfied) to Thomas Robert Smith, a Birmingham manufacturer. Smith must have reassigned to Briody sometime between 1866 and 1872 since Briody was declared to be in default of the mortgages and an unsuccessful attempt was made to sell the land, the Hall and, by this time, two houses, by auction. On the 1st July 1874 the building society rid itself of the property to Edward Charlwood, a grocer and druggist, from the neighbouring area of Ward End, in return for £360; John Jelf the Arden Road lessee was the witness to the transaction. Charlwood immediately mortgaged his purchase back to the building society for £360 and interest. Three years later he died and his wife Ann Charlwood took over. She paid off the mortgage on 7th June 1879 but remortgaged it on the 9th June to the Birmingham Benefit Building Society No. 1 (whose trustees were a taxidermist, a chandler maker and a gentleman) for £218.15.0. In 1880 Briody reappears, he purchases the property off Ann Charlwood for £200 but he obtains a mortgage from her for £150 at 5% interest rate. Part of the deal obliged Briody to pay off Ann Charlwood's mortgage to the building society. In 1883 Briody had paid off most of the money owing to Ann and so she surrendered the property to him. On 21st April 1890 the Birmingham Benefit Building Society No. 1 declared itself paid off also. On the 12th May 1890 Briody surrendered the lease to Adderley paying Adderley £50 to do so. Only two houses had been built. Thus financing and building was a very precarious business even under Adderley's careful control.

Once the houses were complete the builder either assigned his leasehold interest direct to the landlord or he created an underlease for an improved ground rent.

> [There] were no big landlords in Saltley. Some owned more than 50 houses, generally of the poorer sort but the majority took over one or two blocks from a builder. In the better roads with bigger houses, ownership was even more fragmented. Often a railway driver or clerk would own his own house and the house next door, or the other two or three in the block. Top drivers on the local Midland Railway, the labour artistocracy, were paid around £2.10s a week with overtime in 1904 when Ellesmere Road was built. From the beginning one fifth of the houses in the better roads like this were owner-occupied by railway drivers or clerks. The majority of poorer roads were, however, completely rented. In the area as a whole, there were more than several hundred landlords. Generally, they were the traditional petit-bourgeoisie, divided into professionals (schoolmaster, pawnbroker, architect), traders (grocer, dryslater, and especially builder) and manufacturers, not the big local factory owners, but brass-founders and coach-iron manufacturers from the central areas of the city. The three groups were evenly split with wives or spinsters owning about one third of the houses (C.D.P., 1978, pp. 40-41)

> Saltley . . . was considered a solution to the problem of housing the skilled working class. Its byelaw houses were built primarily for skilled artisans and a smattering of clerks, teachers and shopkeepers. It was possible to house them decently because of the general rise in wage levels between 1850-1900 and the emergence of a labour aristocracy in the 'great works' in Saltley. They could afford the minimum rent of 6s 9d which according to H.M. Grant & Co. one of the biggest Birmingham builders, would cover the cost of a house containing "two living rooms, scullery, out-offices and three

bedrooms''. The relation between wage levels and rent was more
explicit then than it is now. The majority of unskilled workers were
poorly paid, earning between 20s and 25s a week. They lived in
back-to-back houses in the older slum areas nearer the city centre
with rents of between 4s and 5s a week. Even in Saltley the pressure
was on rents: so finely balanced was the equation that death or
redundancy forced householders out or to take in lodgers.
Alderman Williams, a member of the Housing Committee,
questioned the city Medical Officer of Health in 1914: the
conditions in Saltley are rather different (from the low rent areas in
the city centre). The houses put up there, where overcrowding
takes place, are houses at 6s or 7s, and it is in consequence of the
poverty of the people that they are bound close together. (C.D.P.,
1978, p. 41)

Thus by the end of the nineteenth century the building lease had
become a relatively sophisticated mechanism which facilitated the
building process. It was used to organize the elements of production.
Land-owners were able to exploit their land and yet retain an interest in
it. They were able potentially to reap a high reversionary value by setting
a high standard of building, providing a sound infrastructure and strict
management of the site. They were also able to collect a steady income by
this management since they could sustain building in a falling market and
organize the release of the commodities to prevent swamping. The
builder was attracted to the site because he was not obliged to finance the
purchase of the plot nor its infrastructure. He was further assisted by the
concession on the first year's ground rent. Finance for building was not
abundant. Rates of interest seem to have been higher for leasehold
finance than for freehold so the less needed the better. The builder was
interested in building houses which a landlord could let at a profit rent.
He was not necessarily interested in small houses although he would be
more interested in density. The Norton and Hutton estates were
spaciously laid out but there is no evidence of lack of take up by
landlords. The financiers were persons with limited capital rather than
the large institutions which existed but were not predominate. Landlords
wanted houses they could rent profitably. They would not be concerned
that the houses were leasehold since the leases were new and the effect of
the strict repairing covenants would be minimal. The houses provided
one type of tenant with reasonable shelter free of the squalid unhealthy
conditions existing in the inner core areas.
    Although it seems that the use of the building lease minimized the

difficulties of production this statement alone says little of the balance of class forces involved and the effect that this social relation would have on the economic cost of housing. If monopoly land-owners chose to use the building lease in order to maximize their return, then this high tribute would be reflected in the cost of the commodity produced. In theoretical terms they might be able to extract absolute rent. This type of rent, as distinct from differential rent, increases the cost of the commodity produced, and thus is an anathema to industrial capital (see Bruegal, 1975, pp. 34-46; Ball, 1976). Houses in Saltley would therefore be more costly to purchase than similar freehold houses elsewhere, or builders would be obliged to absorb the cost and would be unable to produce. If, however, land-owners had no choice because of either legal or economic constraints then the commodity produced is not likely to be more expensive. It is clear not only that settlements and primogeniture did restrict some land-owners but also that the financial structure of house production in the late nineteenth century was precarious. A land-owner, if he desired to exploit his land ownership through development he would be obliged to minimize these structural problems in order to obtain a relatively high return on his investment. The evidence from Saltley might support two very different interpretations of the land-owner's position: either that they had little choice but to use this system, or that their strength allowed them to use the lease as a way of extracting a damaging tribute. Politically, as the next section shows, land-owners were attacked for their ownership and activities. Leaseholding land-owners were particularly singled out for attack, yet there seems little evidence to suggest that leasehold houses were any more costly than their freehold equivalents. Why then the attack? Although payment to the land-owners generally pushes up the cost of housing, the leasehold relation makes land-owners identifiable as a social relation. Ground rent, which represents rent in its pure form, exposes explicitly the cost of the monopoly of land. Freehold land costs are absorbed into the total cost of housing and merely form a part of that payment called rent which includes the ground rent element. There is no direct social relation. Therefore, it is argued that the particular political attack on leasehold owners was on a class relation as a social relation rather than an economic relation which was generated by exploitation of monopoly strength.

Was Norton obliged to use the building lease system because he was shackled by primogeniture and an entailed settlement? The Norton family structure is relatively simple (See Fig. 5).

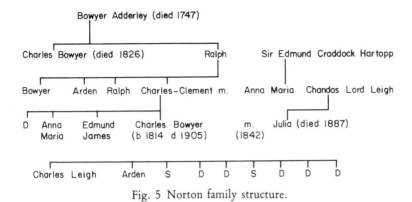

Fig. 5 Norton family structure.

Charles Bowyer Adderley, the developer, inherited his property from his great uncle Charles Bowyer Adderley. Charles Bowyer the elder, although married, did not have any children alive on his death in 1826. Ralph, Charles' brother, was dead; so was Ralph's son, Charles Clement, the younger Charles Bowyer's father. He had died whilst his two sons and two daughters were young children. The family settlement inherited from Bowyer Adderley was tail male: the eldest son succeeded to the estate as a tenant for life; after him his eldest son took the estate. If there was default on this line then the devisee's second eldest son succeeded and after him his eldest son and so on. If all else failed then the daughters of the sons of the original devisee inherited. If even that failed then the devisee's daughters succeeded. The Norton entail male thus bypassed Charles Bowyer, the younger's uncles Bowyer, Arden and Ralph.

Charles Bowyer the elder, on inheriting the property in 1747, obtained a Private Act of Parliament in 1788 to enable him and future tenants for life to grant building and repairing leases of over 21 and up to 99 years duration. Charles Bowyer inherited the estate under the will of his great uncle when he attained his majority in 1838. The family home at Hams Hall and certain other properties were not settled but the land in Birmingham including Saltley, the land in Warwickshire and Staffordshire including the mines, in Northampton and elsewhere were settled in tail male. Uncle Arden and the Reverends William Spooner and William Palmer were entrusted to sell lands and pay debts and expenses. The settled estate was entrusted to the same trio with Uncles Ralph and Bowyer as executors to hold for Charles Bowyer as tenant for life. The rest was inherited direct by Charles Bowyer. Thus he could sell or do what he liked with some land but he could not alienate the other because of the tail male settlement. His relationship with his uncles seems to have been difficult:

> I had troublesome questions about my Staffordshire colliery with Ralph Adderley the executor of my great uncles will. (quoted by Pemberton, 1909, p. 27)

> The three Adderley uncles were all out of my line. It would be unfair to say that all wanted to make something *out of* me rather than *of* me, as they were all friendly and amusing. Arden, the Admiral, was most companionable afterwards to my brothers; and the cleric Bowyer left his pretty place Fillongley, at his death . . . to my second son Arden. (quoted by Pemberton, 1909, p. 27)

If this arrangement had prevailed Norton would have had no choice until 1882 but to grant leases on his Saltley estate but he altered matters early by obtaining a Private Act of Parliament in 1840. This basically switched the settlement from the outlying estates including Saltley on to Hams and others. Thus the unsettled estate valued in 1840 at £120 694 with an annual rent of £3232 became settled. The settled estate valued at £107 801 with an annual rent of £3124.90 was freed from settlement. The Saltley estate was valued at £1004 for 415 acres of primarily farm land. A smaller number of outlying and scattered estates were entrusted to Arden and the reverends to sell off and invest the proceeds in the Bank of England. The money was to be invested in Exchequer Bills temporarily until suitable real estate could be purchased near the other lands. These lands were in fact sold off gradually over a number of years.

In 1840 Saltley was in the hands of Norton to do as he pleased but in 1842 he married Julia Anna Eliza, daughter of Chandos, Lord Leigh of Stoneleigh, which is in Warwickshire some 20 miles from Birmingham. They entered into a marriage settlement. ''In consideration of marriage and settlement on the part of Chandos'' Norton agreed to provide jointure and portions:

> [his] wife would be given a jointure (an annuity during widowhood) in case he should pre-decease her; and [his] younger children, who would not take under the entail, would be given portions [lump sums of money to assist them in their careers and in matrimony]. Jointure and portions would therefore be money payments charged upon the land; the jointure was a rentcharge payable generally out of rents and profits; portions were capital sums which were usually directed to be raised by a mortgage of the

land, so that the mortgage interest was a further charge upon the income of the family property. (Mergarry and Wade, 1966, p. 288)

This involved a sum of £1500 per annum for Julia and £20 000 for any younger children. At the same time Norton granted a mortgage of £5555 to the portion and jointure trustees and Thomas Paine, a solicitor. Land for the first purpose was transferred to the jointure trustees to hold for 100 years. These were his friend and brother-in-law Forster Alleyne McGeachy, his close friend Thomas Dyke Acland and a barrister James Buller East. Land for the second purpose was conveyed to the portion trustees to hold for 500 years. These were a barrister John Robert Kenyon and Julia's brother William Henry Lord Leigh. This settlement in July 1842 was secured on land in Saltley covering most of the eastern side and on Norton the coal area. One can speculate whether Norton had much choice or whether Lord Leigh picked the potentially most promising security. It was possible under the terms of the indenture to secure the settlement on other property, notably stock, but it required the consent of the trustees. Norton did sell some land covered by the settlement in 1852 but he replaced it with new land in Saltley bought from Robert Couchman (see Fig. 6).

Norton and Julia had nine children, four sons and five daughters. Their future wealth caused Norton considerable thought. In 1860 he sought the aid of his solicitors, Paine and company, to devise a scheme to secure the property in their favour. Paine summarizes the position as follows. Hams and the other settled estate was secured for the eldest son as tenant in tail, Saltley and Norton were charged on his marriage with Julia's jointure of £1500 per annum and the portions for the younger children of £20 000 and subject to a mortgage for £5555 to the trustees of the marriage settlement. This left the Uppingham and Peterborough estates. The problem was that, although Julia obtained the rent charge income and the interest on the mortgage, and Charles Leigh the estates, the younger sons and daughters only obtained the return on £2500 which provided an income of roughly £100 per annum. Paine proposed that the Uppingham and Peterborough estates should be devised to the second son, that a younger son should go into the church and obtain the living at Norton in the Moors and that the other children should obtain £300 a year. The solution was to ensure Norton's life for £10 000 and put a further charge by will on the Saltley and Norton estates of £20 000 which would only be raisable after Julia's death. Paine considered that the

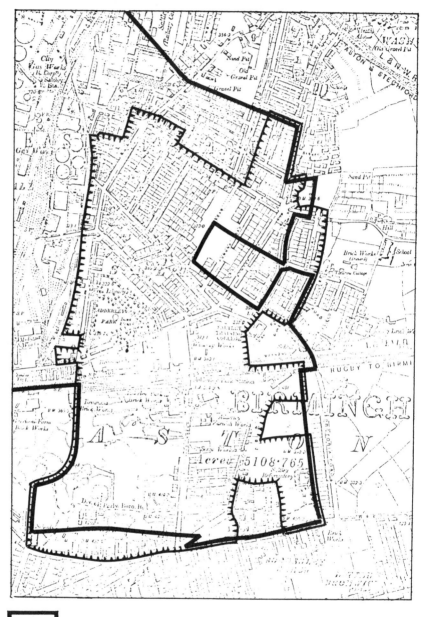

BOUNDARIES OF THE NORTON ESTATE IN 1840

BOUNDARIES OF THE NORTON ESTATE IN 1908

Fig. 6(a). The development of Saltley.

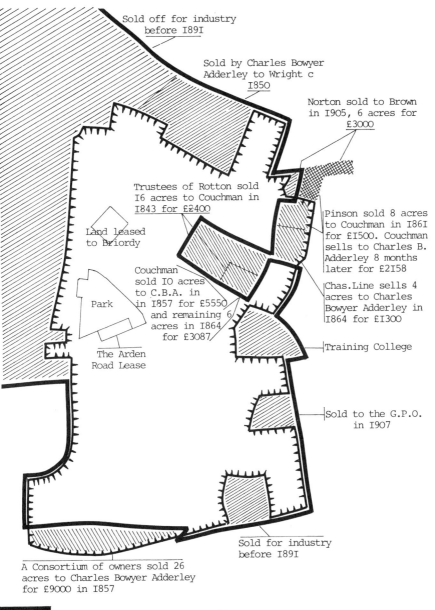

Sold off for industry
before 1891

Sold by Charles Bowyer
Adderley to Wright c
1850

Norton sold to Brown
in 1905, 6 acres for
£3000

Trustees of Rotton sold
16 acres to Couchman in
1843 for £2400

Land leased
to Priordy

Pinson sold 8 acres
to Couchman in 1861
for £1500. Couchman
sells to Charles B.
Adderley 8 months
later for £2158

Couchman
sold 10 acres
to C.B.A. in
in 1857 for £5550
and remaining 6
acres in 1864
for £3087

Park

Chas.Line sells 4
acres to Charles
Bowyer Adderley in
1864 for £1300

The Arden
Road Lease

Training College

Sold to the G.P.O.
in 1907

Sold for industry
before 1891

A Consortium of owners sold 26
acres to Charles Bowyer Adderley
for £9000 in 1857

☐ BOUNDARIES OF THE ESTATE IN 1840

BOUNDARIES OF THE ESTATE IN 1908

Fig. 6(b). Changes in the Saltley estate 1840 to 1908.

Saltley and Norton estates could easily bear this further charge and that the premiums could be paid through income invested in consolidated stock.

These plans were, as far as can be told, carried out by Norton. In 1869 he resettled the land with his eldest son Charles Leigh. The reasons behind this action are described by Megarry and Wade:

> The effect of the original settlement was to render land substantially inalienable until the eldest son became able to bar the entail on attaining his majority. But even then he could create no more than a base fee without the consent of his father, if still alive; and by that time his father would, in his turn, probably regard himself as in duty bound to preserve the property for the sake of yet more distant generations. What often happened was that the son, when he came of age, felt the need of ready money and wished to bar the entail and sell or mortgage his estate in remainder. But his father, instead of consenting to this, would agree to give him some immediate share (perhaps an annual income) in the property if he would join in a resettlement. Father and son would then in collaboration bar the entail, but resettle the property, subject to any outstanding jointure and to the son's annuity, upon the father for life, remainder to the son for life, remainder to the son's eldest son in tail. The land was thus tied up for another generation. (Megarry and Wade, 1966, pp. 288-289)

This process was repeated again in 1894 with Charles Leigh Adderley and his eldest son Ralph Bowyer. Also in 1869 Norton shifted the marriage settlement with the increased charged from the Saltley estate on to the Hams estate. Further dealings occurred through his life to arrange family matters so that in 1907 when his eldest son wanted to convey a six acre parcel of land freehold to Charles Brown for residential development he was obliged to recite a compound settlement involving seven indentures: the four already mentioned plus another three. Each affected some family interest and involved different trustees. Thus, although Norton could, by 1869, have alienated his land in Saltley and sold off freehold for residential purposes, he clearly had in mind the welfare of his nine children and their future status. Land was a way of securing these interests and providing a long term income which was not precarious. The structure of family arrangements were so complex, involving so many parties and trustees that a prosperous estate like Saltley would be a valuable asset in any overall management policy. Norton must have been aware, as will be seen later, that to load all the obligations on to the Hams estate alone would be a risky move. Although its capital value might be considered sufficient in 1860, by 1900 its potential rental growth was negligible. Legally, then, Norton could have chosen to alienate his land, and indeed after disentailment in 1840 he sold off freehold a large proportion of his Saltley land which was not affected by the marriage arrangements, but the social structure which lay behind these complex legal arrangements disposed him to retain most of his potentially high yielding land holdings. He engaged in a tight management and development plan for all his lands. He rid himself of the outlying estates gradually investing the proceeds in stock and concentrated on renegotiating the mining royalties in Norton on the Moors and developing Saltley.

In 1835 the Saltley estate needed a change of management. There were 20 relatively substantial small farmers sharing 415 acres. Joseph Dowler paid £55 a year rent for 58 acres, John Jenkins £150 a year for 173 acres, Thomas Perrins £35 for 51 acres in 1815. But only two of these tenants, Joseph Gaskin and John Standley, had leases, all the rest were at will which presumably allowed Norton to displace them without difficulty. There is no evidence of resistance which seems odd since the records show that some farmers were investing in their land as late as 1835 when, for instance, John Dowler was building a new house for himself. At the same time the Norton family was selling land to the London and Birmingham Railway Company for £1805. It is noticeable in the account of John Dumolo, the agent, that the Saltley, Washwood Heath and Bordesley Green estates were in substantial arrears of rent each half year. Norton changed agents between 1835 and 1840 on the Saltley estate and arrears were reduced. Charles Couchman, the new agent, took a significant part in the future development of Saltley. He later became the senior partner in the firm Couchman Fowler Couchman later Wilmot, Fowler, Wilmot which handled the estate throughout Norton's life. The pattern for development in the early years was to sell off gradually the low lying and sloping land near the railway lines for industrial use, and to consolidate the land holdings in the northern section. Eventually almost half the original 415 acres were sold freehold. The proceeds were invested in stock usually railway stock and later New Zealand Consolidated Bonds.[2] This banking capital was used to finance the residential development. By purchasing strategic land and constructing the infrastructure, Couchman played a central part in the consolidation of the estate. On 13th April 1843 an auction sale took place under the auspices of E.C. Robins, surveyors, of 24 acres of land. The owners were trustees Joseph Stock and Henry Rotten a banker who held on trust for John and

Hannah Rotten to sell the land and invest in stock or other good freehold and leasehold premises. Hannah had inherited the land from her mother. The programme was as follows:

> In the occupation of Mr. Hobday [the tenant] situated in Saltley and Little Bromwich near to Snow Hill and Alum Rock, in the Parish of Aston, well calculated for building houses for persons desirous of a retreat at a convenient walking distance from the centre of the town of Birmingham; an elevated, sound, dry, healthy spot, with cheerful and extensive prospects, and part at least is immediately connected with probable direct lines of thorough fare from Ashted, across the Derby railway and the Bordesley canal towards the communications over the Bridges on the London railway.

The Saltley area which was purchased by Couchman covered just over 16 acres and was described thus:

> A cottage, garden, barn, rickyard and 4 pieces of land lying between the farm houses of Hobday and Dowler fronting the Road leading from thence to Bordesley Green and bounded on all other sides by Saltley Hall and the other estates of C.B. Adderley.

Obviously it was a prime site, Couchman as agent paid £2400, £150 per acre. He did not, however, immediately reconvey to Adderley. He retained the land until 1857 when he sold 10 acres to Adderley for £5550, a mere £550 per acre. In 1864 he conveyed the rest to the portion trustees for £3087, £513.50 per acre. These prices were high despite the rising values. In 1857 Adderley with Couchman acting as a quasi trustee purchased 26 acres of land from a consortium of owners for £9000, £346 per acre. Couchman always made a substantial profit although not of the same order. In 1861 the devisees of John Pinson, freeholder, sold eight acres to him for £1500, £187.50 per acre. Couchman reconveyed to Adderley's trustees eight months later for £2158.75, £269.85 per acre. However it is clear that land values were rising substantially. Adderley purchased four acres direct from Charles Allen Line in 1864 for £1300, £325 per acre. This should have been a sale balanced in the purchaser's favour since Line was in default of two mortgages, of £350 and £1000 respectively, and obliged to sell.

The purchases were important, as Fig. 6 shows, in the consolidation of the Saltley estate. Equally important was the infrastructure. A building map of 1847 shows virtually all the roads planned as they were eventually built. Adderley was as careful with the building arrangements for the roads as he was for the houses. Their construction was undertaken as and when necessary over more than 50 years. They were built by various firms and supervised by Couchman. James Young and Joseph Tatton builders of large parts of Saltley undertook to construct the extension of Hartopp Road in 1899. By· an agreement on 18th April they agreed to build the road before 29th September 1889 to use good materials and drains, ''sewered, paved, levelled, flagged'' to the satisfaction and approval of Lord Norton or his surveyor and the Corporation of Birmingham. They were also to rail and fence off the land. In exchange Tatton and Young were conveyed the land subject to Norton's right to use it. All expenses were to be borne by the contractors except £10.50 for Norton's solicitor and surveying costs.

Norton did, however, pay directly for most of the roads. The trustees laid out £4133 for roads between 1892 and 1899. They seem to cost between £300 and £500 in the 1890s. Bowyer cost £500, Clodeshall £300, Ralph cost £394 in 1905. All the finance came from the sale of stock.

Land values were rising because of the change of use and investment by Norton. The state had also intervened to provide the essential services such as water, sewerage and gas. Adderley then planned the houses along broad streets, in relatively low densities with large gardens, and also provided amenities like Adderley Park, churches and baths. Saltley training college provided an imposing back cloth.

He managed this estate skilfully as well as philanthropically, so that its value increased 20-fold. In 1840 the income from 415 acres was £1004. By 1905 the rental income from the unsold half, containing the residential development, was £8255 a year. The rise in rental income is shown in Fig. 7.

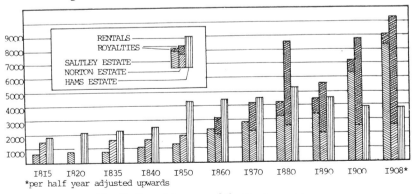

Fig. 7. Rental income of the Norton estate.

By contrast in 65 years the income from the rural estates had hardly altered. For example, the rent from Bemersley Farm at Norton in the Moors, £120 for 111 acres in 1840 had fallen to £106 for 76 acres in 1905, representing only a slight increase in yield from £1.08 to £1.23 per acre. In some cases yields had fallen. In 1840 the tenant of Norton Hall Farm paid a yearly rent of £1.28 per acre. In 1905 the farm had nearly doubled in size to 299 acres but the rent had fallen to £1.02 per acre. At 25 years purchase the whole farm was valued for death duties at only £7600, or £25.50 per acre. The productive outlay on the Saltley infrastructure is in marked contrast to the outgoings on Norton's other estates. The costs in Saltley added to the capital value of the estate in a far more direct manner than the very high maintenance costs incurred on the rural estates. See Fig. 8.

In the short term Adderley obtained substantial increases in rental income with little unproductive outlay. He invested most of the income in stock and generally put his capital to good use. None of his Saltley land was unyielding. One area, on part of which was situated his philanthropic reformatory for boys (see Fig. 6), was mortgaged between 1850 and 1865 first to Richard Horton, surgeon, for £5000 plus interest then twice to John Unett for £4000 plus interest the latter time secured by a smaller portion of land since land prices were rising. This land was at the south end of the estate and scheduled for development at a later stage, for instance 4 acres were sold by his son in 1907 for £6000 to the post office.

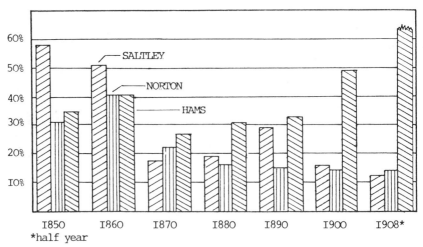

Fig. 8. Maintenance costs as a proportion of Norton's rental income.

The money gained by mortgaging was presumably invested. His financial transactions were many and various as his solicitor and trustee accounts show. In the first half of his life the pattern was to primarily sell land but to consolidate and invest in stock. In the latter half he engaged in a large amount of dealing in stock and few land transactions. Between 1873 and 1905 he sold £28 384 of stock but bought £62 383 worth. He bought no land at all in Saltley and sold £12 372 worth.

Whether Adderley's income was more than he could have obtained by freehold sale is difficult to determine. It is also clear that in the short term he could have obtained more rental income by eliminating the back gardens and doubling the density. He would still have not fallen foul of the by-laws. As it turned out Norton's short-term sacrifices were not great. The land leased to build the earlier, meaner houses in Adderley Road and George Arthur Road between 1860 and 1890 gave a return of £40 an acre, similar to that from the land under the more substantial houses in St Saviours Road built in the 1880s (which Birmingham's Medical Officer of Health noted with approval in his 1889 report). At the turn of the century the return on building land under the most substantial houses of all reached £50 an acre. This represented, according to Norton's surveyor, a value of £1200 an acre, not so very different from some of the best industrial land.

In the long term the estate had a far greater reversionary value with good quality houses. This is the traditional advantage of leasehold development. The retention of a reversionary interest held mounting economic significance with the increase in urban land values. Thus the land-owner could take advantage of the social improvements. Urban land-owners were able to look to the future for their capital return, whilst not being unduly disturbed by any lower return on capital during the subsistence of the lease. Therefore, they could plan carefully so as to reap the future value to its full. Since planning was controlled through the system of covenants, if the land-owner was of lesser economic status the development might suffer as Dyos (1961) points out in his famous example. In nineteenth century Camberwell one estate developed from a meadow to a slum in one generation through the non-enforcement of covenants. In 1905 the valuers for the Norton estate reported as follows:

the ground rents are nearly all secured by small houses at from 6s [30p] to 8s 6d [42½p] per week. The houses are occupied by artisans and are unlikely to survive the life of the lease. We value the ground rents as at the time of the late Lord Norton's death at 28 years purchase when the lease has less than 65 years to run and 27 years purchase when it has more than this term unexpired.

The Saltley estate, which was much reduced in size by freehold sales since Norton inherited it from his great uncle, had nevertheless increased ten-fold in value from £44 398 to £266 780. By 1905 it constituted half his wealth, more than Hams (£82 743) and Norton in the Moors (£115 564) combined. Thus it could be argued that Norton used his monopoly power skilfully to extract as much as possible from the estate and at the same time he satisfied his own family arrangements and his philanthropy. But the material conditions were not all in his favour. The building process was precarious, there were no well organized sources of finance, wages would hardly match housing costs and landlords and builders were anxious to have low cost housing whilst land-owners, wanting to reap as much as possible from their land, tended to force up housing costs. If Norton had decided to off load his estate freehold there is a strong possibility that he would have been obliged to accept a low price because builders could not have afforded the high cost of land and infrastructural development, and because the market would have been flooded. Many houses would have appeared at a time of housing boom and then the market would have stagnated and dried up.

Leasehold building ensured that the market was not flooded as the Town Holdings Enquiry showed. Norton carefully released leases over a number of years. He also stipulated in the leases the building time so that a steady flow of houses were released each year. The relatively high building standards induced reasonably well established builders to undertake the work which reduced the likelihood of bankruptcy and unfinished houses. The local brick works eased the transport costs despite the royalties. Norton also eased the financial burden on the builders by constructing all the access roads. The peppercorn rent for the construction period was a further incentive to builders as was the reasonable ground rent charged thereafter. Norton was obliged to make these concessions so that builders were persuaded to sustain a demand for his land even when the market was slumping elsewhere. By recognizing these material constraints Norton was able to manage a well ordered development and reap its benefits.

The main advantage of leasehold development was that it reduced or at least spread out the land cost element of housing production. The price of land at the turn of the century was generally very high and caused substantial problems. Nevitt (1966) considered that the average cost of land in the London County Council area between 1895 and 1907 was 34.4% of the total housing cost. The resultant high cost of housing had a number of effects, first buildings tended to be of an extremely low standard and secondly there was mounting pressure for higher wages to cover the cost. Costs in London have always been extremely high and land was held by a few very wealthy aristocratic land-owners. Conditions elsewhere were different but the enquiry into urban holdings at the end of the nineteenth century discovered that out of 261 provincial towns 69 were largely owned by great land-owners and 34 by families from the gentry (Sutherland, 1968. p. 33). Thus land costs have formed a high proportion of total cost elsewhere. Leaseholding land-owners were particularly singled out as reaping greater benefit. It was argued strongly at the time that the market could not bear the standards set by the monopolistic land-owners. Land-owners laid down such strict covenants and stipulations for building that builders were obliged to build houses which landlords could not rent out profitably. Evidence from Cardiff, London and Birmingham, although not particularly in Saltley, show the result to be house sharing, overcrowding and in more suburban areas, empty houses. The houses built at this time were primarily to provide shelter for the relatively higher industrial wage earners not for the poor who remainded crammed into the central slum areas. The latter were seen as a social and political problem to be tackled by the intervention of the State. Politically the outcome was an attack on land-owners and leasehold tenure, and State intervention to subsidize working-class housing. Thus leasehold reform and even enfranchisement were major demands in the 1880s and 1890s. These later became incorporated in the Liberal land reforms in a diluted form as the next section will show. But evidence from leasehold estates in Cardiff and Saltley show that land costs were much lower than in London, around 16% of total costs. Daunton (1977) considers still that they caused serious difficulties in Cardiff. It produced "pretentious little houses rather than cottages" and pushed up housing costs generally in the town. Yet it is not clear that freehold costs would have been any less. The Saltley example would tend to suggest that leasehold tenure contained concessions to builders. There is certainly no evidence to suggest that leasehold houses were more expensive than freehold equivalents, although the building system might lead to a different style.

Ideologically, the housing problem was not identified at the time by

Liberal reformers as one of low wages, but was confined instead to the land element of housing costs. Leaseholding land-owners were attacked as the major cause of the problem since they stood out as an identifiable class, unlike those who had sold their land freehold (and as profitably) but reinvested their capital in stocks. Leasehold tenure identifies land-owners as a social relation despite the similar economic relation.

The Politics of Leasehold Development

This chapter has attempted to describe some of the relations which exist in housing where leasehold tenure represents a particular balance of power between the land-owner and other parties. The conflicts manifested themselves ideologically and politically in the late nineteenth century. Housing in London and in the other major cities was viewed as a major problem. In London it was seen as the major social problem. Solutions differed. The radicals in the 1880s sought the abolition or strict control of landlords. Chamberlain sought to make "ownership of insanitary property a crime" and "to transfer the cost of rehousing from the 'community' to 'property'" (Stedman Jones, 1976, p. 225). As will be seen, Henry Broadhurst went further and demanded leasehold enfranchisement. Collins wanted statutory protection for tenants against increases in rents and Dwyer Gray wanted municipalization of the fee simples of urban land. The Trades Council representing artisans was keen to facilitate working-class home ownership. The Conservatives and devotees of political economy, who felt threatened by Henry George, the Social Democratic Federation and 'socialistic solutions', could only contend that the evils were not brought about by deficient legislation but through lax administration. Their solution was viligilance committees to oversee the implementation of the legislation. The Royal Commission on Housing 1884 was a triumph of this last position. What was needed was more efficient administration, not drastic legislation. But by the turn of the century the state was obliged to deal with the collapse of the private housing market in a more fundamental manner by introducing state housing.

The campaign over leasehold tenure was part of this overall concern for housing and figured prominently in evidence to the Royal Commission. The activities of land-owners and their power were attacked by politicians and land reformers in both Parliament and the press. The membership too and activities of the land organizations revived. Bourgeois radicals of the Liberal Party took advantage of this situation to increase the support for a renewal of a campaign against the land-owning aristocracy. The first politician to give public notice of and anxiety at the existence of these problems was Henry Broadhurst, the Liberal-Labour M.P., when he raised the question of leasehold tenure (Broadhurst, 1884, 1885).

Reeder (1961) points out that there were three main reasons for this attack from radicals, socialists and land formers.[3] They saw the prevalence of leasehold land in the hands of aristocratic owners as an abuse of monopoly power which restricted the liberty of townspeople to own their houses. It was the height of laissez-faire concepts but the tenants enjoyed little of it; their economic individualism was thwarted since they were tied to the use declared by the lease. The attack upheld the name of economic individualism. Although they attacked the restrictions placed on urban tenants, the opponents were willing to contemplate similar restrictions if they were imposed by Public Authorities. The Bill before Parliament in the 1880s which provided for compulsory enfranchisement included provisions which would have have kept the covenants in operation after conversion to a freehold through local authority powers of enforcement. The second grievance was that repairing leases increased rents in line with rising land values, thereby providing a tribute for which land-owners had done nothing. As the Fabians declared in 1892 "the princely gift of London workmen to London land-owners in net unearned increment had increased the value of London by a third in twenty years". The impact of Henry George and the single taxers will be considered later. Thirdly, the town holdings of land-owners connected them directly with a number of housing problems, notably leasehold slums.

The political importance of the urban leases was not just to focus on the need for large changes in the ownership of land, but to organize a discontented but unstratified group of tenants in an attempt to abolish the system. Thus the demand was for leasehold enfranchisement. The idea was not new. From the late eighteenth century architects had been troubled by the operation of the speculative building of leasehold houses but by the mid nineteenth century discontent was felt by suburban householders at the defects of the system such as the burden of the land tax, repairs and insecurity. The idea of enfranchisement first appeared in 1848. Attacks were made until the 1870s with little interest from politicians. John T. Emmett, between 1872 and 1885, wrote a series of papers on the system which increased awareness, but the boom came in 1883 when three Bills were introduced into the House of Commons to provide for enfranchisement. The Leasehold Enfranchisement Association (L.E.A.) was formed to rally support in London and the provinces. The main leaders were Henry Broadhurst, H.L.W. Lawson, Secretary to the Metropolitcan Liberal Members Committee, and James Rowlands, M.P. for East Finsbury from 1886. The spark had been provided by the number of leases coming up for renewal in West and North London. Rents increased and evictions occurred. The movement had an essentially middle-class membership although the motives were, like the later land campaign, mixed. Some supported enfranchisement as a lesser evil to the total overthrow of the private property system and an antidote to socialist doctrines. Broadhurst and the municipal reformers in London saw it as a way of striking directly at the town holdings of land-owners and a general measure of social reform, in the same category as the clearance of slums and cheap trains for workers and thus part of the solution to the housing of the working class. Broadhurst and others put forward this view to the Royal Commission on the Housing of the Working Classes in 1884. This body considered the interrelation of slums and leasehold tenure and considered that the latter encouraged slum growth. The supplementary report by ten of the seventeen members declared for enfranchisement. The third group committed to the idea were the bourgeois radical followers of Cobden and Bright. They believed that working-class ownership was good for moral as well as political reasons. The legislation was to give them economic freedom rather than to provide for state intervention.

The heyday of the L.E.A. was in the ten years which followed the first Bill of 1884. They conducted a vigorous, if fruitless, campaign in which representatives toured the country. The support came from towns with large estates of working-class houses such as Sheffield, Devonport, Oxford, Grimsby, Tavistock and Southport and the cottages of quarry towns in North Wales and villagers of Cornwall.

In Cardiff a leasehold campaign did flourish for a while, after the formation of the Cardiff and South Wales Leasehold Enfranchisement Association in 1899. Like elsewhere, the grievance was real but the solution which lay in the resolution of the conflict between wages and housing costs was later sought through council housing. The campaign seems to have made little impact on Birmingham which is surprising.

Both the central slum areas and the outer estates were leasehold. Explanations could lie in the particular structure of Birmingham society. The activities of the Freehold Land Society might have 'creamed' off those elements of the artisan class or lower middle class which might have led a campaign. Also the ruling social structure was very different to that of London. It was not made up of professional and tradespeople instead the Council was dominated by manufacturing interests. (The influence of the professions and trade did not predominate in Birmingham until after the First World War when council house building provided an interest for surveyors, architects and builders.) The attack on the slums was vigorous, carried out by manufacturers on the landlords. Repairs and improvements were insisted upon and enforced by legislation under Chamberlain's improvement scheme. The Housing Committee which was set up in 1901 and whose task it was to supervise these activities, was chaired by J.S. Nettlefold, a leading local industrialist. Thus, although the housing problem was not solved and by 1913 there was a shortage which led to a further special committee enquiry, leasehold enfranchisement was not seen as central to the solution, although the issue of leaseholds contributing to the bad housing conditions did appear in the evidence to the Committee. A leasehold enfranchisement association did exist in the city but its impact was minimal as far as can be detected. Oddly, Henry Broadhurst, who was a stone mason, originated from Birmingham. He won Boardesley at the election of 1885 but left Birmingham for Nottingham. There was also a Midland Land Values League whose first annual report was published in 1910. The objects of the League were "to show the justice and expediency of gradually unrating and untaxing houses, shops, factories, farms, foods, etc. and substituting a rate or tax on land values". Its secretary, Chapman Wright, published along with A. Withy, a pamphlet in 1910 called "A 100 reasons for taxing land values". Reason 54 was that leasehold enfranchisement was unnecessary. No further explanation was forthcoming.

The L.E.A. gave extensive evidence before the Select Committee on Town Holdings which sat between 1886 and 1892 and was constituted partly through the L.E.A.'s pressure. But the L.E.A. did not obtain support from professional bodies like surveyors who were worried about the loss of a steady investment. The opposition was strong as would be expected from the powerful vested interests of the town land-owners and their professional retinue. They formed their own body, the Central

Land-owner Association. Its counter proposal was that building leases were valuable as instruments of good estate management. Opposition also came from the political groupings. The left, usually land reformers, saw it as a petty bourgeois claim. In 1891 the Fabians issued a pamphlet dealing with the issue in which, whilst attacking the system, they also attacked the remedy as a further extension of landlordism:

> Instead of the Duke of Bedford owning Bloomsbury we should have a few 100 little Dukes of Bedford each owning a tiny scrap of Bloomsbury. What good would this do to anybody but these fortunate individuals.

In addition to this opposition the L.E.A. were not aided by some of the changes being made in estate management in the 1880s which had been influenced by the possibility of more drastic legislative action. The ecclesiastical commissioners had converted properties into 999 year leases, the redevelopment of the worst areas were underway and other leading land-owners had sold their holdings. The Spectator of 4th May 1889 suggested that the exchange of ground rents for consols was a wise move. The culmination of the movement came when it was unable to persuade the Select Committee on Town Holdings of its case. The Committee recommended that, where the majority wanted it, the local authority could acquire all the reversionary interests in the area and sell them to occupying leaseholders. They rejected the general concept of enfranchisement. From the 1890s the movement was in decline at the very time when they had convinced leading Radical Liberals that the cause was worth making an item of national policy. From 1891 leasehold enfranchisement was tied up with the policy and fortunes of the Liberal Party. It was used to catch the votes of city workers and provided the important link between land and housing. Ground rents were seen as the embodiment in private hands of the enterprise and industry of the rest of the community through unearned increments. It was not an end in itself as the L.E.A. had envisaged, but part of the larger programme of land reform which was known as the land campaign. It never convinced Labouchere Haldane or Lloyd George who thought the real solution to urban land problems was compulsory purchase enabling the community to acquire what the community had created. The demand was made annually in Parliament but rarely debated. Lloyd George carried out various reforms but, although by 1912 the land reformers had achieved the objective of a national valuation, the single taxers, who took precedence in Parliament, demanded a national tax on full site value. The discussions eventually led to a rift between the single taxers and the others. The Enquiry Committee on the condition of land was set up in 1912 to consider state housing and minimum wages for agricultural workers. Its two reports, rural and urban, published in 1913 and 1914 respectively, coincided with the death throes of the leasehold enfranchisement movement.

Lloyd George launched in October the Land Campaign as a result of the Land Enquiry Committee's first report. The Ministry of Lands and Forests, through the land commissioners, would implement and deal with all matters of wages, rents and tenure. It seemed that some remedies to grievances were underway. At the same time a cluster of London leases fell in. There was more speculation in fag ends by now because the financial syndicates had begun to enter the market for old working-class houses. The professional opinion favoured positive action because covenants tended to fossilize land use in areas of rapid change. The old connection between leases and slum housing was revived encouraged by the publication in May 1914 of the urban report which although it rejected the idea of enfranchisement, did propose security of tenure and the tenants' right to the value of the improvements. The war intervened before any more could be done. Leasehold Bills had been introduced annually and continued to be so even after the war with no avail. By 1914 there had already been 32 Bills introduced. Leasehold enfranchisement was not a productive issue for workers to rally around. It was never a working-class demand, and would have helped only the petite bourgeoise. The political campaign became tied to the issue of unearned increments, and represented intra class conflicts between manufacturing and landed capital. It fell outside the main class antagonisms between labour and capital and gained no political significance.

Notes

1. Waste is defined as whatever does lasting damage to the freehold or inheritance of land or anything which alters the nature of the property (Burke, 1976, p. 346).
2. Norton's biographer praises Norton for not using his interest in colonial matters, particularly in New Zealand, to acquire land in the colonies. He overlooks the quite considerable share capital that Norton held in New Zealand stock.
3. This section relies heavily on Reeder's interpretation of events.

3   Contradiction and Decline

The last chapter described both how the leasehold system was used to organize the production of houses and how the system was attacked politically. This chapter will examine the contradictions surrounding the use of leasehold tenure which evolved in the nineteenth century but which have become clearer in the twentieth century with the more direct intervention of the State. The development of large leasehold estates reflect, as the last chapter shows, a particular balance in the social relations of production. Under the changing market conditions of the twentieth century similar leasehold ventures have not taken place and the main concern has been with leasehold tenure in the circulation and consumption of houses.

Land-owners who used leasehold tenure were accused of creating the city centre slums of late nineteenth century Britain. Because they had demanded high ground rents and building standards, working-class occupiers could not afford their rents and landlords could not keep the properties in repair with such a low profit margin. As the early leases reached their fag ends, lessees had no incentive to maintain the property. There was widespread subdivision and extraction of high rents by middlemen, usually men of straw who, at the end of the lease, disappeared and so evaded the repairing covenants. Yet at the same time, leasehold tenure was being used to create the new improved working-class housing which it was hoped would solve the housing problem. Land-owners on greenfield sites were laying out good quality estates for the workers of Britain's second industrial phase. Saltley's estates are a prime example of this type of development. Land-owners used leasehold tenure as a means of imposing elementary land use control in order to ensure that their properties were well maintained and their reversionary interest protected.

Leasehold tenure has the same contradictory nature in the twentieth

century. It has been used as a means of controlling land use both by
private owners and increasingly by the state. The land question did not
die with the failure of Liberal reforms in the early twentieth century. It
was transformed into a debate over betterment. Betterment is "the
fortuitous increase in the value of land, or unearned increment, which
accrues to the owner of land on account of action of others, often public
authorities" (Ratcliffe, 1976, p. 21). Leasehold tenure has often been
cited as a means by which the state could cream off that betterment.
Thus the increased value of the land would go not to the landowners and
developers, but to the state as guardians for the "community". But the
system has been accused again of causing slums in the better working-
class areas which were built in the late nineteenth century as an
alternative to the old leasehold slums. These areas are now called the
inner-city problem. The leasehold enfranchisement debate which
surrounded the 1967 Leasehold Reform Act, has grappled with these
contradictory elements. The new inner-city problem, coupled with the
plight of would be owner-occupiers, has emerged as the central political
issue in this debate.

   Few large leasehold estates have been created in the twentieth century.
Those that were built tended to be of two types; middle-class estates or
the products of a particular type of industrial philanthropy. In the first
category is the Calthorpe Estate in Edgbaston, Birmingham.[1] The land-
owner's agents actively managed the estates keeping leaseholders up to
the mark with their maintenance, putting down insalubrious activities
and excluding people of dubious social status. Although these mighty
land-owners were not town planners they were "purveyors of a
specialized urban service" who acted as trustees for well-to-do
leaseholders and for future generations (Jenkins, 1975). Their estates
remain today alongside public planning controls rather than inside them
(for further details, see McAuslan, 1975, pp. 329-349).

   The other group was the private philanthropic land-owner cum
employer estates which were forerunners to the public sector garden
cities. Two such were developed at the turn of the century, Port Sunlight
and Bournville. The Bournville Village Trust in Birmingham is a charity
founded in 1900 by Cadbury, "with the aim of showing that good
housing conditions could be provided for members of the working classes
on an economic basis" (McAuslan, 1975, p. 333). An excellent
description of the estate is provided by the report by the Board of Trade
into working-class rents, housing and retail prices in 1908:

the "Garden Village", is situated about four miles to the south-west of the city, and is easily reached by means of the West Suburban Railway and two electric tram routes. The housing conditions here contrast very strikingly with those ruling in Birmingham or any other industrial town. In place of crowded blocks of artisans' dwellings or long monotonous rows of brick houses, the cottages at Bournville, all of which are occupied by workmen and their families, are either semi-detached or built in sets of not more than four. They stand well back from the roads, which are wide and tree-planted. There is a garden in front of each cottage, and another behind, while sometimes a strip runs beside the house. The area of each garden generally averages about 600 square yards. In all cases there are at least three bedrooms in each cottage, and usually two living rooms, besides scullery, larder, and other offices, while in the larger houses there is generally a bathroom as well.... The estate now contains over 600 dwellings and has a population approaching 3,000. The demand for vacant houses is great, but existing tenants rarely leave. About 40 per cent of the householders are employed at Bournville: the bulk of the remaining inhabitants are engaged in occupations in Birmingham.

It is evident from what has been said that the cottages at Bournville cannot be included in a consideration of the rents of working-class accommodation in Birmingham. The rents of most of the cottages range from 4s 6d to 8s per week, exclusive of rates, which are about 6s 3d in all.

The rent for a 6 room house inclusive of rates at the time was 6s 6d. For the usual working-class house of 4 or 5 rooms it was between 5s and 7s 6d.

Bournville can be seen as part of the garden city movement for the Trustees were enpowered also to provide sites for schools, churches and museums.

These original aims have been slowly changed:

> Over a period of nearly 70 years since its foundation, the aims of the Trustees have evolved so that they are now attempting to produce a balance community containing a wide variety of different income groups and providing proper communal facilities. (Bournville Village Trust)

What this means in practice is that while some of the older residents and houses may be working-class and some again let on weekly tenancies, at a low rent, the more modern houses and developments on the estate are clearly and deliberately designed for the professional middle-classes. (McAuslan, 1975, p. 333)

All the major estates are now run by professional agents and employ a wide variety of personnel.

> At Bournville for instance. — an estate containing 6,000 houses on approximately 1,000 acres of land including open spaces, clinic and schools, etc. — there is a staff of around fifty which includes an estate architect and building and maintenance department. (McAuslan, 1975, p. 330)

Subsequently there have been no large private leasehold developments with these corporate aims. Leasehold development has been limited to flats, where freehold ownership is technically difficult to accomplish, and to some estates built in traditionally leasehold areas like South Wales and the West Midlands. Here the developers are able marginally to reduce the price of new houses to "first time home buyers" but thereafter obtain a further tribute from owner-occupiers until they can raise the cash to purchase the freehold. There seems to be no opposition from the freeholder to speedy purchase.

The leasehold system has also been used in the public sector to facilitate land use control and to recoup betterment. Letchworth founded in 1903 and Welwyn in 1920 were developed on 99 year leases. Leasehold tenure was also the form favoured for the New Towns in the Reith Report (1964) since it was essential that the agency should retain as much control as possible over present use and future development. Positive covenants were considered to provide far more effective control over use than negative covenants imposed on the purchasers of freeholders. Leases were to be arranged so that they fell in at about the same time in order to afford the only certain way of ensuring that any given area could be redeveloped as a whole. The control exercised by virtue of ownership was seen as more certain than control by by-laws or by planning acts. These recommendations were carried into effect by the New Towns Act 1964 which provided for the creation of New Towns through the agency of development corporations formed and financed by the Government.

At a political level the state's use of leasehold tenure has become confused with the separate issue of the fate of the earlier private estates produced under this system. These houses are now nearly a 100 years old and have weathered substantial physical and economic transformations. The high cost of houses generally as commodities has caused problems in the sphere of consumption. The contradiction between housing costs and wage levels has brought state intervention in a number of ways, first through the direct subsidy of council housing and secondly through indirect subsidies to house consumers in the private sector. One consequence has been a shift in the dominant tenure form, from letting by private landlords (themselves either freeholders or leaseholders) to council housing and owner-occupation (again either freehold or leasehold). The estates like Saltley have themselves been transformed tenurially. They are also no longer greenfield sites salubriously distant from the city's slum core but have themselves been reclassified as social problem areas which need either to be knocked down and redeveloped or, latterly, improved. Tenurial form and location have each contributed independently to the overall problem and have led, throughout the century, to political initiatives which attempt to resolve their peculiar contradictions.

During the nineteenth century, generally working-class housing was provided by private landlords. Rents were fixed by the level of wages which was relatively low. Housing was of a low standard until it was recognized in the mid century that the conditions created were unacceptable to capitalism as a whole. Not only was the workforce unnecessarily weakened by illness and death but infections fostered in the slums could easily spread to the middle class. By-laws successively introduced in the late nineteenth century to raise housing standards also raised economic rents so that a high proportion of workers' income was consumed on rent.

At the same time landlords raised about two-thirds of the value of their properties on mortgage and so their costs were very sensitive to changes in interest rates. If they were unable to pass on the increases by raising rents, their profits were easily eroded. As the century progressed investment outlets for small savings increased. Most landlords were of the small capitalist type as in Saltley and, when no longer restricted to housing for investment, used the freedom to invest in the Stock Exchange, government and municipal debts and building societies.

Thus before rent control was introduced, the private rented sector was under pressure and failing to provide suitable housing for the working class. Rent control, which first appeared in 1915, was a state response to this problem not an attempt to force the private sector into decline at a time when the private landlord in 1915 provided 90% of the housing. The history of the 1915 Rent and Mortgage Restriction Act has been told elsewhere (Beirne, 1978; Watchman, 1979). The imposition of rent control and restrictions on mortgage interest rates were the start of state intervention in the rented sector which has never ceased. Rents in the private sector increased by 40% after the war when decontrol was permitted in 1923. By 1937 half the houses were decontrolled and, despite a decrease in building costs in the 1930s, the private rented sector did not experience, unlike other sectors, a house boom.

After the First World War the failure of traditional building for rent coupled with the changing balance of class forces, obliged the state to intervene directly in the provision of houses. Wages could no longer sustain the level of rents which landlords needed to extend the provision of new suitable houses to the entire working class.

Council housing had been possible administratively since 1890 but it only became a reality in 1919 with the launching of the first national house building programme, the aim of which was to build 500 000 houses in three years. The local authorities were to ensure that the housing stock expanded without rents escalating. The 1919 Addison Act provided a "no limit per house" subsidy to the local authorities. In 1920 lump sums were also made available for private building but it had little significant effect. The subsidy was abolished in 1921 but introduced again in 1923 and 1924 with the Chamberlain and Wheatley Acts. These Acts provided subsidies in the form of lump sums per annum per house for both local authority and private house building. The control of council rents passed to local authorities and subsidy from the rates was allowed. The result was a major expansion in the council rented sector during the twenties. Between 1919 and 1934, 31% of new houses were built by local authorities, although half were either built for sale or sold to tenants. Standards were high but rents were generally higher than the private sector. During the thirties the emphasis shifted from the provision of "general needs housing" to that of clearance and subsequent rehousing. The Wheatley and Chamberlain subsidies were abolished and rent rebates were introduced along with rent pooling. Rent pooling is a system which averages out notional rents based on the historic costs of different local authority stock. By 1938, 112 authorities were providing rebates.

The 1930s also saw a big increase in the private building of houses for sale and renting to the middle classes. This increase is associated first with decreasing building costs and secondly with the rise of the building societies. At this time also owner-occupation for the working classes began to emerge in areas like Saltley where the effect of rent control had pushed private landlords into capital sales and alternative investment. Blanket rent control for the private sector was reintroduced on the day war broke out. After the war there was a massive surge in new council building. The 1945 Labour government gave council housing a high priority, through a system of building control, large exchequer subsidies and a statutory rate subsidy. The councils had a duty not only to rehouse but also to add to the stock for general needs. The aim to build 300 000 new houses a year by 1947 was constrained by the financial crisis. But the Tories, who were returned in 1951, achieved this quota in 1953 and exceeded it in 1954. Their aim however was not to provide council housing as a priority but rather as set out in the 1953 White Paper "Houses — the Next Step", to promote owner-occupation and to build a property owning democracy. State housing of a lower standard was for those in "need" particularly those subject to slum clearance. In 1956 the general subsidies were abolished and the rate subsidy made non-compulsory. Subsidies were provided only for slum clearance and for higher blocks of houses. In 1955 the cost of financing local authority housing increased when the councils were obliged to rely on the capital market and not the Public Works Loan Board.

The Tory policy brought a rapid decline in new local authority construction which in 1959 was half of the 1953 level whereas owner-occupation was increasing significantly from 27% in 1947 to 42.3% in 1961 to 53% in 1971. As the percentage increased so did the social composition of the sector. Owner-occupation came within the reach of substantial numbers of working-class people in the 1950s and 1960s.

Despite the shift in emphasis and the significance of the local authority sector, the private landlord still played an important part in the mid 1950s. The Tories were keen to rejuvenate the private sector. Their efforts were not successful. The sector shrunk from 58% in 1947 to 22.5% in 1966. There were two attempts at bolstering the private landlord. The first was to encourage an improvement in standards, which were often low, as cheaply as possible. In 1949 and 1954 grants were made available to landlords for improvement. They were not a great success and the emphasis shifted to decontrol in order to obtain greater rental income to spend on repairs. The 1957 Rent Act allowed decontrol immediately for property of higher rateable value and decontrol on vacant possession for the rest. The effect was not to stimulate repairs but to speed up the withdrawal of the private landlord from the market. Winkling and Rachmanism were the type of methods used to remove tenants to facilitate sale of the property to owner-occupiers. Winkling involves the use of financial persuasion, Rachmanism the threat or use of violence to persuade tenants to leave. Small landlords under pressure also tended to sell out to larger landlords.

When the Labour Party returned to power in 1964 they reimposed security of tenure and rent control following the Milner-Holland report (1965). The 1965 Rent Act which is the foundation of the present system and allows the fixing of a fair rent for a property did not, however, halt the move to owner-occupation.

In Saltley the great surge into owner-occupation took place in the immediate post war years so that by 1955 more houses were occupied by payment of a premium than by a weekly rent. By 1964 the Labour Party was converted to owner-occupation as an ideal. Specifically working-class owner-occupation had its first statutory recognition with the option mortgage scheme which introduced mortgage interest relief for non taxpayers. Since then the emphasis for both the Tory and the Labour Parties has been on owner-occupation for the majority. The council sector is posed as the sector for those with problems, peculiar needs, and unsuited for owner-occupation.

While supporting owner-occupation in general the State has been obliged to tackle the specific problem of owners occupying the rapidly deteriorating nineteenth century housing stock now enclosed by the interwar suburbs in the inner city. Though the slum problem had existed on a large scale for a 100 years, the complicating factor of fragmented owner-occupation has emerged only in the last 15 years. The massive comprehensive redevelopment programmes in British cities between 1955 and 1970 were primarily of weekly tenanted houses. Residents were moved into council flats in central tower blocks or out to council estates on the periphery. Their landlords were minimally compensated. But the tide changed in the late 1960s when opposition to living in tower blocks with high rents or miles from the city centres had increased.[2] State funding for council houses was cut back leading to longer and longer waiting lists. Just as important, the older houses next in line for redevelopment were not only better than the recently cleared slums, but substantially owner-occupied. A new policy was called for and the state introduced two kinds of protection for working-class owners.

First, legislation protected the exchange or market value of owner-occupied houses in slum clearance areas. Normally compensation to owners had been minimal site value, though the use value of an exceptional, well maintained house was recognized by the payment of a supplement which brought compensation up to a market price. The 1973

Land Compensation Act made the payment of that supplement mandatory upon the State, whether or not a house had been well maintained. This measure protected the idea of owner-occupation as a secure investment but it did not prevent a tenure change in a direction contrary to the policy of successive post war governments: most owner-occupiers, despite the compensation, could not afford to buy another house and became instead council tenants.

Secondly, the massive programme of comprehensive redevelopment was halted, largely eliminating the specific exchange value problems of owner-occupiers. The 1969 Housing Act extended improvement policy significantly. Grants for house improvements had been available since 1958. But these improvements were usually cheap jobs done under the standard grant procedure introduced in 1959; a patching operation to provide basic sanitation before ultimate clearance. The 1969 scheme was for more long term improvements. Neighbourhoods were to be designated as General Improvement Areas (G.I.A.s). The standard of improvement was to give them a thirty year minimum life. Even so the 1969 legislation was aimed specifically at the better built Victorian terraces and recognized that improvement grants would only appeal to those who already had savings of their own which they were prepared to spend on home improvements. The 1974 Housing Act is based on no such recognition. At best it can be seen as a naive attempt to meet criticism that nothing was being done in the areas of worst housing (housing stress) now that slum clearance was grinding to a halt, or alternatively, as a blatant attempt to shift a much higher level of housing cost on to the working class, especially the owner-occupiers. The 1974 Act sets up Housing Action Areas (H.A.A.s). These are areas which would have been cleared with redevelopment but which now will, in the main, be retained. Grants are available at a higher level than for General Improvement Areas. Improvement is mandatory: failure to comply results in compulsory purchase. After 5 years the H.A.A. is supposed to be reclassified as a G.I.A. At this stage environmental improvements to the area are added.

Owner-occupation may have replaced private renting as the dominant tenure form, but it is no panacea since it merely rearranges the contradictions inherent in capitalist housing provision, as Ball argues:

> The gradual removal of the housing landlord represents the removal
> of one group of agents who appropriate surplus value from the

provision of housing. One contender in the distributional struggle for surplus value has been displaced. (1978, p. 92)

But both owner occupation and local authority systems enable the appropriation of surplus value by loan capital. The State subsidizes both tenures in order to finance a part of those interest charges. Local authorities are obliged to finance their building programmes through loans. The need to pay interest represents a major mechanism through which surplus value can be acquired by private loan capital.

> It obviously benefits those capitals who lend in this way but it operates against the economic interests of the rest of capital, which has to forego surplus value as a result: either through the need for higher wages to pay the rents or through the taxes required to finance the State subsidies. (Ball 1978: 93)

Owner-occupied houses are purchased in commodity form and can be resold at any time. The price is determined by the current cost of a newly constructed house and the state of the market. As commodities houses have developed into an investment; a hedge against inflation from which to work up to bigger, better and more expensive types. The appropriation of surplus value is diverse, first to the various agents in the exchange process, solicitors, estate agents, surveyors; secondly to financial institutions since mortgage funds are usually needed for purchase. This finance involves payment of interest and the distribution of surplus value to loan capital is again subsidized by the State through tax mechanisms. Thus the subsidies are aimed at reducing the cost of loan finance. "State subsidies facilitate the political acceptance of a tenure structure requiring loan capital" (Ball 1978: 94).

If both major tenures allow for the extraction of surplus value why has owner-occupation been favoured? Owner-occupation has distinct advantages for capital. First, it can been seen as a solution to the problem of cost in the local authority sector. There is no need for the State to face the longer term problem of the cost of comprehensive state housing provision. Secondly, it has ideological advantages. As Engels pointed out and the Conservative and now Labour parties recognize, owner-occupation gives the worker 'a stake in the economy' a valuable piece of private property.

> The man who has something to protect and improve — a stake of some sort in this country — naturally turns his thoughts in the direction of sane, ordered and perforce economical government.

> The thrifty man is seldom or never an extremist agitator. To him
> revolution is anathema: and as in the earliest days, building societies
> acted as a stabilising force, so today they stand in the words of the
> Rt Hon. Barnes, as "a bulwark against Bolshevism and all that
> Bolshevism stands for". (Bellman, 1927, p. 54)

It allows also the imposition of higher housing costs without creating the
dissatisfaction which leads to political or economic struggles to lower
these costs. People will 'scrimp and save' to pay for a house. This aspect
is starkly highlighted in the Saltley context. Loans are necessary for the
exchange of second hand houses as well as on purchase of new ones and it
is possible to suggest that more loan capital circulates in the owner-
occupation sector and therefore more surplus value is extracted. When
owner-occupation is coupled with large capital costs of renewal, as in
Saltley, this extraction is even greater.

The diversity of tenure also has a political function. Subsidies are posed
by the State as benefits to the working class and much debate centres on
who benefits the most. Much conflict is produced between the tenurial
groups making any united action around housing *per se* very difficult.
Part of the ideology of owner-occupation is that such ownership is a
sound investment for capital gain (and a necessary condition for trading
up into a bigger, better more expensive house). The neo-Marxist school
associated with the Political Economy of Housing Workshop, together
with Saunders (1979) and others, questions whether this is so. In general
their calculations are complex and their conclusions are ambiguous. But
it is clear that specifically leasehold owner-occupation does not provide
owners with long term capital gains. The occupier purchases a term of
years in exchange for a premium. It seems to be home-ownership but it is
very different. In the early years there are the convenants to worry about,
in later years the end of the lease. If the repairing covenants are not
complied with the leaseholder can be evicted. Contractually, when the
lease runs out the tenant must leave. The campaigns for leasehold reform
in the twentieth century have reflected the changes in housing provision
generally. In the early part of the century the emphasis was on reducing
the land-owners' powers to enforce repairing covenants and dilapidation
orders. By the 1950s when a substantial number of inner-city leasehold
properties were becoming owner-occupied, pressure for reform built up
and resulted, as the next section shows, in the Landlord and Tenant Act
1954 which gave some security to occupiers but in line with Tory policy
towards private landlords at the time, this was security as tenants once

the lease had expired rather than freeholder status. By the 1960s the ideological contradictions of leasehold owner-occupation were clearer. The leases were short, most had less than 30 years to run, the houses were no investment, no commodity from which to trade up, no security with which to carry out the substantial repairs now required by the new state policy of renewal after years of disinvestment by landlords. The use value was declining rapidly both economically as security and physically, yet the purchase prices were not offsetting the costs of repairs and the declining asset value. The campaign in the sixties has to be set against this emerging background of owner-occupation at any cost. The paradoxes of leasehold reform perhaps become clearer. While the leasehold tenure system had become increasingly important both in state development activity and in various abortive nationalization attempts, which had obtained substantial bourgeois backing, at the same time moves were made to obtain leasehold enfranchisement culminating in the Leasehold Reform Act 1967.

The leasehold reform movement started again in earnest in the second decade of the twentieth century. The issue, which became increasingly complex, led to considerable divergence over the type of reform required. Two strands can be distinguished, the earlier which saw the problem in terms of security of tenure, and the later which recognized the economic "right" of the leaseholder to enfranchise. Early campaigns, recognizing unfair bargaining power, called for a social reform to enable leaseholders to remain in the premises after the expiry of the lease, although they would be obliged to pay a weekly rent. They would then have the same protection as that given to the great majority of working-class tenants. The economic injustice in this situation was not considered since ideologically at the time it would have conflicted with the dominant ethos of sanctity of contract and would have been seen as an interference with property rights. The security approach triumphed in the 1954 Landlord and Tenant Act. The economic injustice of a leaseholder paying rent for his own house was recognized but, until owner-occupation had emerged as the main tenure form, was not a significant feature.

The thrust was to alleviate the worst effects of the unfair bargaining position which was not recognized in the term sanctity of contract. This phrase assumed that the lease was a "bargain" made between equal parties able to negotiate and haggle freely. This was obviously unrealistic when applied to the building lease and was recognized as such by academic lawyers and politicians. An influential member of the former profession wrote:

> It is evidently absurd to speak of freedom of contract in relation to such a system . . . . The landowner dictates his terms to the building lessee, who in turn dictates them to the occupier making the occupier's obligations, for his own protection exactly follow those of the original lease. In this way the population of whole cities may be said to live at the will of a few great landlords. (Pollock, 1885, p. 155)

Consequently, a reapportionment of the obligations in the agreements were seen as necessary. The landlord's right to terminate the lease if the tenant fails to pay the rent or is in breach of a covenant, has long been subject to the tenant's right to claim relief against the forfeiture. As an action for forfeiture is one of the main sanctions that a landlord can impose on his tenants, the tenant's right to claim relief represents a substantial curb on the landlord's powers. The Law of Property Act (LPA) 1925 prevented a landlord from demanding a payment for the grant of his consent to an assignment or subletting proposed by the tenant. The Landlord and Tenant Act 1927 (LTA) made covenants against assignment and underletting without consent subject to a proviso that such consent would not be unreasonably withheld. This Act also added provisos to covenants against making improvements or changes of use without consent, thus further limiting the landlord's ability to interfere with the tenant. The LPA 1925 and the LTAs 1927 and 1954, and in particular the Leasehold Property Repairs Act 1938, imposed a complex statutory procedure for the enforcement of repairing covenants, through which formerly landlords had been able to exploit tenants. These measures, in addition to measures in the Housing Act 1957 and 1961, which are unsuitable for building leases, illustrate the trend of landord and tenant legislation: the limitation of the landlord's rights and powers and a reapportionment of some of the obligations of the agreement.

This recognition of the myth of sanctity of contract did not challenge the further ideological concept of interference with property rights. Thus the measures were overlaid by a formulation of the problem as socially undesirable. The aim was to provide security of occupation, but not ownership for the leaseholders when the lease expired. The Land Enquiry Committee in 1913 did not recommend enfranchisement rather that the leaseholder, with a lease for more than 21 years, should have a right to an extension not only on expiry but any time before. It was never implemented. Legislation to give tenants security of tenure was first introduced for tenants of low rateable value houses on leases of less than 21 years in 1915, as a temporary measure under the Increase of Rent and Mortgage Interest (War Restrictions Act 1915) but it did not cover long leaseholders. The position was considered again in 1919 when a departmental committee under Lord Salisbury looked into the 1915 measure and in 1920 by the Select Committee on Business Premises. Both heard voluminous evidence on leasehold enfranchisement from the Town Tenants League and other supporters. In both cases the conclusion was that security of tenure was required.

The opposing strand which saw enfranchisement as the solution gained one victory in 1920 with the enactment of the Places of Worship (Enfranchisement) Act which concerned certain ecclesiastical leasehold premises. Annual Bills were introduced until 1929 and then another in 1937. After this, activity died down until 1946 when the new context brought renewed interest. A considerable amount of property had been destroyed in the war and the leases granted in the boom time of the 1950s were about to expire. Something had to be done. In 1948 the Lord Chancellor appointed a Departmental Committee under Lord Uthwatt, to consider leasehold tenure. Among the terms of reference was a consideration of the desirability of enfranchisement. They reported finally in 1950, after issuing an interim report on rents and tenure of business premises in which they recommended that a sitting tenant of business premises should be treated as having a right to renewal of his tenancy. This measure was restricted to occupying tenants and the onus was on the landlord to instigate the procedure for renewal. In assessing the general effect of the evidence for enfranchisement the committee considered that, for the freeholders, this would involve a fundamental interference with property rights and freedom of contract. It would cause grave hardship to the freeholders through their inability to find alternative sources of investment, the difficulty of estate management, the loss of unified control and through the inadequacy of the compensation if it were fixed on any basis likely to be attractive to lessees. They found difficulty in establishing the opinion generally held by tenants

> owing to their lack of organisation as a class. One or two local or
> national organisations were committed to political demands like

enfranchisement but these would not claim to be fully representative of ground lessees as a class. (1950, p. 20)

There was "no identity of interest among leaseholders as there was among freeholders". Therefore, it was

> fair to say that only a minority of tenants desire enfranchisement in relation to residential premises. Support comes from organisations representing small traders who live on the premises and even here most are interested in security of tenure, not enfranchisement. (1950, p. 21)

They did admit that "a considerable degree of local support for the principle exists in South Wales". They refused to consider the original monopoly situation: "at this distance in time it is obviously impossible to adjudicate upon charges of unfair conduct on the part of the original landlords in granting leases" (1950, p. 23). Professional opinion was heavily against the measure. The view of the majority was that:

> the inconveniences and injustices formerly associated with the leasehold system have been substantially removed or mitigated by legislation and that any outstanding defects still demanding attention could be adequately dealt with by further legislation within the framework of the existing law. (1950, p. 24)

Government departments and other public authorities were unanimously opposed for reasons of management and planning. The trade union movement advocated the right of compulsory purchase for tenants of all types "as an encouragement to a sense of domestic and civic responsibility".

The committee considered the general trend of legislation over the last 65 years to have, in some respects, weakened the case for enfranchisement as it stood in 1884. They recognized the tendency to use the system as an instrument of planned development. They stated that: "we ourselves take the view that the leasehold system is a convenient and even an essential feature of our real property law" (1950, p. 30). The majority conclusion was then that they did not find sufficient grounds for holding that a measure conferring on building lessees the right to purchase the freehold is warranted as a matter of fairness between the parties. "We are satisfied that the typical building lease is by no means the one sided affair that the advocates of enfranchisement assume" (1950, p. 34). The recommendations were that there should be no right to purchase but wherever practicable the occupying tenant should be given first refusal.

The protection of the Rent Act should be extended to occupying tenants within the rateable value limitations.

The minority report produced by Hale and Ungoed Thomas took a different political and social outlook:

> We consider nowadays, in general, that the landlord's interest is an investment of a financial interest whereas the tenant's interest is for use and occupation; the landlord's interest is in what he can get out of the property, the tenant's interest is in the property itself. (1950, pp. 126-127)

They went on to state that:

> We do not believe that our committee sufficiently appreciate what fierce resentment the history of the building lease system has engendered in these [industrial] areas. (1950, p. 139)

They considered the concept of nationalization of the reversions and stated that, where necessary, private ownership should yield to public, but:

> where a thing is owned not for business but for personal use and enjoyment, it should serve that purpose. The whole object of ownership is that the owner should be able to do exactly as he likes with it. (1950, p. 139)

Their recommendations were that the occupying tenant should have the right of enfranchisement, although flats and fag ends of lease (last 10 years) were excluded. Compensation was to be the fair market value of the reversion assuming that there was a sitting tenant protected by the Rent Restriction Acts subject to deductions for improvements made by preceeding and present tenants.

In 1951 the Labour Government passed a temporary measure, the Leasehold Properties (Temporary Provisions) Act, which introduced a standstill for two years. This had the effect of extending leases due to expire before mid Summer 1953. In the second reading debate the Government proposed to set up a committee of officials under the Chairmanship of a Minister of Cabinet rank to study the matter of the expiring leases and to prepare legislative proposals. The Government changed in 1951 and in 1953 the Conservatives introduced their White Paper on the subject. This strongly favoured the 1950 majority report rejecting enfranchisement mainly on grounds of alleged practical difficulties.

The conclusion reached by the Government is that the cost to the lessee and the various exclusions necessary in order to prevent (which they only partially do) the dangers and inequalities which might result from the scheme would in practice limit the number of enfranchisements to something well below what would justify so complex and controversial a measure. (1953, p. 10)

The alternative was:

In the Government's view, the main practical need for long lease-holders the expiry of whose leases is in sight is for security of tenure rather than for freehold ownership and more good can be done by protecting the right of occupation than by giving a new right of ownership. (1953, p. 10)

The Landlord and Tenant Act 1954 implemented this policy by giving sitting ground lessees the right, in certain circumstances, to remain as statutory tenants and giving them the protection of the Rent Acts. This right to remain is severely qualified since the landlord can obtain immediate possession if he proves that he needs the premises for redevelopment or any reason under the Rent Act provisions. The tenant is still responsible for the whole cost of the dilapidations. He also pays a different standard of rent to other statutory tenants since it is based on the condition of the house after the initial repairs (dilapidations) are done. Therefore, the leaseholder faces the heavy burden of paying an open market rent and the cost of the "initial repairs".

In 1954 the security aspect predominated. The tenant's economic claims were not allowed to interfere with the ownership of property. Tenants were seen to want security, not owner-occupation and the supposed freedom of property ownership. The sub-committee of the Society of Labour Lawyers endorsed this view. They considered that enfranchisement was not a satisfactory way of giving people the security they needed. People of small means acquiring the freehold would not be able to keep their property in repair. Therefore their report (1953) preferred a statutory tenancy at a low rate. A further option put forward by James McColl, Labour M.P. for Widnes, in the 1953 debate, was that where estates were not well managed it would be better if they were taken into public ownership rather than being split up.

The pressure for reform died down again until the early 1960s by which time many old leasehold houses had become owner-occupied. The immediate cause for activity was once again the imminent falling in of leases, this time in South Wales. The issue was now couched in different terms since the idea of a property owning democracy had become important. Leaseholders no longer needed mere possession obtainable through security of tenure, they required the economic right to own along with everybody else. Thus by the 1966 General Election both bourgeois parties were committed to relieve the social hardship and consequent political problem through the ideological framework of enfranchisement. The emergent battle revolved around the leaseholder's economic rights when looked at in terms of compensation and rateable value limitations. Property rights were no longer sacrosanct, compensation was now the issue.

Considerable changes had also occurred in the national property ownership structure. The post war period brought a property boom in which institutional investment dominated the market. In the 1950s entrepreneurial property companies emerged financed primarily by insurance companies who lent money on fixed interest terms. The 1960s saw the growth of pension fund activity. Together with insurance companies they took on ordinary shares and equity stakes in companies and engaged in partnership on specific projects. All urban land values increased but most dramatically in the commercial sector. The new capitalist land-owner sector

> is distinguished from that of former landed property by the fact that it operates completely within capitalist terms. By this is meant that land (and property) ownership is here just another sector to invest in. (Massey and Catalano, 1978, p. 67)

They were not interested in the residential sector of the property market. It was neither profitable nor politically acceptable for the pensions of workers to be made from other workers' rents. But they were interested in redevelopment. Thus leasehold interests came into the hands of these owners who used them for reversionary investment purposes alone when ground rent returns had lost any significant economic value. At the same time the large landed estates had lost their significance as urban landholders (see Massey and Catalano, 1978). As the Sunday Times reported:

> Tax and mismanagement have eroded the great estates leaving Government bodies and public institutions as the last of the great landowners. Of the top ten landed gentry in Britain now only one is the head of a truly private estate. (the Sunday Times, 2nd February 1975)

Economic considerations had pushed them in two directions. First to seek alternative investment in commercial dealings, secondly to sell off their leasehold estates into freehold owner-occupation to obtain lump sums to reinvest and to avoid further management costs. As Marriot (1967) has pointed out the great London estates in the 1960s attempted to improve their economic position by joining in partnerships with development companies whereby they would redevelop parts of their estates. Similarly the church commissioners were persuaded to sell off their residential estates and engage in commercial activities with developers as partners.

There had been three private members bills between 1959 and 1962. In a debate on 12th July 1961 in the House of Commons, it was claimed that leaseholders were suffering considerable hardship because of the onerous terms which landlords were asking either for the sale of reversions or extension. The Ministry of Housing and Local Government examined 50 cases which, they thought, failed to substantiate these claims. The Government decided to seek the help of the professional bodies most experienced in the field. They asked the Law Society, Royal Institute of Chartered Surveyors, Chartered Auctioneers and Estate Agents Institute and the Incorporated Society of Auctioneers and Landed Property Agents to examine and report on the present practice of ground landlords, particularly in South Wales. The Law Society concluded that support for leasehold enfranchisement was confined to South Wales and it was limited even there with a considerable volume of positive opposition to it. There was some support for legislation to give lessees a statutory right to a new lease, but there was considerable opposition to both enfranchisement and renewal on a compulsory basis because it was "repugnant to the principle of freedom of contract". The other bodies felt that there was nothing fundamentally wrong with the leasehold system. There was widespread ignorance among lessees as to the limited nature of their interest and it was this lack of understanding rather than any inherent defects in the leasehold system which was the difficulty. They suggested that the Government should publish a new booklet designed to inform lessees more adequately about their rights (Summary Report, 1962).

Yet in the same year the Times published an article on the leasehold system. It concluded that few reports have become so quickly obsolete as that of Jenkins in 1950, and that there was a substantial body of opinion within the Conservative Party now in favour of enfranchisement: the Wales and Monmouth Conservative Association had passed a resolution in favour of the right of a lessee to purchase his freehold compulsorily at a fair price. Professional opinion was no longer against the measure:

> a questionnaire was recently sent to all solicitors practising in Swansea, Cardiff and Newport asking their views on the subject and the balance of opinion is now reversed, at least in those areas. Those solicitors are now heavily in favour of leasehold enfranchisement ... Estate agents in those three towns were also consulted, and their views were similar. (the Times, 16th May 1962)

The Times suggested that in addition to the recognized social effects of the leasehold system that short leases had a marked effect on the values of property and mortgages were unobtainable, there were a number of new considerations. First, the leasehold system itself was beginning to spread rapidly in a number of the largest cities; secondly, the Conservative Government had adopted as one of its objectives the theme of "a property owning democracy" and was encouraging home ownership; thirdly, the Government had instituted a policy of improvement. As a result:

> It may not unfairly be said that if the Government's policy is truly property owning democracy then it must will the means to a full implementation of that policy. Not until a house owner is free from the difficulties and hardships of the leasehold system can it be said that the Government has taken all the steps which it reasonably could take to implement its own policy. (the Times, 16th May 1962)

The paper went on to reflect the current attitude to the new property owners who sought to make the maximum profit out of their investments.

> This is not legally improper but whether this should be allowed is a matter of high social policy, it is no longer a matter of law or finance. These new ground landlords have invested in a type of security that has a very special importance to the lessees concerned. They have invested in the right to receive money by way of an annual payment from a property that is in fact the home of another British citizen. (the Times, 16th May 1962)

The practice of harsh landlords had led to a feeling of rankling injustice, "which any Government ignores at its peril". Skeffington (1963) echoed later the same fear, "It cannot be good for the nation that this social friction between lessee and freeholder should continue." Both dismissed the sanctity of contract argument as outdated.

With this rousing support by the Times, the Labour M.P. for Small Heath (which covers half of the Saltley area) Dennis Howell introduced his private members Bill into the House of Commons. It received a second reading on 7th December. The Economist had accused him of introducing a Bill of a "blatant political character", but once again the new freehold ownership was attacked with talk of "very shady operators" and the problems of mortgages were discussed. The Conservative Party maintained on the whole the concept of sanctity of contract, and the Government spokesman refused to concede to enfranchisement even at market value so the Bill was defeated.

In 1964 the Government changed hands. The Labour Party had been pledged to leasehold reform since 1951. The issue appeared in their election manifesto which stated briefly but firmly that the government would change the leasehold law to enable householders with an original lease of more than 21 years to buy their own houses on fair terms. The White Paper on the proposed legislation did not appear until February 1966. In the intervening period there seemed to be a growing consensus for leasehold enfranchisement. In 1963 Skeffington reissued his 1956 Fabian pamphlet which was strongly in favour of the measure. Even the Inns of Court Conservative and Unionist Society committee on leasehold enfranchisement in its report in 1965 did not deny the concept, although it was very cautious. It heralded the arrival of a new issue. Their recommendation was that, if leasehold enfranchisement was necessary, it must be at market value with no rateable value limits and cover flats but not business premises. The only major dissenting voice was the Town and Country Planning Association which heard a paper at their National Conference in 1965. The economic consequences of the leasehold system were outlined but enfranchisement was rejected as a means of overcoming the problem. Instead, the paper supported the proposition, which had support amongst those concerned with land use planning, that a reformed leasehold system should be widely expanded to cover all urban land.

Behind the scene, however, all was not well. The problem arose from the difficulty of translating a simple electoral pledge of enfranchisement on fair terms into a firm legislative formula. Crossman (1975) then Minister of Housing who initially had responsibility for the legislation, describes it as an "inordinately complicated measure" on 2nd November 1964 and "an appalling political embarrassment" on 1st July 1965. Heavy pressure was put on Crossman by the Welsh Labour Members of

Parliament, including James Callaghan then Chancellor of the Exchequer, to give the measure top priority. Crossman managed to stave off pressure for a while and pass the responsibility on to Fred Willey at the Ministry of Land and Natural Resources. By October 1965 Willey had come up with some "new and radical proposals" but the cabinet meeting on 23rd December 1965 was completely taken up with a deadlock on the issue.

> Fred Willey on the one side and the Law Officers, Lord Chancellor and Minister of Housing all on the other. The lawyers were profoundly shocked by Fred's proposal that we should give every leaseholder the choice between a 99 year lease — tantamount to confiscation of the property — and an improved rent. I was shocked because this would apply not only to the private leaseholder but to the local authorities, public corporations and nationalized industries. An important issue of socialist principle was at stake here though few people seemed to bother about it. For many years the Labour Party's view on leasehold has been that it is an excellent way for public authorities to retain their basic rights while permitting owner-occupation, thus ensuring good physical planning. (Crossman, 1975, p. 420)

After a great struggle the paper was referred back to the committee. By the cabinet meeting on 10th February 1966 the terms of the Bill had been settled except for one outstanding issue.

> The lawyers demanded a rule that no one should be allowed to get the confiscation of site value which is implied in leasehold enfranchisement unless (a) he had lived in the house for five years, and (b) (this was the difference) he or his father had held the lease for more than twenty-one years. Willey and I were united in objecting to this. (Crossman, 1975, p. 452)

Willey and Crossman won the day, but not before their colleagues had become "nervous about whether the Cabinet was not being asked to play politics *too* flagrantly" (original emphasis). On 17th February 1966, the eve of the publication of the White Paper, Crossman described the drafting of the Bill as "ghastly". "Afterwards Fred Willey told me he had had to do the work himself because Bruce Fraser (his Permanent Secretary) had just refused to co-operate" (Crossman, 1975, p. 459). Crossman had the same reaction from his own civil servants. The "Dame" as he describes his Permanent Secretary, detested the whole idea and used the ministerial committee to fight a running departmental battle against it.

The White Paper appeared on the 18th February and was debated on the 28th, the day on which the General Election was announced. The White Paper stated that in the Government's view:

> the basic principle of reform which will do justice between the parties should be that the freeholder owns the land and the occupying leaseholder is morally entitled to the ownership of the building which has been put on and maintained on the land. (1966, p. 3)

The document went on to state the short term purposes of the proposed legislation. Two circumstances made the reform a matter of urgency. The first was the mortgage problem. A purchaser on a mortgage may pay virtually the freehold price for a lease but as he reaches the end of his mortgage term he feels a "sharpening sense of injustice". He realises that after he has discharged the mortgage he will have an interest of far less value than it was when he bought it and will have difficulty in selling it because a subsequent purchaser may not be able to obtain a mortgage. The second reflects the increasing pressure from South Wales on the Government:

> A great many leasehold estates were built in the second half of the 19th century when landowners used their monopoly power to prevent development taking place on other than leasehold terms. This occurred particularly in South Wales and in some English areas. These leases are beginning to fall in and the leaseholders are experiencing the full harshness of the leasehold system. (1966: 3)

The White Paper excluded flats, since "different conditions of equity apply and there would be many practical difficulties"; it proposed rateable value limitations; and suggested a price mechanism. The White Paper justified its position in the following way:

> It is important to ensure that the price paid for enfranchisement is a fair price. But present market prices reflect the position under the present law which is inequitable to the leaseholder and the price for enfranchisement must accordingly be based not on present market values but on the value of the land itself including any development value attaching to it. The price of enfranchisement must be calculated in accordance with the principle that in equity the bricks and mortar belong to the qualified leaseholder and the land to the landlord. (1966, p. 6)

The debate reflected, first the imminence of a general election, and secondly support for enfranchisement as a measure.

Until the White Paper and the Bill based on it there was considerable commitment to enfranchisement as a solution to the social evils of the leasehold system. Support came from those groupings wedded to the property owning democracy. Within this consensus, however, a struggle emerged around the freeholder's economic right to compensation. The legislation was proposed with a major new element which lost their support and led to rejection of the measure itself. This was the recognition of some sort of economic assessment between the parties which was represented in the rateable value limitations and the basis of compensation. The measure was to benefit 'poor' leaseholders only (although only 1% of leaseholders were excluded by the limits) and was to be viewed from an historical perspective which recognized the economic inequalities in the late nineteenth century.

The Labour Party, which won the election, issued a pamphlet (1967) supporting its measure. It argued that the reform starts at the very root of the leasehold problem based on the principle that the leaseholders' rights are to the house itself while the freeholders' lie with the land alone. Opposition came swiftly from the Conservative Party. Their Monday Club's view was predictable:

> From any objective stand point, the Government proposals are patently unjust and unfair. The consensus of opinion of all the professional bodies connected with the land is against them. (Housing Study Group, 1967)

They recommended another commission to investigate the whole leasehold system. The National Federation of Property Owners mounted a nationwide campaign to lobby M.P.s and other interested parties. They claimed that they were faced with a "monstrous threat to individual freedom" and stressed the financial outlay to the land-owner involved in the leasehold system. The right approach was for enfranchisement on a voluntary basis at full market value. The Town and Country Planning Association (1966) considered the White Paper unsatisfactory and that there was good reason for suggesting that enfranchisement was an anachronism. Their proposal was for extensions only. The Chartered Surveyors Joint Committee declared that: "Enfranchisement represents the forcible transfer at less than market value of one individual's property to another individual" (the Times, 28th February 1966), and recommended that the system should be reformed by improving the security of tenure.

The professional journals expressed their disapproval of confiscation.

The Conveyancer article considered that the provisions concerning compensation "mar an excellent bill. For all the White Paper's talk of 'equity' there is undoubtedly a strong element of confiscation in the Bill". It called for full market value compensation. The New Law Journal sounded a cautionary note, "A civilised society must promote the concept of social obligation attaching to property whilst avoiding arbitrary confiscation" and considered that market value was the only acceptable principle. The Estates Gazette followed the same line.

The Times also reflected the shift in opinion. It considered the White Paper as advocating bluntly "confiscation":

> landlords may be an unpopular class but for a white paper in these circumstances to use the word 'equity' twice in its first paragraph about the plan is to abuse the English language . . . The Government seems more than half way to declaring war on the private investment in leasehold property. (The Times, 19th February 1966)

The paper proceeded to mount almost a campaign against the Bill as it passed through the House and in doing so neatly illustrated the issue: it considered that the Bill bore the marks of legislative extravagance. "Instead of remedying the evils to which it is addressed in the most economical way, it propounds an elaborate and far reaching solution" (the Times, 24th February 1966). This could be done by a right to renewal but, if enfranchisement was considered just, the Bill enshrined terms which were "too biased in favour of the leaseholder":

> These Robin Hood methods can sometimes be justified if the beneficiaries are particularly deserving and their victims particularly undeserving. In this case the victims include charities, pension funds and small investors. (the Times, 24th February 1966)

A very different assessment of property owners and leaseholders to the previous article.

The Bill which was introduced on 22nd February 1967 proceeded through Parliament with the debates reflecting the same divergence of opinion. Fred Willey opening the second reading said:

> If a property owning democracy makes any sense social justice requires that the owner-occupier should have the opportunity of obtaining the basic security which the owner-occupier prizes most, the freehold, with all the liberty and responsibility that goes with it. (1967, 742 House of Commons Official Report 1277)

An excellent account of the Act's Parliament history is given by Ted

Rowlands. He writes of the second reading:

> The official Opposition had avoided for electoral reasons a division
> on the White Paper, but were now to reveal their true feelings on
> the proposals. A reasoned amendment was moved which, while
> accepting the rights of leasehold enfranchisement, condemned the
> bill as "confiscatory". But the Opposition was not unanimous.
> The Government's Bill had Conservative friends from leasehold
> constituencies. Mr. Gurden, a Birmingham Member, frankly
> admitted "I am pleased that the Government had introduced this
> bill. I had a fear at one stage that it might go the way of many other
> promises by the Labour party. But I congratulate them on bringing
> in the bill...". On the division, one South Wales Conservative,
> Mr. Gower, voted with the Government and at least three of the
> Opposition Members abstained. The Government had an unusually
> large majority of 122 (319-197). (1971, pp. 336-337)

The valuation section was largely neglected

> Only one member, Mr. Rossi, warned of the possible confusion
> that might arise: "On the proposals as put forward by the
> Government the leaseholder and the freeholder cannot escape
> having to employ professional valuers... Anyone who has any
> dealings with this matter knows that valuers, like experts, often
> disagree. There can be endless and tedious arguments, calculation
> and possible litigation... This kind of situation and the expense of
> employing these people will be inevitable in using the methods
> proposed by the Minister in the bill...(Rowlands, 1971, p. 337)

Rowlands, commenting on the committee stage of the bill, says that

> Straightforward political confrontation on Second Reading lines
> replaced, for the most part, any dispassionate scrutiny of whether
> the Government's intentions were adequately and effectively trans-
> lated into legislative terms. (1971, p. 340)

The rateable value limits which were removed at committee stage were
reintroduced at the Report stage. Here again none of the issues which
have pre-occupied the Lands Tribunal, valuers and leaseholders after the
passing of the Act, were considered. The Act acquired Royal Assent in
October 1967 without any debate on the substance of section 9, which
deals with the valuation of the freehold interest.

The measure was abused throughout its Parliamentary history by the
national newspapers; the Times now considered that enfranchisement
should be limited to South Wales and the industrial North-West. So the
Act appeared on the statute book amid fierce hostility from former

grudging supporters. Richard Crossman reflected:

> What worries me (on the home front) is whether we shall work out
> a satisfactory solution to a number of our central problems. Indeed
> it is clear once again that a socialist opposition in this country comes
> into office with very half baked plans. True this time we have done
> far more work than the 1945 Government on social security, but
> the incomes guarantee is not nearly sufficiently worked out to be
> put into practice. I strongly suspect the same is true of steel
> nationalisation and I know it be true of leasehold reform and the
> land commission, where at first glance in Whitehall the Party
> policy was seen to be unworkable or futile. (1975, p. 118)

The Financial Times reported likewise: "Officials at the Ministry of
Housing were privately apologetic. 'This,' they would explain, 'was a
fudged up piece of electioneering' " (quoted by Rowlands, 1971, p.
340). The social objective had been recosted. Freehold owner-occupation
was the ideal but the price was too high to pay for those immediately
involved as landholders or the professionals representing them. Yet the
system created by the Act for enfranchisement was a reflection of market
conditions. It relied, as Hugh Rossi pointed out in the Second Reading
debate, for its enforcement on those groupings who had rejected the
measure, the land-owners and professional bodies. Apart from this
obvious problem the system was set up inadequately even in its own
terms. Very little thought had gone into the valuation clause. The
columns of the professional journals were full of extensive debate over its
interpretation. Should account be taken, in assessing a freehold price, of
the possible inflation over the period covered by the proposed 50 year
extended lease? Was the leaseholder bidding in the open market for the
freehold? If so in both cases the effect was to push up the freehold price
much in excess of the examples quoted in Parliament. The Lands
Tribunal rejected the first but supported the second. One year later
Section 82 of the Housing Act 1969 had to re-establish the principle of a
fair price. Section 9 was fodder for professional valuers. The Law Society
soon stepped in to announce its position. The leaseholder ought to go to
a solicitor or he may serve ineffective notice or serve notice when it
would not pay him to do so. The legal costs may be a high proportion of
the total enfranchisement price for some leaseholders but "solicitors are
not going to grow fat as a result of the Bill because most of the legal
work will be comparatively unremunerative" (the Times, 27th October
1967).

At a political level the issue of compensation caused heated argument. Both 'market' and 'fair' forms of value involve assumptions about the rights of owners. Both assume that a landowner has a right to compensation for loss of the land, but the latter restricts the freeholder's right to compensation for loss of the house. The legislation adopted a 'fair' value and gave rise to cries of 'confiscation' or 'expropriation'. Yet if the leaseholder loses a home there is no such outcry, even though he has paid not only for the house but also for the use of the land over and over again. (Nor, one might add, is similar compensation payable for the worker's only source of income, a job.) The issue of compensation can be taken further. Why compensate a freeholder for even the land if its only real value is for development? A leaseholder is entitled to remain in the house after the lease has expired. The freeholder can then collect a weekly rent but the evolution of the relations of property and tenure forms hardly suggest that this is their main incentive. The new property owners had bought their leasehold estates for their potential reversionary value. This is a product of private ownership of land but surely not one for which leaseholders are obliged to pay. It is a form of betterment not an object of compensation. Yet the issue was never couched in this way but in terms of private property rights at a time when the state was intervening to curb the excessive profits made out of development by the same urban landholders.[3]

The Land Commission Bill, which vied for priority with the Leasehold Reform Bill, concerned the means of transferring these profits to the state. Its method involved a form of public leasehold tenure, crownhold. Subsequently the White Paper, "Land" (1974) which preceded the Community Land Act 1975, also suggested a similar approach (see Massey and Catalano, 1978). Development land would be bought by the local state and leased out to builders. It seems paradoxical that a leasehold system was advocated by the state to cream off betterment whilst the Leasehold Reform Act required working-class leaseholders to compensate the same land-owners for loss of it.

The Act seems to represent the triumph of an ideology of the property owning democracy based on individual property rights and achieved at whatever cost over rational management of the housing stock. It was never explained how fragmenting ownership of worn out housing estates would be in the public interest at a time when the idea of co-ordinated area improvement was replacing that of redevelopment nor even in the long term interests of house owning lessees. Perhaps working-class lessees' call for the right to enfranchise was based on the desire for security and a recognition of the investment they have made in their homes not on a desire to be part of the property owning democracy for its own sake since, in their case, it involved a heavy future financial burden to purchase a freehold and to improve. Their interests could perhaps have been furthered by transfer of the freehold interest to the State, in line with Labour Party policy at the time to introduce some measure of public ownership of land under a leasehold system. Lease-holders would then not have had to purchase their freeholds but would still have had the security of the public sector, their investment could have been compensated through a local authority sponsored improvement scheme, and a coherent area policy for improvements could have been worked out using the advantages of a state run leasehold system.

Notes

1. The industrialists of the late nineteenth century lived in Edgbaston. Their twentieth century counterparts still do. The Calthorpe Estate houses many of the dominant West Midland bourgeoisie. The residents association is highly influential and managed to exert enough pressure to bring about the amendment to the Leasehold Reform Act 1967 which is now incorporated in the Housing Act 1974. This allows the 1% excluded by high rateable values to enfranchise. The other 1¼ million leaseholders have had more trouble in lobbying for reform as will be seen later.
2. Rent rebates were introduced in the 1950s to deal with this problem. It is the same conflict. Decent housing is too costly for some sectors of the working class. The rents of the new council houses were too high and thus had to be subsidized. Birmingham introduced rent rebates in 1955. The schemes were voluntary until 1972 when the Housing Finance Act made them mandatory.
3. The outcry did not stop with the passage of the Act. As late as January 1979 the issue was still stimulating opponents to seek remedies. In an article in the Estates Gazette entitled "Even Freeholders may have Human Rights" Harry Kidd lately bursar of St John's College, Oxford, urges "some John Hamden among freeholders" to appeal to the European Court of Human Rights. His argument is as follows:

Writing of the Leasehold Reform Act 1967, in the Law of Real Property, Megarry and Wade observe, ''When the ground lease of a house needing repair neared its end, a purchaser could usually acquire it for little or nothing, yet the Act gave those who had done this the right to acquire the freehold for the price of the site at the expense of a reversioner who until then had a valuable and appreciating asset ... the Act of 1967 ... expropriated the reversioner without compensation''. In a footnote they say, ''Since this was for the benefit of the tenant rather than for any public purpose, it may have been a breach of article 1 of the First Protocol (1952) to the European Convention on Human Rights (1950), which provides that 'no one shall be deprived of his possessions except in the public interest' ''. (1979, p. 31)

4 The Act and How They Thought It Would Work

The aim of this chapter is first to describe the provisions of the Act, and then to set out the practices which have evolved. It does not attempt to provide a comprehensive guide to, or explanation of, the Act since it is not an exercise on legal interpretation and writing. The Act is the background to a struggle over housing in Saltley and so only the provisions which are particularly relevant to Saltley houses are outlined here. Secondly, it attempts to point out how the conflict, which evolved with the Act, has been perpetuated in its mechanisms, and how this, coupled with bad drafting, has led to abstruseness in the Act itself, confusion and amendment. As the last chapter showed the two main parties clashed over a number of issues, the most significant of which were the rateable value limitations and the level of compensation. The rateable value limitations gave rise to a caustic comment by Taylor in the Estates Gazette which represents a strongly supported view: "This marvellous concept of equity for the tenant who was alleged to have paid for his house was nevertheless limited to houses with low rateable values" (1977, p. 795).

In 1974 the Housing Act increased the rateable value limits. The result is a complex test for assessing eligibility and in many cases an arbitrary outcome. In addition a different process of assessing compensation is required for higher rateable values. But the main problem with the Act has come over fixing a price. To quote Willey M.P. on the problem of price:

> I can do no more than say that this is a clear distinction which has divided the two sides since we began our discussions not on the White Paper — there was no Division on the White Paper — but on the Bill which implements the White Paper. We say that the price for the freehold should not be on present market values, but

the fair value, including the development of the land alone. (Hansard, 248 House of Commons Official Report 1486).

Technically this contentious concept of fair value had to be translated into a mechanism to achieve that objective. The Act does not state what is a fair price and it does not set out a formula which could be applied to each property. If a price, for instance, had been fixed by relating it to a multiple of the ground rent or the rateable value there would be no technical valuation problem. Both sides would be presented with a *fait accompli*. The procedure for obtaining the standardized freehold interest would consequently be simple. The freeholder could notify a tenant of his right and offer the freehold at the known price. Instead the Leasehold Reform Act artificially creates a ''free'' market in which the interested parties, on the initiative of the tenant, engage in negotiations and bargain over a price. The market is, however, artificial for three reasons. First, the freeholder is obliged to respond to the initiative; secondly, the parties must take account of the principles and assumptions about price which are contained in sections 9 and 15 of the Act; thirdly, if the parties cannot agree the matter is referred to the Lands Tribunal who, whilst adopting in their procedure the idea of a ''free'' bargain, ultimately fix a price. Although professionals complain that there is no real world with which to compare freehold valuations, the Act mechanisms have created their own commodity market. Dealers are able to buy freehold interests (or ground rents as they are commonly called) and sell for a profit to tenants just because there is no clearly agreed free price. The lack of political will to provide a fixed formula has now created a business of leasehold reform. The problems can be seen throughout the procedure, in the tenant's responsibility to establish eligibility, in the system of negotiation and primarily in the valuation method. Inevitably the combination of procedural weakness, abstruseness and bad drafting has caused major problems for efficient implementation of the Act.

In an attempt to combat the hostility and bad drafting, the Act was amended by the Housing Act 1969. The Lands Tribunal has tried to evaluate and arbitrate on the practices built up by the professionals and the Court of Appeal has attempted to interpret the sections and produce guidelines for the experts. The Leasehold Reform Act 1979 closed a loophole and both the Labour Housing Bill of 1979 and the present government's replacement suggested further amendment. But the weaknesses in the technical and procedural elements cannot be divorced from the weakness in the substance of the Act. The creation of a market based system makes the determination of a fair value impossible. The chapter is divided into two parts, first how do residents in Saltley tackle the process of buying their freeholds and secondly how much will they have to pay for them?

When residents came to see us because they were worried about being leaseholders we told them that there were three possible options open to them: either to do nothing about their position, or to use the rights given by the Leasehold Reform Act to either extend their lease or to buy out the freehold.

The first option allows the lease to expire. Originally, when this happened, the land and buildings on it reverted back to the freeholder and the leaseholder could be evicted. But, as a previous chapter has shown, the Landlord and Tenant Act 1954 provides some statutory protection for the tenant. Part I enables a leaseholder occupying a dwelling or part of a dwelling under a ground lease to remain in occupation when his ground lease comes to an end. The former long tenancy is converted into a statutory weekly tenancy which is given security of tenure by the Rent Act 1977. All long leaseholders are eligible provided that they are still living in the dwelling at the end of the long tenancy but a tenant is not covered if his landlord is the Crown, a local authority, the Commission for New Towns, the development corporation of a new town or certain housing associations or trusts. The long tenancy is assumed to continue until it is either surrendered by the tenant or by the land-owner. If the tenant decides to leave he must comply with any dilapidation order (see later). If he stays the type of notice given by the landlord depends on his intentions: he can either allow the tenant to stay on new terms or require the tenant to leave. If it is the former the notice must, when served, specify the date of "termination" on which he wishes the tenancy to end and contain a warning to the leaseholder that any rights he possesses under the Leasehold Reform Act 1967 will be lost if not exercised within two months of the date of this notice. (So the leaseholder does not lose the right to buy or extend the lease until two months after the land-owner has initiated the procedure to change his status.) The tenant then replies, within two months, stating his desire to stay. The notice will have contained proposals as to rent and repairs including "initial repairs". The landlord and tenant can negotiate on the proposed terms and come to agreement in writing. Either the landlord or the tenant may apply to the rent officer for registration of a fair rent if they cannot agree on the amount of the rent. An application cannot be made until the other terms of the statutory tenancy have been agreed, the most important of which concerns the "initial repairs". These may be carried out by the landlord or by the tenant to comply with a dilapidation order. If the landlord does them he is entitled to recover from the tenant the reasonable cost of the repairs and the reasonable cost of a survey to ascertain what repairs were required. The payment may be made by the tenant either in a lump sum or by instalments. The responsibility for the initial repairs must have been set out in the landlord's statutory notice and agreed upon in writing between the two parties. In default of agreement the landlord can apply to the county court for a decision.

If the landlord serves notice to resume possession the notice again must give the termination date and the availability of the tenant's rights under the 1967 Act. It must also contain the grounds on which the landlord considers himself entitled to possession. The tenant then has two months within which to reply stating his desire to remain and contesting the grounds for possession. After that the landlord must, within two months of the tenant's reply, apply to the county court for a possession order. This procedure and the grounds for possession are similar to those under the Rent Act 1977 (see Partington, 1980). If the land-owner is successful and lawfully repossesses the house the leaseholder must comply with the dilapidation order and put the house in a state of good repair. Obviously residents are placed in a vulnerable position when they take this option since it involves paying a weekly rent and for additional repairs at best, and eviction and repairs at worst.

The second possibility is to extend the existing long lease. Section 4 (1) states that,

> the landlord shall be bound to grant to the tenant and the tenant to accept, in substitution for the existing tenancy a new tenancy of the house and premises for a term expiring fifty years after the term date of the existing tenancy.

The tenant can apply for an extension any time during the subsisting tenancy. It will be added to the existing tenancy on its term date. Extension does not operate to prevent a tenant buying his freehold. It is permissable to extend the lease and then purchase the freehold provided that notice to enfranchise is served before the end of the original long tenancy. Section 16 (1) (b) provides that the right to extend can be exercised only once.

Extending the lease is not a popular option. There are various reasons for this. First, a tenant must have complied with the repairing covenants contained within the original lease before the landlord is obliged to grant an extension. The cost can be prohibitive in physically decaying areas. Secondly, although the terms of the new lease are similar to those of the original long lease, the rent payable is a modern ground rent which, as section 15 stipulates, is an assessment of the site value at present use. There is a clause allowing a rent review after 25 years. Only two cases have ever appeared before the Lands Tribunal in 11 years. In one the reasons put forward were that,

> no well advised tenant would prefer to pay a rent for a house as postulated in Section 15 [finding that rent out of taxed income] if he had the opportunity instead of either purchasing the freehold or of paying a modest ground rent coupled with a capital sum for a long lease. It is understandable, therefore, that tenants to qualify under the Act have apparently with one accord hitherto, elected to purchase rather than take extended leases. (*Carthew and Others v. Estate Governors of Alleyn's College of God's gift (1974) 231 E.G. 809*)

Thirdly, the security provided by an extension is not all embracing. The landlord can obtain possession during the term if he satisfies the grounds laid down in section 17:

> Where a tenancy of a house and premises have been extended ... the landlord may at any time not earlier than twelve months before the original term date of the tenancy apply to the court for an order that he may resume possession of the property on the ground that for purposes of redevelopment he proposes to demolish or reconstruct the whole or a substantial part of the house and premises.

This section applies to any tenancy during the last year including those which have been extended or with registered notices.[1] If the county court is satisfied of the grounds it will grant possession to the landlord and compensation to the tenant. These rights will arise on the same date and are fixed subsequently after the amount of compensation due to the tenant is settled. The tenant can defeat the landlord's application by giving notice to enfranchise. Then only an order for costs can be made on the landlord's application to court. There are two exceptions to this;

(a) if the tenant serves notice after the date for termination has been fixed;

(b) if the landlord's application is made within 12 months after the tenant gave notice claiming the extended lease.

Thus the tenant should allow more then 12 months to elapse between service of notices to extend and enfranchise, the first being made more than a year before the end of the original tenancy.

Compensation to the tenant is assessed as the amount the house would be expected to realize in the open market, when sold by a willing seller to a willing buyer; with the assumption that the tenant has the right to extend if this has not been done but no right to enfranchise. The Lands Tribunal fixes the amount in default of agreement and this sum is payable on a date determined by the county court once the amount is known. These provisions are contained in Schedule 2 of the Act (see further 245 E.G. 768.).

The best option (the third) open to the leaseholder is to enfranchise. A tenant is entitled to purchase the freehold anytime during the subsistence of the existing lease and also, in circumstances already referred to, after the lease has terminated. He is not obliged to have complied with the covenants contained within the lease before he makes his claim and is not debarred from acquiring the freehold (or an extended lease) simply because the premises are out of repair. See *Central Estates (Belgravia) Ltd v. Woolgar; Liverpool Corpn v. Husan* [1972]. Enfranchisement effectively terminates all obligations on the part of the leaseholders to the freeholder, with one exception. The landlord is able to insist that the freehold should be subject to any restrictive covenants in the lease which benefit other property in which he has an interest. The price to be paid is laid down in section 9 as amended by the Housing Act 1969 section 82 and the Housing Act 1974 section 118. For houses with rateable values below £1000 in Greater London and £500 elsewhere it is the amount that the house would fetch on the open market at the date the tenant serves his notice, if sold by a willing seller, on the assumptions that:

(1) there is an extended lease;
(2) the right to enfranchise does not exist;
(3) the tenant and members of his family residing with him in the house are not seeking to buy (added by s82).

The land-owner cannot normally prevent the exercise of these rights. But it has already been noted that a landlord can prevent an extension of lease by an application for redevelopment rights. The landlord can also exclude both extension and enfranchisement by claiming residential rights.

> Subject to subsection (2) below, where the tenancy of a house and premises has not been extended under Section 14 above, but the tenant has a right to acquire the freehold or an extended lease and has given notice of his desire to have it, the landlord may, at any

time before effect is given to the notice, apply to the court for an order that he may resume possession of the property on the ground that it or part of it is or will be reasonably required by him for occupation as the only or main residence of the landlord or of a person who is at the time of the application an adult member of the landlord's family (Section 18 (1))

Subsection (2) limits the right to landlords whose interest was purchased or created before 18th February 1966. The landlord is obliged to prove to the satisfaction of the county court during the subsistence of the original lease;

(a) that he wants the house for occupation;

(b) that it would cause the landlord more hardship to be denied possession at that time than having to leave the house would cause the leaseholder.

The latter condition is a matter entirely within the court's discretion. It must have regard to all the circumstances including whether the landlord or the tenant has alternative accommodation available. The landlord also has to compensate the leaseholder for his loss on the same basis as for redevelopment.

Purchase of the freehold gives the resident the greatest benefit. However there are other considerations to take into account. First the resident must be eligible to use the Act and secondly he has to consider the cost of purchasing.

The right to enfranchisement (the ability to acquire the freehold) or extension is contained in section 1 (1):

> This part of this Act shall have effect to confer on a tenant of a leasehold house, occupying the house as his residence, a right to acquire on fair terms the freehold or an extended lease of the house and premises where
>
> (a) his tenancy is a long tenancy at a low rent and the rateable value of the house and the premises on the appropriate date is not (or was not) more than £200, or if it is in Greater London, than £400 [Amended subsequently by Housing Act s118].
>
> (b) at the relevant time [that is to say, at the time when he gives notice in accordance with this Act of his desire to have the freehold or to have an extended lease, as the case may be] he has been tenant of the house under a long tenancy at a low rent, and occupying it as his residence, for the last five years or for periods amounting to five years in the last ten years.

Thus to qualify for the right to enfranchise or extend, the leaseholder must occupy the house (within certain rateable value limitations) as a residence, for 5 years on a long tenancy at a low rent. To take each part in turn. To occupy the house as a residence the tenant must have occupied for the five years immediately prior to the application or it must be the tenant's only or main residence for five out of the last ten years. This provision is designed to exclude speculators. However, the tenant can occupy part only. Hence a person does not become ineligible if part of the house is sublet provided he resides there and the original lease covers the entire house. Thus houses in multiple occupation fall within the scope of the Act. The tenant's widow or other member of the family will qualify if they have been resident during the appropriate time (section 7(1)). The meaning of house is defined in section 2 (1) it ...

> includes any building designed or adapted for living in and reasonably so called, notwithstanding that the building is not structurally detached or was or is not solely designed or adapted for living in, or is divided horizontally into flats or maisonettes and,
> (a) where a building is divided horizontally, the flats or other units into which it is so divided are not separate ''houses'' though the building as a whole may be; and
> (b) where a building is divided vertically the building as a whole is not a ''house'' though any of the units into which it is divided may be.

The aim was to exclude flats and maisonettes. It follows that, if a building as a whole is a house and contains the tenant's only or main residence he remains eligible even though part is used by him for a business or other non-residential purposes. For example, a flat above a shop is covered.

The tenancy must be a long tenancy at a low rent. Long tenancy is defined in section 3 (1) as a tenancy granted for a term of years certain exceeding twenty one years. A few residents in Saltley are excluded because they own an underlease created by a headleaseholder when less than 21 years of the original term are unexpired. If a long lease comes to an end but the land-owner has not yet exercised his rights under Part I of the Landlord and Tenant Act 1954, the original tenancy is assumed to continue as we have already seen. Low rent is defined by section 4 (1) as,

> at any time when rent is not payable under the tenancy in respect of the property at a yearly rate equal to or more than two thirds of the rateable value of the property on the appropriate day or, if later, the first day of the term: (appropriate day is 23 March 1965.)

The rateable value limits have been the subject of two legislative amendments and a number of cases in the courts. For many people they are extremely complicated but for Saltley residents there are no problems. They all fall within the lowest limit of £200 assessed on the 23rd March 1965.

Most residents in Saltley are eligible or will be once they have satisfied the five years residential period. Once eligibility is established the main question remains, how much will it cost. This central problem merits a separate section and is dealt with later in the chapter. For the moment we must assume that the resident decides to go ahead. What must he do? As we have seen the method used by the Act was to reproduce the market arrangements. These can be divided into five separate stages.

The leaseholder must make the first move. He must serve a notice of leaseholder's claim which must be in writing on the form prescribed by the Act and may be served on any person having a superior interest in the

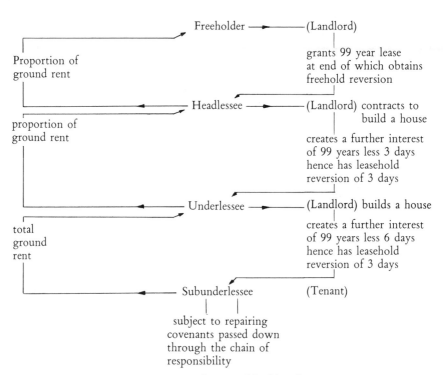

Fig. 9. Structure of a typical building lease.

house. He must also serve copies of the notice on any other person whom he knows or believes to have an interest in the house superior to his own (Fig. 9 describes the structure of a typical Saltley building lease). If the landlord cannot be found then the tenant may apply to the High Court instead of serving notice and if the court still cannot find the landlord but finds that the tenant is entitled to enfranchise it can make an order to secure his rights to him. Service of notice by the tenant operates like a contract: it binds both landlord and tenant to complete the purchase of the freehold. It also provides the reference date on which a fair freehold price is based. Once a notice has been served a tenant cannot withdraw except within a month after the price has been determined, but then he is obliged to compensate the freeholder for his losses.

If the notice is served directly on the freeholder he is obliged to give notice in reply on the prescribed form within two months. In the case of a subtenancy where the person receiving the notice is not the freeholder, the recipient must serve a copy on anyone else he knows or believes to have an interest in the house superior to that of the tenant who has not already been named. The person or persons who receive this notice must do likewise. Each time the tenant must be notified. This procedure continues until the notice is received by the 'reversioner' who is obliged to serve the counter notice on the tenant. The reversioner is the person entitled to a tenancy having an expectation of over thirty years possession most immediately expectant on the termination of the tenant's subtenancy or, if there is no such interest, the freeholder. In most cases there are no such interests and the freeholder will automatically become the reversioner who is then responsible for the negotiations and for the subsequent division of the compensation. Other landlords, if they wish, may act independently. Figure 10 describes the process.

When he replies, the reversioner or freeholder may require the tenant to pay a deposit of three times the ground rent or £25 (whichever is the greater) and to furnish evidence of title by means of an abstract of title. Whosoever is entitled to serve the counter notice must do so within two months of receipt of the notice. The counter notice can:

(a) accept the leaseholder's eligibility;
(b) dispute this right; or
(c) claim possession or redevelopment rights.

If the landlord disputes the tenant's right he must state grounds on which he does so. The dispute is determined by the county court although various matters normally within this jurisdiction can be transferred to the

Lands Tribunal when it considered the price to be paid. However, proceedings to establish eligibility cannot be dealt with concurrently with determination of price. They have to be brought in the county court. If the landlord claims possession or redevelopment rights the proceedings follow the steps outlined previously.

Once eligibility is established the parties proceed to negotiate a price. This task is performed by valuers or experienced solicitors retained by both parties. The outcome of the negotiations can be threefold: first, the tenant and landlord can agree on a price in which case the parties proceed to the conveyancing stage; secondly, the tenant can withdraw within a month of the landlord's offer whether a Lands Tribunal action has taken place or not, but he is obliged to pay the cost incurred by the other

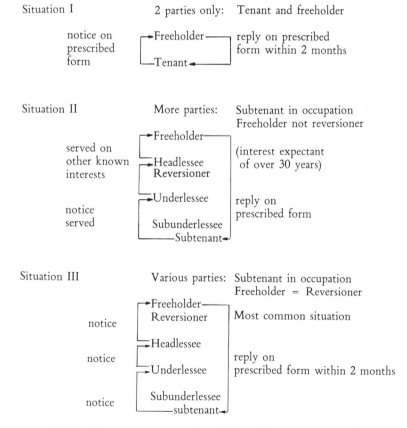

Fig. 10. Notification processes under the Leasehold Reform Act.

parties and is barred from using the Act for a further five years; thirdly, if the tenant and landlord cannot agree, the Act provides that the dispute can be settled by the Lands Tribunal, which has jurisdiction to fix the price payable under section 9.

If, before the tenant's notice is carried into effect a notice to treat is served on either the landlord or tenant by a person or body with compulsory acquisition powers the tenant's notice ceases to have effect although compensation is assessed and divided as if the notice were effective.

The obligation to repair permeates the relationship between landlord and tenant. At any time during the long tenancy a landlord is entitled to serve a notice relating to a breach of repairing covenant otherwise known as a schedule of dilapidation. If there are more than three years left on the lease the tenant can claim the protection of the Leasehold Properties (Repairs) Act 1938 as long as the notice relates to repairs which are the tenant's responsibility during the currency of the lease. The protection available and procedure involved are as follows. The tenant must serve a counter notice within 28 days. The landlord can then take no further action without the court's permission. The court will only give the landlord permission to either obtain possession of the premises or claim damages if the landlord can prove one of the grounds set out in section 1 (5).

(a) that the immediate remedying of the breach in question is requisite for preventing substantial diminution in the value of his reversion or that the value thereof has been substantially diminished by the breach;

(b) that the immediate remedying of the breach is required for giving effect in relation to the house to the purposes of any enactment, or of any byelaw or the provision having effect under an enactment relating to the safety, repair, maintenance or sanitary condition of houses, or for giving effect to any order of a court or requirement of a local authority under any such enactment, byelaw, or other provision as aforesaid.

(c) In a case in which the lessee is not in occupation of the whole house that the immediate remedying of the breach is required in the interests of the occupier of the house or part thereof.

(d) that the breach can be immediately remedied at an expense that is relatively small in comparison with the much greater expense that would probably be occasioned by postponement of the necessary work;

(e) special circumstances which in the opinion of the court render it just and equitable that leave should be given.

If the landlord is given permission to proceed he may still have to go through the courts to seek to enforce his rights. In such proceedings the court may grant the tenant relief against the full consequences of a breach of his obligations. Any damages which the landlord may ultimately obtain cannot exceed the amount, if any, by which the value of the landlord's asset is diminished by the the tenant's breach of covenant.

If there is less than three years to run, the tenant is obliged to carry out his responsibility but can challenge the amount if it is excessive in the county court. The procedure is similar to that when a tenant is claiming the right to extend.

Enfranchisement is not normally affected by dilapidation orders but a tenant claiming the right to extend is obliged to put the property into a state of 'good repair' before the landlord is obliged to grant the extension. 'Good repair' includes both structure and decoration having regard to the age, character and locality of the house. But it only covers repairs, not improvements, so that major work to roofs, for example, would not be covered. At most the dilapidation order should not exceed the difference between the property as it stands and the value of the property if it were well maintained. For example, if the house is worth £2000 as it stands and needs £1000 spent on repairs which would increase the value of the property to £2500, the dilapidation order can only be for £500, not the £1000. Any dispute can be settled by the county court.

The most important question which the resident asks is how much will it cost. This, we explain involves two different types of cost. First is the price of the freehold and any intermediary interest, second is the professional costs which both sides are presumed to incur in transferring these interests, but for which the resident is responsible. The provision of costs for enfranchisement are contained in section 9 (4). They are the reasonable costs incurred by the landlord in pursuance of notice of or incidental to:

(a) the landlord's investigation of tenant's right to enfranchise;
(b) any conveyance or assurance of any outstanding estate or interest in the house and premises;
(c) deducing evidencing, and verifying the title to any estate or interest in the house or premises;
(d) making out and furnishing such abstracts and copies as the tenant requires;
(e) any valuation of the house and premises.

Costs for extension are contained in section 14 (2). Again the tenant is liable for the reasonable costs of or incidental to:

(a) the landlord's investigation of the tenant's rights to an extended lease;
(b) the extended lease;
(c) any valuation obtained by the landlord to fix the rent payable under the extended lease.

The resident, then, has to pay the freeholder's and any intermediary leaseholders' legal and valuation fees in addition to his own costs, any stamp duty or other out of pocket expenses. As there can be as many as three intermediary interests on one lease, this amounts to ten sets of fees over eight of which the resident has no control. Negotiations over price, as we have seen, are assumed to follow a free market approach: the leaseholder applies, the freeholder responds with a price and the leaseholder bargains with the freeholder. If negotiations break down the Lands Tribunal decides a correct price. Negotiations are presumed to bear the statutory assumptions in mind. The Lands Tribunal, however, reflects the market process in both its procedure and the substantive issues involved in arriving at a price.

The Lands Tribunal are established in 1949 by the Lands Tribunal Act to replace various panels of arbitrators, referees and others all with disparate jurisdictions. It is a permanent judicial body composed partly of lawyers and partly of valuers and it exercises wide jurisdiction over all matters relating to land. This includes rating assessments on appeal from local valuation courts; assessment of compensation for compulsory acquisition of land where there is no agreement between the acquiring authority and the property owner and the determination of price and rent payable under the Leasehold Reform Act. The membership consists of a legally qualified chairman and seven other members. The president hears substantial or novel points of law. The other members are lawyers and surveyors. They go on circuit where necessary and frequently sit alone. Their decisions are almost invariably reserved to be read at a later date. The Tribunal is the final arbitor on points of fact and evidence but there is appeal to the Court of Appeal on point of law. Unlike virtually all the other tribunals the legal aid scheme is available for hearings before it. The procedure to be adopted is laid down in the Lands Tribunal Rules 1975 (S.I. 1975 No. 299). The tribunal is very court-like although only one tenth of the cases it disposes of come to a formal hearing. The proceedings are fairly informal by High Court standards and the strict rules of evidence do not seem to apply. Evidence can be given orally or by affadavit (rule 39). Legal representation is customary, and although rule 44 allows audience from anybody with the leave of the tribunal, this is not often granted. In most cases expert witnesses, which are limited to one each by rule 42, are present on both sides. The Tribunal fixes a price after considering the evidence which is presented by both experts on the basis of their market experience. This price is usually independent of both unless the strength of the case presented by one side is overwhelming. Each side usually submits a sealed offer, as set out in rule 50.

(1) An unconditional offer of any sum, or of readiness to accept any sum, as compensation shall not be disclosed to the Tribunal until it has decided the amount of compensation to be awarded to the party to or by whom the offer was made, but a copy of the offer enclosed in a sealed cover may be sent to the registrar or delivered to the Tribunal at the hearing by the party who made the offer and shall be opened by the Tribunal after it has decided the amount of the compensation.

(2) Where the proceedings relate to the price payable on the acquisition of a freehold property or the rent to be paid under an extended lease in accordance with the provisions of the Leasehold Reform Act 1967 (a) and that the price or rent is or has become the only issue in the proceedings, the provisions of paragraph (1) above shall apply to an unconditional offer of readiness to agree to a specified price or rent.

Much hinges on the sealed offer since it is usually the basis for an allocation of costs: the person whose sealed offer is nearest to the Tribunal price wins the costs. The Tribunal seems to be plagued by delays with its cases. This is brought about mainly by the method of approach to the issues. Until recently, once the valuations and supporting documents had been lodged, time could be extended before a hearing indefinitely. This process is to enable "settlement out of court". There can be frequent grants for the extension of time or stay of proceedings to enable settlement to be reached and, even during the hearing, adjournment was often granted at the request of the parties or on the Tribunal's own initiative if it appears that this could resolve the dispute or even narrow its area. Since 1975, in order to speed up the process, it is possible for the President to dismiss the proceedings or for the registrar to order a hearing if the parties have not been duly diligent.

In leasehold reform cases expert witnesses argue about valuation methods before the Tribunal. I spent some time reading all the reported Lands Tribunal cases on the subject in an attempt to learn the relevant valuation procedure. It was clear from this study that a very high proportion of freeholders were corporate institutions whereas only one leaseholder had that status. It is also obvious that interests differ. Freeholders are dealing in investments using freeholds as commodities, leaseholders want secure roofs over their heads. Experts seem to take a cynical view of leaseholders motives, attributing them to a desire to increase their investment by marrying their leasehold property and freehold interest together. There is no doubt that this is the consequence of the activity whether, as V. William Taylor suggests, it is the motive is highly questionable.

> No doubt many tenants were pleased with the bargains they made, and the concept of preserving the family home has long since been overtaken by the chance of converting a low-value leasehold into a valuable freehold for sale at a quick profit. Cynical as this view may be, a few years experience in private practice had confirmed it in the minds of many practitioners. One has only to deal with the probate value of leaseholds to find that district valuers are not unaware of the concept of regarding such interests as merely a species of deferred freehold subject to minimal profits and a certain amount of trouble. (242 E.G. 795)

Thus the scene is set for the possible battle before a highly professional body. Determination of the freehold price is regarded as a technical exercise argued about by professional practitioners who perhaps regard the job as involving minimal sums and only a little trouble, the purpose of which is to maximise the investment value of the commodity. It is an exercise which is far removed from the realities of how much a leaseholder can afford to pay for the security of freehold owner-occupation.

Any explanation of the valuation method tends to be technical and complex. It is, however, of the first importance to any leaseholder and to anyone advising or acting with leaseholders groups. The following section is an attempt to set out the main elements involved in the process of arriving at the prices. First the purchase of the freehold interest.

It is salutory to begin with a quotation from the Tribunal in *Custins* v. *Hearts of Oak Benefit Society* [1969] 209 E.G. 239:

> Presumably some one persuaded the majority of both Houses of Parliament that these provisions provided a reasonably clear basis of valuation. Alas they underestimated the ingenuity of lawyers and surveyors.

Practices have evolved and certain patterns can be discerned. The devices bear little relation to financial reality: for many calculations taxation and inflation are deemed not to exist. The Tribunal is attempting to compensate the freeholder for the loss of the ground rent for the remaining term and also the expectation of the reversion. Section 9 of the Act provides that the price payable shall be the amount at which the house and premises would sell in the open market.[2] Various assumptions are added: first, that the freeholder is selling his interest subject to the existing tenancy; secondly, that the tenant has no right to acquire the freehold but has been granted a 50 years extension of his term. Thirdly, that the 50 year extension is at a "modern ground rent" defined as the rent for the site without the buildings, with the land being used only for the purposes to which the house and premises have been put since the commencement of the existing tenancy and, lastly, that the sitting tenant and members of his family are not buying or seeking to buy. This last assumption was added by S82 Housing Act 1969. How is a figure achieved?

Where the lease has a long term remaining the dominant element in valuation is the ground rent payable under the current lease. The reversion will not take place for a long time and so the loss to the landlord is small. More important is the loss of the right to collect ground rent for a substantial period. The current ground rent is capitalized at a certain rate of interest to arrive at its market value. Put another way, if the capital sum is invested at a certain rate of interest it will give an annual income equivalent to the annual ground rent. Thus the market value of a ground rent of £4 for a lease with 36 years left is £46, if an interest rate of 7% is used. The only dispute is about what interest rate is most appropriate which involves two possible bases for valuation, the money market method which relies on evidence as to the rate of return that an investor-purchaser would expect in other parts of the capital market and the land market approach which relies on evidence of yields in comparable property transactions. The Court of Appeal in *Gallagher Estates* v. *Walker* (1974) considered that the land market approach was more appropriate for all types of valuation under the Leasehold Reform Act. But recently Tribunal members have recognized the nature of this market and the unreality of the Court of Appeal's position. In December 1977 one member stated that:

> I think it is generally agreed that the investment market for long reversion ground rents has for many years been a far from lively one. Speculators are interested in blocks of ground rents at low prices in the expectation of holding in order sooner or later to make

a profit out of sales to the sitting lessees. (*Ugrinic* v. *Shipway Estates* [1977] 244 E.G. 893 at 895)

When the lease has a relatively short number of years unexpired, say less than 30, the land-owner's reversionary interest is more valuable than the current ground rent. The reversionary factor increases in importance as the term shortens.

The method of valuation is explained in *Mimmack* v. *Solent Land Investments Ltd* (1972). It is a three stage process, involving four main valuation variables. The first stage is to assess the current ground rent. This has already been dealt with and the only variable is the rate of interest at which it is capitalized. The next two stages calculate the reversionary interest. The value of the land to the freeholder is limited both by the tenant's right to occupy it at a low rent for the remaining years of the current lease, and the tenant's further right to extend the lease for 50 years. The second stage therefore is to estimate the rent which would be payable for the house and premises on expiry of the original term. This is termed section 15 rent or modern ground rent. The third stage is to capitalize this section 15 rent as if in perpetuity,[3] deferred for the period of the unexpired term of the existing tenancy. This third sum produces the freehold price when added to the first sum.

In calculating the section 15 rent two major and one subsidiary variables are involved: site value; the rate of interest at which to decapitalize the estimation of "use" and development potential. Valuers generally use one of two ways to calculate site value. First, where the subject house is likely to remain standing for the foreseeable future, valuation is by reference to the value of the whole premises as they stand. This is called the standing house method. Secondly, where the subject house is nearing the end of its economic life in the foreseeable future valuation is by reference to the prices of sites for development or redevelopment for comparable users. This is called the cleared site method. In Saltley we use the standing house method which derives section 15 rent by first estimating an "entirety" value which represents the value of the subject property in good condition and fully developing the potential of the site and then estimating site value as a proportion of that figure. This proportion varies, outside London between 25% and 33%. Our method of achieving a standing house valuation is to check the price of freehold house sales in the immediate area and then take a 25% proportion since the houses are very narrow fronted terraces with small front gardens and the site contributes a materially below average proportion of the entirety value.

Until recently the standing house approach has been almost universally used. It has now come under a stinging attack in *Miller* v. *St John Baptist Oxford* [1977] 243 E.G. 535. The Tribunal member thought the standing house approach "quite inappropriate". His reasons are as follows:

> The standing house basis is an artificial basis. *A fortiori* is this so in the present case, because the basis requires the employment of a fiction as well as a certain amount of guesswork. It requires the use of a fiction that the house has been repaired, improved and modernised notwithstanding that the cost of putting it into that condition is quite unknown and maybe of major proportions. It appears to me that the selection of a percentage attributable to site value is a matter of guesswork, albeit intelligent guesswork. (535-7)

The practical alternative is the cleared site method. This has been restricted to houses nearing the end of their economic life. Here the current use value and site value for redevelopment purposes are beginning to coincide. The assumption is that in the reasonably near future the site value will attract a developer considering a more profitable use for the site to bid for it. Thus a cleared site method uses a site value from sale prices realized for other sites sold for a similar development. The problem in using this method as an alternative is spelt out by the Tribunal member so opposed to the standing house method in a recent case:

> The selection of the percentages representing the relationship between site value and entirely value is particularly arbitrary. It requires a guess. For these reasons I would not be willing to apply the standing house approach except in the last resort. I am willing to apply it in the present case only because I have been satisfied by the valuers that they have sought evidence in the locality of a market in land for residential development and have found none. (*Embling* v. *Wills and Lampdon Charitable Trustees* [1978] 247 E.G. 909)

In this case the lease still had 13 years left. It would be reasonable to expect this method to be adopted in Saltley. However, there is no market in land for building. Nothing has been built in Saltley since the turn of the century except the vicarage and the local authority houses necessary to replace bombed houses. Once the value of the plot has been established, a rate of interest is applied to it to acquire the modern ground rent. This gives an estimation of the rent which would become payable after the expiry of the current term. It is called decapitalization. The rate of interest remained at 6% for many years but has risen recently to 7%. It did reach 8% in 1975 but fell with the market yields on property investment.

The third stage in the process is to calculate what amount of money invested now will give, after the number of years remaining on the lease, the modern ground rent for 50 years on that plot which has already been established under stage 2. This is called recapitalization. The convention was to use eight per cent to recapitalize. Thus the rates of interest used were stage 1 7%, stage 2 6% (now 7%), stage 3 8%. The difference between the latter two stages is known as the adverse differential. This phenomenon has had a long troubled history. The differential is commonly 2% and is "adverse" because it reduces the price to be paid to the freeholder. The four cases reported prior to 1969 had decided that the sitting tenant was a bidder in the market for the freehold. Obviously because the resident was especially interested this raised the price. Section 82 of the Housing Act 1969 passed hastily to exclude the tenant from the open market and thus reduce the price to be paid by him. From then the adverse differential appeared and has been presumed to be the valuation method by which Section 82 was implemented although it has been regarded as a quantification of the other statutory assumption that the site is lease-encumbered. It has been attacked in the Court of Appeal in *Official Custodian of Charities* v. *Goldridge*. The view of Lord Denning M.R. was that unless the evidence of a particular case showed it to be justified or

> reasons are forthcoming, I think the Lands Tribunal should give up using the adverse differential and the special incentive. They should adopt the same percentage for recapitalisation as for decapitalisation. ([1973] 227 E.G. 1467 at 1469)

The Lands Tribunal subsequently showed marked reluctance to follow the Court of Appeal's line, and it has reappeared in a few cases. The Tribunal considered that the use of the differential was justified because it reflected existing professional practice.

Since comparables are of great significance in the "provable" land market approach, the Tribunal has expressed itself strongly and at length over their use. If a market process is used, then similar transactions must form the basis of valuation and must be selected carefully. The problem is that there is virtually no open market comparable to the one required under the Act. First the tenant is excluded from any bid and secondly, a single freehold ground rent is a very undesirable commodity. There is little to compare it with except freehold purchase settlements which, of course, include the tenant's presence. Valuers following their market approach tend to offer long lists of houses scattered over wide areas such as quoting a Birmingham house as a comparable for a London case. They also quote different types of sales such as in auction and private transactions to substantiate an "open market transaction". The Tribunal has refused to consider much of this type of evidence and they consider that offers from the tenant are not relevant. For standing house comparables the Tribunal likes evidence of freehold values in the immediate vicinity. Likewise for its cleared site method the Tribunal looks for similar sites in the same locality. It requires evidence of the value of sites for residential development. Again the Court of Appeal has intervened with its view. Lord Justice Sachs in *Gallagher* v. *Walker* (1974) quoted in the Lands Tribunal in *Finkel* v. *Simon*

> In the Leasehold Reform Act cases the assumptions postulated under Section 9 of the 1967 Act coupled with the exclusion of the tenant's bid by Section 82 of the Housing Act 1969 means that, in practice, directly comparable open market transactions are unavailable and the comparables cited to the Tribunal have taken the form of prices which have been agreed, under the 1967 Act as amended, in respect of neighbouring freeholds, an approach described by the Tribunal in *Delaforce* v. *Evans*. ... (1970)
> 'In the present case the transactions on which the landlords rely seem to be analogous to settlements in cases of disputed compensation for compulsory acquisition. They are not true open market transactions, for the tenant is in effect acquiring under compulsory powers. But there never will be true open market transactions which can be used as direct comparables in the kind of case ... It seems to me that in this situation settlements under the Acts of the enfranchisement price of nearby and similar properties afford perfectly legitimate comparables ... subject to ... one qualification.'
> (The neighbouring tenant's anxiety to settle). [1974] 231 E.G. 329 at 331

The Tribunal is very cautious with settlement comparables and requires detailed contextual knowledge. They cannot be relied on if the tenant has settled without professional advice or despite it; secondly, if there is no clear evidence for the basis on which the settlements were negotiated; thirdly, if the valuer producing the settlement evidence was not personally concerned in the negotiations; fourthly, if there is market evidence which puts into doubt the site value contended for; and lastly, if the evidence afforded by the settlements is readily displaced by other evidence. *Delaforce* v. *Evans* (1970) also made another point about settlement comparables: that a tenant, anxious to obtain his freehold, is more likely to go up than is the landlord to come down to achieve settlement. Therefore, some downward adjustment should be made to the figure which would otherwise result from the direct application of comparables. This has become known as the ''Delaforce effect''. Like the adverse differential the significance of the Delaforce effect has been gradually eroded. It is now necessary to provide evidence in each case of a particular anxiety to settle. The amount usually deducted seems now to be between £25 and £50. Sometimes this figure is offset against costs: the landlord will pay some of the tenant's costs which he is not obliged to do instead of reducing the price. An example of the standard valuation method arrived at is given below for a terraced house with a 12 foot frontage built in 1885 in what is now an inner city area.

The lease was created in 1885. At the time of the service of notice there was an 8 year unexpired term. The annual ground rent is £5.

	£	
current ground rent	5.00	
years purchase for 8 years at 7%	5.97	
capitalized current ground rent		29.85
freehold value in entirety	4000.00	
site value: 30% of entirety	1200.00	
decapitalized at 7%	84.00	
years purchase in perpetuity deferred 8 years at 7%	8.31	
capitalized modern ground rent		690.04
	Total price =	719.89
	say =	£720.00

The purchase of intermediary interests has not occupied much of the Tribunal's time. Only one case *Hameed* v. *Hussain* (1977) has come before the Tribunal. The author has detailed knowledge of this case because it came from Saltley and was sponsored by Norton Residents Association. (The background will be discussed in a later chapter.) Mr. Hameed paid £3.50 ground rent a year. This sum was collected by Mr. Hussain who simply passed it on to Mr. Leonard who passed £2.97 on to the free-holders. The dispute concerned how much Hameed should pay Hussain. The interest is represented by the capitalization of the difference in rent payable until the expiry of the lease. In this case the profit rental was nothing but it was important to establish the valuation method. We worked it out as follows:

	£
Rent received	3.50
Less rent paid	3.50
Profit rent	0.00
Years purchase for	
(25¼ years at 9%, 3% tax at 37p in £)	7.60
TOTAL	80.00

Our valuer argued that the purchase of an intermediate interest required a different set of tables to that used for the freehold. A leasehold interest is finite: it expires at the end of a number of years, in this case 25¼. However, an income can be achieved from it in the meantime. Thus if the sum equivalent to that income is invested now it must take account of the finality of the interest and provide for a sinking fund to cover the loss. This lowers the level of yield and the fund must be provided out of the income which is itself taxed. The Tribunal agreed with the method and only ordered Hameed to pay £1 to Hussain whilst Hussain was obliged to pay the £365 costs. (This figure was subsequently reduced to £275.) This case may seem bizarre but the aim of the case was to acquire approval of the method so that it could be used as a basis for other intermediary valuations. Although the Tribunal does not have a doctrine of precedent in that it is not bound by its own decisions it does follow closely its own guidelines wherever the evidence is sufficient to justify it. Unfortunately because the landlord did not appear or submit evidence the Tribunal did not report the method of valuation.

Cases are rare because the costs of bringing a case are absurdly dispro-portionate to the figure involved because, until recently, an alternative method of dealing with these interests has been available. The Leasehold Reform Act permits the creation of a rent charge to pay off these interests.[4] Schedule 1, paragraph 8 states that:

> In the case of a tenancy having an expectation of possession of not more than one month, the consideration payable in accordance with Section 9 of this Act shall, if the claimant by written notice given to

the reversioner so requires, consist of a rent charge to be charged on the house and premises by the conveyance to the claimant.

This rent charge was payable until the term date of the immediate superior tenancy and was an amount equal to the profit rental. The Rent Charges Act 1977 prevents the creation of new terminable rent charges including those under the 1967 Act. It also provides a statutory formula in section 10 for the redemption of already existing rent charges.[5] The Law Commission in their report included the 1967 Act rent charges in the list of exemptions thus permitting their creation, but the Bill removed them.

Could leaseholders make use of the formula in Section 10 to fix a price for their intermediary interests? The debate on this issue expose some of the assumptions upon which the Act is based. The early position taken by the Department of the Environment seemed clear:

> What is now a bargaining counter which is sometimes used in negotiation could become the standard means for fixing the price of one particular interest — possibly a different price from that which would have been agreed, or from that which a Land Tribunal might have determined. Furthermore it would be difficult to justify using a fixed formula in the situation to which paragraph 8 applies and a different method of valuation [agreement or reference to the Land Tribunal] in others. It would seem to cut across the principles underlying the Act whereby if the parties cannot agree terms they can go to the Land Tribunal. (David Glover, June 1977)

But in 1979 the formula appeared in the Labour government's Housing Bill as an amendment to the 1967 Act. It has subsequently been incorporated into the Leasehold Reform Act 1967 Section 7A by schedule 21 paragraph 6 of the Housing Act 1980. The next question to ask is why can there not be a formula for both freehold and intermediary interests? An early statement comes from Denis Howell:

> You suggest that a fixed price should be put on freeholds enfranchised under the Act. This, however, would be quite inequitable. Even the person whose property is compulsarily bought by public authorities for public purposes is entitled to receive a price related to the value of what he is compelled to sell. (Dennis Howell, May 1975)

A more recent one comes from the civil servants at the Department of the Environment.

> I will explain the justification for the formula in the previous Government's Bill for valuing minor intermediate leases. The inter-

mediate leaseholder to whom this would apply has no reversionary interest, he merely receives a net ground rent for the remainder of the lease. Consequently in his case no question of valuing land arises and it is simply a matter of compensating him with a capital sum for loss of a known income. (Robin Sharp, November 1979)

The objection has changed from one of procedure to one of substance. But both show how closely the two are related since it is assumed that a market approach based on negotiation will produce a price related to the value of the reversionary interest. It is not clear, however, why a formula cannot achieve a fair price. This can be done. In Eire the Landlord and Tenant (Ground Rents) (No. 3) Act 1967 and Landlord and Tenant (Ground Rents) (No. 2) Act 1977 provide formulae and eliminate all legal and valuation costs for a very small payment. (See section 18 of the 1967 Act and sections 15 and 23 of the 1977 Act.)

The market process relies on the use of the professionals who then engage in complex technical debate over an interest which must be defined by both sides in financial terms. The professional valuers must assess these interests as investments but they find the process difficult because the statutory assumptions prevent a real market from existing. So they argue about the technical methods of offsetting the statutory assumptions. Can it be done by an adverse differential? Does a land market have to be invented? How quantifiable is a Delaforce effect? These technical market terms define reality. The resident wants security for two reasons, first to avoid the necessity of paying a weekly rent to the freeholder when the lease expires and secondly to obtain the necessary economic ability through ownership of a freehold asset to undertake expensive repairs. In Saltley when a working-class leaseholder weighs up the cost of purchasing the freehold he is unaware of the professional valuation jargon and his only concern with investment and marriage values is to obtain sufficient equity in the house to support further loan finance. Although his main concern is with use-value considerations, in order to negotiate and if necessary dispute the price the resident must employ a valuer who will transform the calculation into a market method which will exclude the tenant's bid and anxiety to settle. Thus leaseholders are caught in the market process. They can only purchase security by engaging in a debate about the financial market and transforming this desire into a form of exchange.

Notes

1. The tenant can register his right to extend against the freeholder's title before a modern ground rent is ascertained in the last year of the lease.
2. Although the Act refers to the house and premises as the object of valuation, the statutory assumptions are supposed to reflect the equitable allocation of bricks and mortar to the leaseholder and the site to the freeholder. Thus house and premises seems to be a misnomer for site.
3. This practice of capitalizing as if in perpetuity was brought into question in the most recently reported case of *Haresign* v. *St John the Baptist's College Oxford 1980*. The lease had 3 years unexpired term and the Tribunal accepted 7% deferred for 53 years instead.
4. To quote the Law Commission Report No. 68: a rent charge is an annual or periodic sum of money payable to someone who is not entitled to the reversion to the land charged with its payment.
5. The formula in Section 10 is as follows:

   10 — (1) For the purposes of section 9 above, the redemption price shall be calculated by applying the formula:-

   $$P = £\frac{R}{Y} - \frac{R}{Y(1 + Y)^n}$$

   where:-

   P = the redemption price;

   R = the annual amount of the rent charge to be redeemed;

   Y = the yield, expressed as a decimal fraction, from 2½ per cent Consolidated Stock; and

   n = the period, expressed in years (taking any part of a year as a whole year), for which the rent charge would remain payable if it were not redeemed.

   In calculating the yield from 2½ per cent, Consolidated Stock, the price of that stock shall be taken to be the middle market price at the close of business on the last trading day in the week before that in which instructions for redemption are served.

5 The Struggle to Enfranchise in Saltley 1972-1975

In 1972 Saltley took on the status of a "multiply deprived area" with the intervention of the Home Office sponsored Community Development Project (C.D.P.). The following extract from "Gilding the Ghetto" provides a brief description of the C.D.P. programme.

> The Home Office, with James Callaghan as Home Secretary, embarked on CDP in 1969. The idea was to collaborate with local authorities in setting up local projects, each with a five-year lifespan as "a neighbourhood-based experiment aimed at finding new ways of meeting the needs of people living in areas of high social deprivation". There were to be twelve projects, and these were eventually located in Batley, West Yorkshire, Benwell, West Newcastle, Canning Town, East London, Cleator Moor, Cumbria, Glyncorrwg, West Glamorgan, Hillfields, Coventry, Vauxhall, Liverpool, North Shields, Tyneside, Clarksfield, Oldham, Paisley, Glasgow, Saltley, Birmingham, Southwark, South-East London. Their brief rested on three important assumptions. Firstly, that it was the "deprived" themselves who were the cause of "urban deprivation". Secondly, the problem could best be solved by overcoming these people's apathy and promoting self-help. Thirdly, locally-based research into the problems would serve to bring about changes in local and central government policy. (C.D.P., 1977c, p. 4)

Chapter 1 described the way C.D.P. workers arrived at their analysis of Saltley's decline. Our analysis of why the leasehold system was a problem evolved through work with residents wishing to purchase their freeholds and through our investigation of the identity of freeholders and intermediary landlords. The pattern seemed to be clear. Traditional land-owners were either being superseded by property companies whose aim was to profit not from estate management but from the redevelopment of

128

valuable inner-city sites or the same land-owners were transforming themselves to share similar aims. The problem for redevelopment was that existing houses stood in the way.

Since their first intervention in Saltley, London City & Westcliff (L.C.&W.) gradually consolidated their holding by buying in as many outstanding leasehold interests as possible, marrying them with their freehold interest to give a clear title. When in 1966 the Leasehold Reform Bill was being discussed in Parliament they (through their agent) effectively intimidated many leaseholders by serving dilapidation orders. These were schedules of repairs required under the leasehold covenants, costly to carry out. Some leaseholders, owner-occupiers and elderly landlords, surrendered their leases for nominal sums. Most schedules were resisted by the newly formed Norton Residents Association with the help of local M.P. Dennis Howell. The 1967 Leasehold Reform Act must have been a bitter blow to L.C. & W. Occupying leaseholders now had the ability to block comprehensive development of the estates by buying individual freeholds before their leases fell in. The company decided to obstruct this process and they were very successful.

Our analysis was based on the balance of forces as they manifested themselves in 1972. On the one hand there was a blockade by freeholders to prevent enfranchisement at any cost because redevelopment was the prize, on the other residents wanted to buy their freeholds to increase their security (and in some cases, mobility) and to prepare themselves for large-scale repair and improvement of their homes. Therein lay the conflict of aims between the ''sides'' although, at the time, the implications of the clash of policies between redevelopment and improvement was not clear to either C.D.P. workers or residents. Renewal was analysed merely as an additional incentive to the desire to purchase freeholds. There was a need to break a blockade by a large company on behalf of poor residents who happened to be potential owner-occupiers. Individual members of the working class had to fight a big bad property company for a legal right. Thus our strategy was based on a desire to enforce a legal right through positive intervention which would offset the economic inequality of the protagonists. The Act and its administration seemed to be vitally important and all the debate ultimately hinged on the attitude of professionals to it, the nature and cost of its enforcement, whether it worked or not, and if not, the ingredients to make it work. Its purpose, which was to make working-class residents into real home owners, was assumed and not considered to be problematic in itself.

This chapter will show that our analysis consisted of three separate but linked elements. First, procedurally the onus was on the leaseholder to take all the initiatives in order to enfranchise; secondly, the Act assumed professional legal and valuation services; lastly, there was no recognition of the effects of economic inequality between the parties. This focus on procedure excluded an analysis of the local housing market. Intermediary leaseholders, generally estate agents or property companies (which were later uncovered as important economic interests) were seen in relation to the main battle merely as the forces of confusion which prevented lease-holders finding freeholders. The legal profession was seen as inefficient and unsympathetic to but separate from, the process of enfranchisement. They did not work well for leasehold clients because leaseholders were not property owners. Occasionally solicitors seemed to be more directly linked to freeholders or intermediary landlords in which case we considered that they did not fulfil their professional role as independent advisers but were colluding with freeholders or were corrupt. Their class positions in the local housing market were not analysed. Chapter 6 will show this to be a major error although it must be made clear that at the time, the situation was dominated by L.C. & W.'s blockade and all the inadequacies of the Act and its implementation by professionals remain correct.

What follows is the analysis which we developed then and what we did to overcome the problem. But first we were obliged in our campaign to show that the Act was not working. We learned of the leasehold problem from three sources; a detailed household survey, an in depth survey of one street and from residents. Information concerning the operation of the Act was obtained from a household survey conducted by Oxford University in June 1973. The Social Evaluation Unit, which had previously been responsible for the Educational Priority Area action-research programme was chosen for the research element within the Birmingham Project. The survey involved extensive interviews with a sample of one in eight households. The aim was to establish what residents felt were the problems in the area, the trends in mobility and, if this mobility were significant, the reasons for the phenomenon. A major section of the questionnaire involved an investigation of problems associated with leasehold tenure and the operation of the Leasehold Reform Act. The main findings are given in the course of this chapter. The survey estimates that owner-occupation accounted for 53% of the household tenure in the area (see Table I).

TABLE I

Household Tenure in Saltley C.D.P. Area

	1973 Oxford Survey %	1971 census %
Owner-occupied	53	48
Council tenants	16	17
Private unfurnished tenants	25	30
Private furnished tenants	4	5
TOTALS	100.0 (497)	100.0 (-)

Of the 53% owner-occupied, 80% were leaseholders which represents a weighted total of approximately 1750 households. Five per cent of owner-occupiers at the time had bought their freeholds since buying the leasehold house but only 3% had done this since the Act was passed in 1967 (see Table II).

TABLE II

Percentage of Owner-occupiers

	Percentage	Number
Bought house as freehold	14	(38)
Bought freehold since purchase	5	(13)
(pre-1967)	(2)	(4)
(post-1967)	(3)	(9)
Leaseholders	80	(212)
TOTALS	99	(263)

The survey figures show a very low take up of freeholds in the seven years up until 1974. It could be as low as 0.5% a year because only 3% of existing owner-occupiers have actually bought their freeholds separately. Or it could be a maximum of 2.7% if the 14% who have bought the house freehold since 1967 are added. The maximum rate includes the process whereby the freeholder buys in the lease (usually of a tenanted property), marries it with a freehold and sells it off to a new owner-occupier. In addition it includes the process whereby a landlord leaseholder buys in the freehold, marries it to his lease and, when the house becomes vacant, sells it freehold to an owner-occupier. C.D.P. experience suggested this occurred frequently. Hence the take up of freeholds by owner-occupiers themselves was estimated to be approximately 1% a year.

This lack of take up became more significant when seen in conjunction with other findings. First, 62% of leaseholders were potentially eligible by residence qualification. Secondly, it might be expected that a considerable number of leaseholders would be anxious to buy since the unexpired terms were short: 48% under 25 years (see Table III).

TABLE III
Length of Unexpired Term

	Percentage
10 years or less	1
15 years or less	4
20 years or less	17
25 years or less	26
30 years or less	28
35 years or less	7
More than 35 years	8
Don't know	8
TOTAL	% 100
	(N) (212)

Thirdly, leaseholders had tried to purchase: Table IV shows that 14% had already tried and failed. Another 12% were trying at the time of the survey.

TABLE IV
Attempts to Buy Freeholds

	Percentage
Never tried	70
Tried but failed	14
Trying now	12
Offered but refused	4
TOTAL	% 100
	(N) 212

Although the survey showed that 70% had not tried it was necessary to define "try". For the purposes of the household survey this described a fairly formal initiative such as contacting the freeholder or his agent.

Finally, nearly half wanted to buy their freeholds and another 17% would have liked to under certain circumstances (see Table V).

TABLE V
Attitude towards Buying Freehold

		Percentage
Trying to buy freehold at present		12
Wishes to buy freehold		33
Would like to buy freehold under certain conditions*		17
Does not wish to buy freehold		37
TOTAL	%	100
	(N)	(212)

*The majority of conditions involved considerations of cost.

This evidence does not in itself provide a comprehensive view. The area can be subdivided into specific sectors. The two largest areas were owned by London City & Westcliff Property Company and C. & P. Estates. The remaining area contained another large estate, that of the Hutton Estate Trust, and various other smaller freehold owners. (See Fig. 1, p. 20)

The London City & Westcliff Area covered about one quarter of the Project area. It contained 810 leasehold houses. As Chapter 2 described, the freeholds were owned by the Norton Estate which laid out this area towards the end of the last century and granted 99 year leases on the bulk of the houses. Hence the leases had between 15 and 35 years unexpired in 1973. In 1962 London City & Westcliff Property Company bought this part of the freehold estate for £80 000. There was considerable controversy at the time over local authority intervention. The Labour majority on the Council wanted to buy the estate in order to manage the estate in its entirety and to prevent it passing to another private freeholder. The Conservative group were extremely upset at the idea and publicly announced in the Birmingham press that they considered such a move as creeping nationalization by a backdoor method. The Council did put forward a bid of £60 000 but withdrew this one month prior to the auction on the grounds that they could not afford the expenditure. London City & Westcliff (L.C. & W.) obtained the estate at a price which they considered to be very cheap. The press recorded their spokesman as saying they were "cock-a-hoop". They successfully resisted all attempts by residents to enfranchise until 1974 when a resident shopkeeper finally accomplished it after four years of legal battle. Her purchase had involved an action both in the county court and the Lands Tribunal. The Birmingham Post described her as "the Joan of Arc of Saltley" in an article the paper thought worthy of a full page spread.

Though at the time we had not uncovered the great extent of their freeholdings, it is now clear that C. & P. Estates similarly resisted residents' attempts to enfranchise before 1973. Only on the Hutton Estate had some residents bought their freeholds. The nine found in the household survey were shown to come from this area when the analysis was conducted on a street basis. A further survey was carried out on one road in this area. The aim of this smaller survey was to provide an in depth study of leasehold problems and to discover whether the difficulties found in the L.C. & W. area were atypical of the whole. I carried out the study in March 1974, by which time it was possible to draw on substantial information from the C.D.P. experience. Membury Road was the most appropriate street because it had a high number of leasehold properties, was of manageable length and the proportion of immigrants was low since the cultural and language problems would have made it impossible for me to talk to a large number of Asian households.

There were 94 houses in the street, 77% of which were owner-occupied. Of this form of tenure, 86% were leasehold. Although 70% of households were eligible on residence grounds to use the Act only 5 out of a possible 67 had bought their freeholds which amounts to 7% of the total. Here again leaseholders had tried to buy their freeholds as is demonstrated by Table VI.

TABLE VI

Attempts to buy Freehold in Membury Road

	Percentage	
No attempt	47	(31)
Attempt made/offered	47	(31)
Not known	6	(4)
	%	100
TOTAL	(N)	66

The interpretation of "trying" was wider than that of the household survey. It included approaches made to neighbours, ground rent agents and intermediary landlords as well as to solicitors and other professional bodies. Yet leaseholders wanted to buy their freeholds: 62% stated that they would have liked to purchase (see Table VII).

TABLE VII
Attitudes to buying Freehold in Membury Road

	Percentage	
What to buy	62	(32)
Do not want to buy	31	(16)
Would like to under certain conditions*	15	(8)
Don't know	2	(2)
TOTAL	% 100	
	(N)	(58)

*The conditions imposed were usually cost.

The survey material was supported by C.D.P. experience of over 200 cases of difficulty which had arisen during the year 1974. In addition to individual cases C.D.P. staff had dealt with groups of leaseholders in four different streets and attended a general meeting of leaseholders in difficulty in this area arranged by one of their local councillors.

The evidence showed that leaseholders were not managing to buy freeholds or, at best, they were having considerable difficulty in doing so. This suggested that the Act was not working although it could be argued that it shows only that leaseholders were not using the 1967 Act procedures. A further possibility was that the implementation of the Act by third party professional advisors was deficient. The test which we adopted for the efficacy of the Act was whether eligible residents, who wanted to, were enfranchising. They were not, and government officials were not correct in asserting that there was a distinction between the efficacy of the Act and its implementation. They argued that the Act worked but that residents were not implementing it correctly. It follows that to understand the causes of failure it was necessary not simply to look at the Act but at the entire leasehold structure. The leaseholder's working-class position affected both their attitude towards legal processes and their relationship with the legal profession and their relative economic weakness affected their ability to fight. The procedural structure of the Act failed to take account of the class relations of the leasehold system. Because working-class leaseholders did not possess the familiarity with the professional practices which the Act makes obligatory they attempted to carry out the transactions involved in enfranchisement informally. Because they held a leasehold interest, leaseholders were expected to realize the need for the available legal services. But that assumed relationship between professional services and property holders did not exist for many working-class residents (see for further details Mayhew and Reiss, 1969). Leaseholders in Saltley were not institutionally integrated with these professional services although they possessed a property interest. They probably had contacted a lawyer prior to the present negotiation in order to make the assignment of the lease but the association did not continue. The explanation could be the novelty of home ownership for this socio-economic group coupled with the lack of financial resources available to engage legal services or a different perception of the need for legal help. Hence there was a conflict between the formal requirements of the Act and the social organization of leaseholders. The Act, which was used merely as a backcloth to inform the transaction, was open to obstruction.

Evidence of the leaseholders' informal initiatives was found when we looked at whom they contacted in order to obtain the information and assistance required to initiate the process of enfranchisement. A leaseholder would not necessarily be well informed of the rights and procedures involved and there was no mechanism available to aid him, for instance he would not be notified after five years of residence that he was now potentially eligible. The person chosen varied according to circumstances. In the London City & Westcliff area there was a certain awareness of the identity of the freeholder as a result of the Norton Residents Association. Members of the Association had some familiarity with their rights and with the company so they tended to make initial contact with the agent for the company who was known to many for his visits occasioned by service of schedules of dilapidations in 1967. Most members did not pay their ground rent direct to the freeholder so some had contacted agents employed by intermediate landlords. Non-members were often uncertain of whom to approach. In the remaining area even more leaseholders were unsure of their freeholders' identity. The survey of Membury Road established that leaseholders were confused about their freeholders and about the most appropriate person to contact to find out information. Four of the five successful attempts were made as a result of direct contact between a freeholder and leaseholder. This freeholder was resident in the street and known to the leaseholders. He was contacted directly by the leaseholder, negotiations took place with no third party involved and an offer was arrived at. The landlord's solicitor was used by both sides to convey the freehold interest. Of the other residents in the street who made some sort of formal contact, eleven approached their ground rent agents, one a surveyor, one the Citizens' Advice Bureau and three a solicitor.

Solicitors did not figure significantly in the leaseholders' actions. Estate agents acting for themselves as intermediary landlords or as agents for the freeholder would not seem to be the most appropriate person to contact for impartial advice or assistance. This was borne out by the experience of leaseholders. Of the 16 people involved in formal approaches, four discovered that they were ineligible but eight of the remaining 12 were given evasive replies or were positively deterred by the person contacted. The agents replies varied from none at all to positively misleading. Two replied that the freehold was not for sale to them (the agents) so the leaseholder also would not be able to buy. Another replied that the process would have to be carried out through them. Others stressed the complexity of the transaction. One replied that the procedure would be complicated because one of many interests involved lived in South Africa. The lack of assistance was not limited solely to agents. The Citizens' Advice Bureau replied that the leaseholder would waste his time in attempting to buy and that it would cost a great deal in legal costs. Three leaseholders did contact solicitors but received non-committal replies amounting in the main to vague commitments to "look into the matter". When questioned why they did not use solicitors to act for them throughout the proceedings both successful and unsuccessful leaseholders replied that it would have been premature to involve solicitors at this stage. The solicitor's function was not one of advisor or initiator of action but rather that of technician. Only when the transaction was well advanced between the leaseholder and his freeholder was a solicitor seen as essential to convey the freehold interest.

Most leaseholders initially attempted to purchase without professional assistance and without using the formal provisions of the Act. Being unfamiliar with the complexities both of the law and the leasehold system, they encountered considerable difficulties. One has been seen already. They obtained dubious advice from the people they contacted which often had the effect of deterring them at the earliest stage. Once the leaseholder had obtained the necessary information he moved on to the stages involved in the transaction of purchase. These involved contacting the freeholder or his agent, acquainting him with the lease-holders desire to purchase, establishing through negotiation a fair price and then arranging the transfer of the freehold interest. In addition many leaseholders were involved in a complex chain of interests which obliged them to discover and buy out all other parties involved. By not using the provisions of the Act, the leaseholder took on the burden of initiating all the action and because the Act is structured around the assumption of professional legal assistance and formal procedural stages, when these were not used the rights contained within the Act are open to obstruction by the parties to the transaction.

The leaseholder's informal efforts can be obstructed throughout by the freeholder. First, freeholders were elusive. Many deliberately hid their identity from the leaseholder by using agents who refused to divulge their principal's name or whereabouts. London City & Westcliff had even transferred applicants' houses to a subsidiary company, Lonwest, which resulted in confusion for the leaseholders. With no property register in England it was often extremely difficult to find out who owned the freehold. It required pertinacity on the leaseholder's behalf to contact agents and insist on knowing his principal if he declared that he was a mere intermediary. The applicant was then obliged to discover the identity of a superior landlord and so on. Given that the leaseholders involved were not familiar with the intricacies of the business world they often found this process beyond their capabilities. Once the leaseholder had discovered the identity of his freeholder he informed him of his desire to purchase. In the main this was done by letter as the freeholder was not normally resident in the area. These letters could be ignored. C.D.P. experience was that repeated applications were ignored. If the freeholder or his agent did eventually reply, the communication could be non-committal, such as "we will consider the matter and contact you in due course", and then there was no further contact for several months. L.C. & W. had acknowledged a mere handful of claims made from the entire estate.

The freeholder could at this stage, claim that the leaseholder was ineligible. The burden of proof fell to the leaseholder. Many had little idea how to satisfy this. Building societies or the local authority hold many assignments of under-lease on security for mortgages and would not pass them over to leaseholders. It often required considerable protocol to obtain the assignment and even then the leaseholder did not possess the legal knowledge to extract the required information. In Saltley the high proportion of immigrants from rural Mirpur in Pakistan increased the problem not just because of language difficulties but also because the extended family system tended to defeat eligibility on residence criteria. For example, an uncle may have bought a leasehold house and then given it to his nephew who had recently arrived from Pakistan. A transfer by assignment may not have been made. The nephew after five years could not prove his eligibility. C.D.P. experience, particularly in the L.C. & W. area, showed that this and many other problems arose with immigrants who failed to understand the complex land tenure system. To contest his eligibility a leaseholder might have had to support an action in the county court for which he would have been obliged to use formal procedures and professional assistance. This was a lengthy and costly business. The leaseholder might have been awarded costs if he succeeded with the action but the threat of legal action often was sufficient to deter him.

Some freeholders did not contest eligibility formally and did make offers but some tried to impose conditions. An example of this is a leaseholder in a block of four houses who was told that she could purchase the freehold if she bought the other three. Leaseholders were worried and confused about such conditions and allowed the application to drop. The most common obstruction open to freeholders during these procedural stages was to offer a totally unrealistic price. They could offer whatever figure they chose for it falls to the leaseholder to contest the fairness of the offer. L.C. & W. offered a blanket figure of £600 for most applications. This was frequently three times the fair price. Many leaseholders were deterred by the figure and gave up their attempt at this stage since they did not have the adequate resources of knowledge or money to fight.

If the leaseholders decided to fight, formal mechanisms are provided. The Act provides for the parties to file an action in the Lands Tribunal. It is the leaseholder who must decide on such a course since the burden of challenge rests on him. Once again the leaseholder is obliged to obtain professional assistance and use formal methods. These take time and money and form a daunting prospect to most leaseholders. The freeholder's bluff to uphold his unreasonable offer in the Lands Tribunal acted as the final deterrent in most cases. Very few leaseholders managed to struggle to the conveyancing stage. When it is reached it is the simplest stage for the leaseholder. The only difficulty is that he is obliged to employ a solicitor to carry out the conveyance which adds legal fees to the overall cost.

It would be misleading to suggest that all the problems of the informal methods employed by the leaseholder arose out of the ability of freeholders to obstruct. He was not the only person negotiating with the leaseholder. In Saltley it was possible for each of the intermediary lessees, who had to be bought out if the leaseholder was to secure the whole chain of interests, to be just as obstructive as the freeholder. The Act again fails to prevent this. They were often extremely difficult to identify. The head lessee was obscured from the leaseholder in possession by the underlessee. They frequently acted through agents who refused to divulge their principal's name. Many of these estate agents were the intermediary landlords. In Saltley most of the interests which were once owned by landlords have been bought out by small property companies. A considerable number of transfers between different companies had been observed by C.D.P. The leaseholder was not normally notified of these transactions. Occasionally he was instructed to pay his ground rent to a different agent but he was not informed of the change of ownership. These transactions and the structure of the property industry tended to give the leaseholder the impression that the agent acted for an independent principal but most acted for their own holding companies, for instance the intermediary interest in Parkfield Road was held by Frederick Yorke Brooke and Co., for Mr. Frederick Yorke Brooke; the intermediary interest in Membury Road was held by L.H. Martin for Larkcroft Properties, a Mr. Nelson is director of both. In the L.C.&W. area Ray Investments acted as agents for Asho Property Company which is the same concern. These agents often refused to reply to letters or to give information about their clients. If they had recently sold their interest they were not obliged to divulge the identity of the purchaser. For instance Dennis Fell & Co. acting on behalf of a Dennis Fell holding company in Parkfield Road refused to identify its new owner. With no register of property it was a daunting task to establish and contact these interests.[1]

The intermediary landlords could also set grossly inflated prices for their interests. C.D.P. had many examples of this, for instance, one landlord claimed £100 for an interest worth £12. They also could and did use the threat of a Lands Tribunal action to deter the leaseholder. The reply to a letter claiming that £12 represented a fair price was: prove it to the Lands Tribunal. So a leaseholder with two intermediary interests could be faced with contesting three interests in the Lands Tribunal.

Hence this complex leasehold system with its chain of interests created additional responsibilities for the leaseholder. The chain obscured the identity of the freeholder. The leaseholder would not normally worry about the identity of the freeholder or the activities of the intermediary landlords until he took steps to enfranchise. The entire process of discovery could be an immense task. A case study of Membury Road shows this. As Fig. 11 shows there were only three freeholders in the street, two of whom were of minor significance yet the leaseholders did not realize that the majority of them rented their land from one freeholder. This was a result of the multitude of intermediary agents. There were 11 agents involved in the collection of ground rent in the street, ten of whom acted for the Hutton Estate Trust. To give an example of the complexity, Yorke Brooke collected the ground rent from the leaseholder in possession. They paid this improved ground rent to Smallwood Jones who then paid a proportion to Fleetwood and Co. who actually paid it to the trustees. A mere £5 was involved. Leaseholders were unaware that Fleetwood gathered all the head rents. Although there was a mass of estate agent activity in buying and selling these blocks of intermediary leasehold interests, the freehold ownership remained relatively stable. Thus what appeared to be a chaotic property shuffling was merely a peripheral activity which screened the freeholder.

Eventually a leaseholder would be forced to recognize the need for legal assistance. First, if he had managed to obtain a satisfactory offer he was compelled to use professional services to convey the freehold interest to him. Secondly, if he had been unsuccessful, he had a choice either to admit defeat or to contact a lawyer to aid him. As there were few leaseholders in the former category, the most common initial contact between solicitor and leaseholder occurred after the leaseholder had failed to purchase by his own efforts and now needed professional assistance to provide a formal initiative. If the Act procedures had been used many of the possibilities for obstruction would have been removed. The leaseholder should have instructed his solicitor to serve Notice of Leaseholders Claim Form 1 on the person responsible for the collection of ground rent, that person would in turn, serve it on any other person known to him to have an interest. The procedure takes its course and a

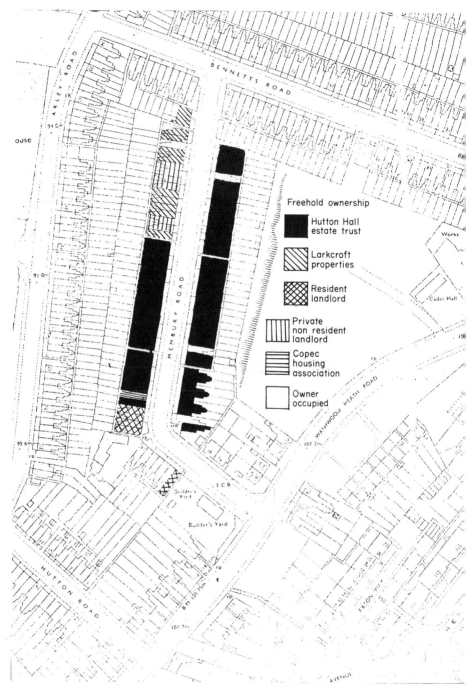

Freehold ownership

◼ Hutton Hall estate trust

▨ Larkcroft properties

▩ Resident landlord

▥ Private non resident landlord

▤ Copec housing association

☐ Owner occupied

Fig. 11(a). Freehold ownership.

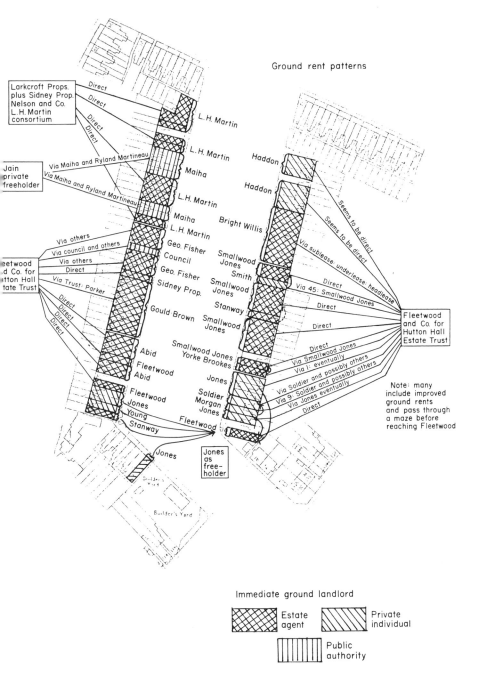

Ground rent patterns

Larkcroft Props.
plus Sidney Prop.
Nelson and Co.
L.H. Martin
consortium

Jain
private
freeholder

eetwood
d Co. for
itton Hall
tate Trust

Direct
Direct
Direct
Direct

L.H. Martin

L.H. Martin   Haddon

Via Maiha and Ryland Martineau
Via Maiha and Ryland Martineau   Maiha   Haddon

L.H. Martin

Maiha   Bright Willis
L.H. Martin

Via others
Via council and others   Geo. Fisher   Smallwood
Via others   Council   Jones
Direct   Geo. Fisher   Smith
Via Trust: Parker   Sidney Prop.   Smallwood
Jones

Gould-Brown   Smallwood
Jones

Direct   Abid   Smallwood Jones
Direct   Yorke Brookes
Direct   Fleetwood
Abid   Jones

Fleetwood   Soldier
Jones   Morgan
Young   Jones
Stanway   Fleetwood

Jones   Jones
as
free-
holder

Seems to be direct
Seems to be direct
Via sublease: underlease: headlease

Direct
Via 45: Smallwood Jones

Direct

Direct

Direct
Via Smallwood Jones
Via 1: eventually
Via Soldier and possibly others
Via 9: Soldier and possibly others
Via Jones eventually
Direct

Fleetwood
and Co. for
Hutton Hall
Estate Trust

Note: many
include improved
ground rents
and pass through
a maze before
reaching Fleetwood

Soldier's Yard

Builder's Yard

Immediate ground landlord

Estate
agent

Private
individual

Public
authority

Fig. 11(b). Ground rent patterns.

considerable number of the problems would be eased by efficient informed legal advice.

Solicitors, in practice, fulfilled neither requirement. They were reluctant to use the Act and, in many cases, they did not provide an efficient service. Many of the problems which were experienced by leaseholders in their relationship with professionals resulted from this failure to use the procedures laid down by the Act which was the reason for leaseholders contact with them. Leaseholders had usually failed by informal methods and required the formal procedures which the Act assumed would be carried out by solicitors. As Johnson (1972) has suggested various factors can prevent the client from exerting the necessary control over the professional to persuade him to act formally and effectively. A leaseholder would often not discriminate between solicitors in order to pick one who was both sympathetic and familiar with the type of work involved. Again he would be mystified by the use of jargon such as "enfranchisement", "intermediary lessees", "reversion in possession" and feel unable to control the process or question the procedures which the solicitor was adopting. Individual leaseholders waited for solicitors to act but lacked the common background knowledge necessary to challenge the method of action or its effectiveness. Thus they felt helpless and incapable of suggesting formal methods when faced with opposition or lack of concern from solicitors.

But an analysis which rests solely on social distance fails to take account of two further interrelated factors which make the need for the leaseholder's control more essential but less likely. As a result of the organization of the profession to service property interests lawyers tend both ideologically and institutionally to be more sympathetic to the freeholder.

The leaseholder required both sympathy and efficiency from his advisor. Efficiency was extremely important in the particular context. The complexity of the leasehold system has already been described. Instead of using the formal procedures solicitors continued with an approach which leaseholders had demonstrated to be ineffectual. This inefficiency can be linked to the institutional framework of the legal profession. Arguably there were two competing property interests but it is a strong supposition that the leaseholder's right was not seen as a normal property interest. The result was that the Act procedures were not used to provoke a situation which solicitors define as conflictual. Clients were persuaded against this course because solicitors failed to inform them of its availability. For example, a letter stating that "they are not willing to enter into voluntary negotiation for the sale of their interest" did not suggest that the Act procedures could be used. Alternatively residents were warned of the consequences of its use, "You will have to decide what expense you are prepared to be involved in, in order to enforce your rights under that Act".

However, there are notable differences between the informal approaches of a trained professional and a leaseholder from Saltley. Solicitors are relatively well informed and possess a professional status which enables them to obtain information. Informal networks of contacts exist among such groups which facilitate the ready exchange of information. Conceivably three or four telephone calls could have established the interests involved on most leases. This was particularly so in the L.C.&W. area as the company seems to have been infamous throughout the Birmingham business world and well-known to the majority of solicitors. These efforts were not made, so establishing identities took a considerable length of time. Two year periods of delay in obtaining this information were not uncommon in the area. The negotiation stage did not seem to take place at all since solicitors tended merely to receive an offer from the freeholder and pass it on to their clients. There did not seem to be any attempt to challenge the validity of the offers. Hence one would expect the third stage to be reached speedily. Instead the process was extended for many months or, in some cases, for years.

Institutionally solicitors are not organized to act on a one-off basis. As a result leasehold work is not as lucrative as other work. Leaseholders do not form the traditional type of client. They are not long standing account holders. They do not retain a solicitor to deal with their property interest and hence build a stable relationship with their lawyer. So solicitors tended to allocate leasehold work a low priority. For instance, an acceptable offer received by a solicitor on behalf of his client was not passed on to that client for a year. This example could have been amplified by many others in the area. Inefficiency coupled with the non use of the Act procedure inevitably led to enormous delays. Leaseholders who had contacted solicitors after being thwarted in their own attempts became disillusioned because they heard nothing from their solicitors or, having made enquiries, found that they had made little progress. If the leaseholder did persist and eventually received an offer he was was often so astounded by the professional fees that he gave up at this final stage.

Although the leaseholder required sympathy from the solicitor, there were ideological barriers. Professional loyalties lie with the prevalent property industry ethos of the maximization of profits on assets which are represented here by the freeholders. The principles behind the Act were not popular with the private legal profession. They saw it as amounting to private compulsory purchase at less than market value. Many solicitors still oppose the Act as unjust and find it difficult (thought financially worthwhile) to represent leaseholders. The substantial group of solicitors who are Conservatives and those who are involved in the property industry must feel the conflict even more acutely. In the Saltley area the only solicitor practising nearby is a Conservative M.P. and a director of property company holding freehold and leasehold interests. After declaring these interests during the second reading debate on the Bill he went on to argue strongly for full market compensation (although he abstained on the second reading vote, contrary to his party's policy). Yet it was to him, because of his proximity, that leaseholders naturally but unwisely, in the circumstances, turned.

The consequences of this antipathy are obvious. In many instances solicitors failed dismally to serve the interests of their leasehold clients. This was seen in their lack of efficiency but they also failed to sense the leaseholder's frustration at failing himself and the consequent need for urgency. They agreed to act for the leaseholder and then delayed for months. They failed to take any positive action except to write to somebody suggested by the leaseholder. They did not feel the need to offer positive advice. They did not set out a full picture of the possibilities open to a leaseholder, such as explaining the advantages of buying the freehold prior to the intermediary interests so as to reduce the bargaining power and thereby the price of the latter; the availability of council mortgages for financing the purchase of freeholds or the relative merits of buying rather than extending the lease, particularly in potential clearance areas. The leaseholder's position was not put in context. The solicitor failed to explain what constitutes a fair price and whether the offer made was reasonable. He tried to act merely as an impartial third party, although by so doing he may easily have advantaged the freeholder. The most obvious failing in this situation arose over advising on offers. For instance, in response to a freeholder's offer of £700 for an interest worth not more than £250 a Birmingham solicitor wrote to his client "we enclose a copy of a letter from the landlord's solicitor and await your further instructions''. The leaseholder found it impossible to act on this non-committal statement. Solicitors failed to negotiate or even to suggest the procedure in the Lands Tribunal by which a fair price could be settled. Leaseholders were warned heavily against an action even if they themselves suggested it. They were advised on grounds of likely expense. By deterring their clients from this step, solicitors, one could suggest by collusion, inflated settlement prices way above comparable tribunal assessments. Between them they were able to set a market price.

Valuers are the other professional group involved in the enfranchisement process. The solicitors often have their own ''rules of thumb'' on the correct value of the interest, but occasionally it was thought necessary to retain a qualified valuer. The chartered surveyors have the same links with the property market as solicitors. They are socially organized to service the dominant property interests. They are dependent on this sector for their existence and inevitably share its values. Hence, unless compelled by a tribunal, valuers have a tendency to accept their own fair price which may accord more with the freeholders concept than with their leaseholding clients.

The two groups of difficulties covered so far have focussed on the legal process; the third, we saw at the time as an economic problem. We thought an understanding of the economic inequality between freeholder and leaseholder which provide the context of the transaction was vital since it contributed crucially to the freeholder's ability to obstruct while the leaseholder's economic strength not only determines whether he could afford the freehold but contributed independently to the outcome of the negotiations. There are two potential outcomes to the transaction: the leaseholder may anticipate that the negotiations with the freeholders will run smoothly towards a fair settlement or, realistically, he may anticipate difficulty in achieving a fair settlement.

In the first situation the leaseholder must weigh the cost against his ability to afford the freehold price. Leasehold enfranchisement requires capital outlay unless the leaseholder can obtain a mortgage to finance the transaction. Private mortgage facilities are not available to leaseholders not already mortgaged with the company in question. Private loans involve very high interest rates so the only viable alternative is a council mortgage. At the time these were for five years at 11% interest. Eligibility was limited: no one of 60 or over could apply and the total outgoings in credit transactions could not exceed a quarter of gross income. Both resulted in a considerable number of ineligible leaseholders.

The Pakistanis often had too many commitments and the whites were too old.

Residents who could afford to buy their freehold (with cash or on credit) had also to decide whether it was worth it, bearing in mind their other priorities. Many want the security it offers and the economic advantage but others have to make the best of externally imposed planning policy. In a clearance area the main consideration is compensation for demolished houses under the provision of the Land Compensation Act. Almost inevitably houses in clearance areas are old and have short unexpired terms. Compensation to a leaseholder can be negligible, as low as £75 but, if he serves notice to purchase, his compensation will increase as much as six-fold and if he purchases he will be classified as an ordinary freeholder. Thus a leaseholder was obliged to weigh up whether the purchase of the freehold would be less than the compensation subsequently received. In most cases the service of notice prior to notice to treat is the best solution.[2] In a Housing Action Area the leaseholder is obliged to carry out substantial improvements to the house which tends to have a short unexpired term. In order to carry out such a heavy burden of improvements, the leaseholder is compelled to enfranchise. Grants are not available to leaseholders with less than five years lease remaining. The economic burden is enormous with the additional cost of enfranchisement arising before improvements. Because the area is secure, leaseholders in General Improvement Areas are in the best position and enfranchisement can take a high priority without economic deterrents.

Both ability to afford and priority given had to be weighed against actual costs. These involve the freehold and intermediary interest prices plus professional fees. Table VIII shows some average prices for 1975 worked out by a valuer and solicitor.

The freehold cost varies according to length of lease and freehold values in the area. Intermediary interest costs depend on the portion of the ground rent retained. Legal and valuation fees vary considerably: some were as low as £90, others were as high as £300. Professional fees deterred a considerable number of people. Residents could not afford the sum of all these interests and all the legal and valuation fees.

Independently deterring the leaseholder was the possible additional cost of an all out fight with the freeholder. If the freeholder was obstructive the total cost as outlined above could have easily doubled. The case had to be taken, possibly to the country court, to establish the

TABLE VIII
Normal cost of Buying A Freehold in 1975

Cost of Freehold Interest		Legal and Valuation Costs	
Freehold £250	£250	Freeholder's legal costs	£30
		Freeholder's survey fees	£25
		V.A.T.	£5
		Resident's legal costs	£40
		Resident's survey fees	£10
		V.A.T.	£5
Head lease £25	£ 25	Legal costs	£20
		Survey fees	£10
		V.A.T.	£3
Sub lease £25	£ 25	Legal costs	£20
		Survey fees	£10
		V.A.T.	£3
TOTAL	£300	TOTAL	£181

leaseholder's eligibility and then to the Lands Tribunal. Negotiations at each stage in this sequence might have increased the solicitors' fees by £100. To this must be added up to £50 for representation at the county court, £150 to instruct a barrister and valuer at the Lands Tribunal and, in case of failure, up to £100 set aside to cover the extra legal costs incurred by the freeholder at 1975 prices. This increase had a far greater relative impact on a working-class leaseholder than his middle-class equivalent. For a leaseholder who had only £500 capital (which is probably more than average for Saltley), such an increase would have placed litigation beyond his means.

Hence the leaseholder had to consider two sets of costs, the normal costs and the additional costs of forcing negotiations to a conclusion. The first could be calculated more or less independently of the freeholder, although it involves other considerations such as professional fees and planning policy. The second depended upon the freeholder's resistance and his ability to finance such resistance. If the freeholder was as poor as the leaseholder he would probably not have risked a threat of or actual action in the Lands Tribunal. It was also very likely that he would be eager to sell. The return from ground rent is minimal, usually £5 a year and since redevelopment at the end of the lease would be beyond his limited means he might have been keen to have a capital sum from the compensation. This was seen clearly with the freeholder who was resident in Membury Road. He bought a block of houses in 1970 probably to sell off in order to make a small amount of profit when he needed. He did this in the four years making no difficulty when approached by leaseholders. The economic distance between the parties was relatively small. He was not a rich man. If the freeholder was much richer than the leaseholder he could have well afforded to go to the Tribunal. Even if he thought he might lose, he still could use the potential of his economic strength to bluff. The threat of an action could be very effective. Settlement prices were invariably £50 to £100 above fair prices because the margin of doubt is not worth fighting for in such situations. An economically powerful freeholder was likely to want to fight since he probably owned a large number of leasehold houses which would give a small annual return of ground rents but would have a more important reversionary investment value. The area could be redeveloped. L.C.&W. showed this. The return on their 810 houses, for which they paid £80 000, was a mere £2800 per annum or 3.5%. Yet the area as a whole had an asset value based on residential redevelopment.

There were then two distinctive cost limitations on the leaseholder. It was not only his own economic circumstances which determined his chance of buying but also the relative economic power of the leaseholder and freeholder. In practice freeholders (excluding owner-occupiers) were generally much richer than leaseholders in Saltley. Most of them were companies or trusts. The biggest in the project area then was L.C.&W. a quoted property company with assets of £95 million and a profit of £4 025 052 in 1973. Hutton Trust Estate was not much smaller. Leaseholders who used the Act were by definition individual owner-occupiers. Though the richest of them may have owned the leasehold house next door, this was exceptional and most living in inner-city areas earned less than the national average. Clearly the economic difference between the two sides was great, making the leaseholder's bargaining position weak.

However, leaseholders are not typically the poorest members of the community: generally they are not on social security or receiving other community help. As stable skilled working-class people, one of their major priorities was to buy their freehold and many had saved up to cover the basic cost of the freehold if not the professional fees. This capital made them ineligible for legal aid to offset the additional costs of a fight. The most frequent disqualification for effective legal aid was the capital which the leaseholder must have in order to cover the normal costs of purchasing his freehold. Would this sum fall within section 11(3) of the Legal Aid Act 1974?

> The regulations shall include provision for securing that the resources of a person seeking or receiving advice or assistance or legal aid shall be treated as not including the subject matter of the dispute.

Yet the Law Society suggested in discussion that the capital sum would not be exempted by this provision. In other legal disputes, differential wealth (over a certain minimum) is recognized as inhibiting the case of the poor man. Legal aid is supposedly provided by the state to give him relatively equal access to the law. In the present case neither side was considered poor enough to create any inequality before the law although the state seems to have thought the situation sufficiently unjust to provide legislation to deal specifically for this purpose.

From 1973 to 1975 we tried to tackle these types of obstruction by land-owners. Our strategy involved conducting test cases in the London City & Westcliff area through Norton Residents Association. We also campaigned in the Saltley area more generally and assisted other groups with their battles. At a policy level we discussed the problem with local M.P.s, the Home Office, the Department of the Environment, the Lord Chancellor's Office, national pressure groups, local councillors, council officials and the press.

The idea of a test case strategy was developed in 1973 once C.D.P. had decided that leasehold enfranchisement was important. Norton Residents Association (N.R.A.) had been in existence since 1967 but had become weak and inactive after the original problem of dilapidation orders had been suspended. It was, however, a structure which existed and it did have contacts. The President was Dennis Howell who had been interested in leasehold reform for some years and was the local Member of Parliament. The residents' association also retained a firm of solicitors who had contacts with a valuer. I set about preparing the test cases during the autumn of 1973. We were keen not only to break the obstruction but also to establish the procedures and get reasonable levels of prices and costs. Once we had learned how to fill them in, the appropriate forms were completed and sent off by ourselves without using professional assistance. The freeholders replied accepting the claims.

Negotiations then took place over the price. These were hard and protracted. The whole process took until late 1974 when the agent for L.C.&W. agreed to the prices for the ten test cases. Subsequently he agreed to negotiate over prices for entire streets in 1975.

It was not, however, such as easy process as it sounds. It involved three firms of solicitors, two firms of valuers and a great deal of bargaining with the Home Office, Lord Chancellor's Office and Department of the Environment. It became clear to us early on in the process that the firm of solicitors retained by N.R.A. were not sympathetic to our strategy. The crisis came when the valuer suggested by them produced valuation figures which we knew to be too high. However I had gained considerable expertise in leasehold valuation and could, therefore, check the valuation proposed by using Lands Tribunal guidelines. Both valuer and solicitor felt unable to produce and support lower figures. We tried another firm of solicitors. We picked a firm which had acted very successfully for a residents group on the other side of the city. It was a very different type of area but we felt that the firm had built up a knowledge of the Act and would be able to make a positive contribution. This did not materialize. It became extremely difficult to exercise any degree of control over the solicitor and we felt that he became obstructive. Again the crisis came when we required his support for our attempts to use C.D.P. money for financing the test cases. He felt unable to give it. We tried a third firm. This time we decided, with the support of the Association, to use the firm which had completed the only freehold purchase in the area since the Act was passed. The solicitor agreed and the relationship has been fruitful. He has agreed to act on behalf of a considerable number of the groups which have been formed subsequent to his retention by N.R.A. We picked a second valuer ourselves. We decided to use a small firm which we thought would be less likely to be involved with large freeholders and which would be in need of work. We attempted to keep his influence to a minimum and to use him only for the formal valuation calculations which are necessary for a Lands Tribunal case. We chose the test cases carefully ourselves, bearing in mind the need to fix a blanket of prices. The attempt was to cover the area as comprehensively as possible. The relationship with the valuer has not been highly successful. He insisted on maintaining a freedom to negotiate which we felt was too wide. The professional relationship between himself and the freeholder's valuer seemed to be as strong, if not stronger, than his relationship with his clients. The concept of a freehold interest as a financial asset as described in Chapter 4 is a strong influence over the valuation profession as a whole. Negotiation over price takes place under the exclusive control of the two professionals. The association instructs the valuer to negotiate but cannot, for practical reasons, totally restrict his power of discretion over the haggling. He can and does amend his valuations in the light of discussions with his opposite number. Professional camaraderie is strong. It is extremely difficult to question his judgement under such circumstances.[3] Experience has shown that, now our own expertise is highly developed, conducting negotiations without using a valuer at all produces lower figures. Settlement figures produced in 1978, after negotiations with the successors to the C.& P. Estate, have been lower than the figures agreed to for the test cases in 1974.

It is extremely unlikely that these settlements on the test cases would ever have been achieved if C.D.P. had not interposed itself between the professionals and the client residents' group. A great deal of knowledge was used as a relatively effective control over the independence of the professions involved. In addition N.R.A. members themselves became much more familiar and confident with the technical procedures. With knowledge they felt more able to argue and insist on prices.

The other problem encountered for the test case strategy was cost. The freeholder was strong and powerful. They could easily afford to fight an action through all the stages. N.R.A. could not raise that amount of money easily. The amount involved was substantial and the leaseholders were not rich. To feel secure enough to call the freeholders bluff it was necessary to obtain additional funds to cover actual and potential valuation and legal costs. C.D.P. wanted to use part of its £40 000 a year "social action" budget to assist the residents group. This money was not for individuals to purchase their own freeholds or to cover their own legal costs, it was for topping up their resources so that they could go to the county court and the Lands Tribunal. It was to give them the potential to fight. In principle the idea was to give money in order to overcome the difficulties generated, first by the onus to initiate action resting on the leaseholder, and second, by his economic weakness. The claim was for £3000. This was estimated on the basis that it might be necessary to conduct up to 20 cases. From the start the Home Office was reluctant. In February 1973 they refused to sanction a grant stating that:

If we undertake financial assistance in a case like this, it would have the effect of setting up a rival scheme of legal aid to the one which is already established as Government policy.

Later, after negotiations with both the Department of the Environment and the Lord Chancellor's Office, the Home Office granted £400 towards the cost of strategic valuation and general legal advice. The rationale was difficult to understand. At the time it was not actually possible to use legal aid, but because the legal aid scheme existed it was not possible to provide an alternative. This was the only area of expenditure where the Home Office was restrictive. The only possible other remedy was to employ a solicitor. This had a number of potential advantages. First, resident control over the professional services was more possible and, secondly, the costs could have been borne without the difficulties raised by the Home Office. Other C.D.P.s had lawyers attached to their teams. We did see this as a long term alternative and, in fact, after another three years a lawyer joined the Saltley Action Centre (S.A.C.) which was originally founded by C.D.P. but which is an independent resources centre. The disadvantages of this strategy were two-fold. First, the time scale involved was inappropriate; secondly, there were a number of technical difficulties. Waivers from the Law Society practising rules are necessary for public sector lawyers. At the time of the test cases these were causing severe difficulties. The S.A.C. lawyers' waiver contained a condition that the solicitor only engage in "Representation before Tribunals for which a Legal Aid certificate is not available under the Legal Aid Scheme".[4] The Lands Tribunal is one of the few Tribunals for which legal aid is available. In addition, waivers seemed to be granted on the understanding that lawyers do not engage in traditional private practice matters. Leasehold work is part of that bastion of the private profession — conveyancing. After a number of years the waiver position has been settled with a standard waiver for all law centres. It solves the first problem but not the second. A law centre or salaried solicitor cannot conduct a conveyance.

The freehold prices in the L.C.&W. area were becoming clearer by the end of 1975, although only the ten test cases were settled. But the action on other manifestations of the problem was also proceeding at the same time. The first section described the inadequacies of the legal profession as we saw them then. Their services were costly and inefficient. One aim was to expose the worst excesses of their practices. In particular two firms of solicitors came to our notice. One firm consistently acted for both sides in the freehold purchase arrangements. In addition they seemed to have had a standing arrangement with an estate agent to act for the buyer of a property which the agent was selling. To act for both sides has been against the Law Society's practising rules since 1974. As a result of our complaints the solicitors were fined £1500 in 1975 for their activities. The other case involved the former secretary of the local Law Society who was struck off the practising list following an enquiry. We had complained about his activities in Saltley which had included proferring incorrect advice to a client about the relationship between rental purchase and leasehold enfranchisement.[5] The problem of delays and inefficient treatment were tackled by providing knowledge for residents. We found out who owned the freeholds, who owned the intermediary interests, which agent acted for whom and we explained the processes and the technicalities. This was done at public meetings, through leaflets and, primarily, through group organization. Obviously the most efficient method was for residents to use the same solicitor. This would be much cheaper and more efficient. The firm would become familiar with Saltley's leasehold structure and use the knowledge gained in one case to resolve problems created by another. They could build up a standard procedure with the common freeholder and various head leaseholders for arranging the transfers.

A steady flow of work from a succession of residents would enable the firm to plan its work, cut down delays and so reduce costs. As a study on the provision of legal services in Birmingham states:

> Other types of work for the poor or people of modest means, particularly housing, social security, consumer work and debt problems are either not presented to solicitors by clients or are filtered out at an early stage of the relationship with the solicitor.
>
> A firm which depends on legally aided litigation has to be geared up for it. There has to be rapid turnover, with delegation of functions to less qualified staff and standardisation of office working methods to ensure that work can safely be delegated and that, when delegated, it proceeds expeditiously. Such arrangements ensure the economic use of professional man power but they render it difficult to take on new types of work.
>
> This is not to say that it is impossible to take on new types of work. There are three stages. A firm can do a small amount of housing or social security without upsetting its normal routine. Once the amount of this work reaches a certain level it tends to become disruptive and uneconomical. At a third stage, however, a firm will be doing enough of such work to justify new standard procedures

which will enable it to be done in bulk. It is only at this stage that
the work becomes economical. (Bridges *et al.*, 1975, p. 229)

To put this into practice N.R.A. decided to invite tenders from different
firms of solicitors since it was clear that neither of the early test-case
solicitors was willing. Of those that replied, one firm quoted £40 for
handling the freehold purchase and £40 for each intermediary interest;
one quoted £35 and £30; and one quoted £25 for the freehold and £15 for
each intermediary interest. N.R.A. selected the last who besides being
the cheapest was also the firm which was handling the test cases. This
method of cutting costs was not popular with the professions, to quote
"Leasehold Loopholes":

> Solicitors are not, according to Law Society rules [which merely
> express their common interest in putting over a respectable image]
> allowed to advertise. They get their work, and make their money
> from recommendations or connections. Working class owner-
> occupiers, without the tradition of a family solicitor are often
> directed to a friendly solicitor by the estate agent who sells them the
> house. So, for example, the majority of local residents who buy
> from local estate agent Arthur Wood, finish up with a firm of
> solicitors R_____G. W_____. Once the resident is in the
> hands of one solicitor there seems little point in his changing since
> it is normally difficult to judge the merits of others. And the firm
> can encourage them to stay by keeping house deeds in safe keeping.
> If they are lucky, their client will continue to use their services.
>
> Norton Residents' collective rationalised programme disrupts these
> delicate arrangements. It is particularly threatening to a future flow
> of work when residents call in and demand their deeds back from
> their former solicitors. Birmingham Law Society accepted a
> complaint made by (. . . solicitors) that circular letters sent out by
> the Community Development Project to members of the association
> using the phrase "If you decide to use the association's solicitors to
> save costs" was objectionable and amounted to touting on behalf of
> the associations solicitors. (1979, p. 28)

The Law Society decided not to continue with the complaint. The local
campaign extended further than the N.R.A. area. Five leasehold groups
were formed in 1975. Residents from Warren Road negotiated with
Michael Pinney, one of the beneficiaries under the Norton Estate.
Hutton Estate leaseholders struggled to establish a pattern of fair freehold
prices with the trustees. The Parkfield Road and Phillimore Road groups
battled with property dealers Yorke Brookes and D. Fell. C. & P.
freehold fighters contended with C. & P. Estates. The groups followed

the N.R.A. pattern of bulk purchase. They were all serviced by C.D.P. workers and given small £150 grants towards communal expenses. All the groups used the same valuer who also agreed to a reduction in costs

JSB/JB/

Solicitors
CA   K & WAL
Telephones: 021-553 WEST BROMWICH B70

Mr. J.   V.A.T. Reg. No. 276 848,
    Highfield Road
Saltley
Birmingham.
                                    9th January_____19_____

Purchase of Freehold, Headleasehold and Underleasehold Interests in Highfield Road, *Saltley*, Birmingham	VAT @ 8%					
Paid Freehold purchase price			250	00		
Paid Freeholders Solicitors costs			41	58		
Paid Freeholders mortgagees costs			8	64		
Paid Freeholders Agents costs			27	00		
Proportion of Freehold ground rent due to the date of completion			1	72		
Paid Headleasehold purchase price			30	00		
Paid Headleasehold Solicitors costs			18	47		
Paid Underleasehold purchase price			40	00		
Paid Underleaseholders Solicitors and agents costs			45	74		
Paid Land Registry fees			13	70		
Paid search fees			2	00		
By cash you on account					454	57
To our legal charges re: Freehold	2	00	25	00		
To our legal charges re: Headleasehold	1	20	15	00		
To our legal charges re: Underleasehold	1	20	15	00		
	4	40	533	85	454	57
Add VAT			4	40		
			538	25		
Deduct receipts			454	57		
Balance now due from you			83	68		

Fig. 12. Non-reducible costs of freehold purchase 1975.

for bulk purchase, although most groups increasingly decided to rely merely on C.D.P. advice and negotiations.

Nothing could be done to cut the freeholders' legal costs or their valuation costs. Nothing also could be done to cut any intermediary landlords' costs. An example is given in Fig. 12 of the way these costs mount up. The freehold cost £250, the bill is more than double.

C.D.P. also acted on a policy level. The aim was to achieve some reform in the law and its operation. For two years all the channels open in a social democratic mode of reform were tried. Three meetings involving the Department of the Environment (D.O.E.) took place. The first had as its main concern the approval of expenditure for leasehold action and involved D.O.E., Lord Chancellor's Office and Home Office representatives. It was a result of the "special relationship" which existed for C.D.P. workers by which each local project was linked to a section of the Home Office in which civil servants concerned with the administration of the urban programme dealt with any policy recommendations. The other two were arranged by a local Member of Parliament, Dennis Howell, who luckily had special interest in leasehold enfranchisement legislation and was a Minister of State at the D.O.E. The second meeting was a discussion between D.O.E. officials responsible for rent and leasehold legislation and Birmingham C.D.P. The third involved these and also Dennis Howell and Gerald Kaufman, then Minister of State at the D.O.E. responsible for housing. The same difficulties arose each time. The debate concerned not so much C.D.P.'s proposals for reform, as the D.O.E.'s refusal to accept the proposition that the Act is not working.

At the first meeting it was contended by the D.O.E. that the Act worked well if the correct procedure was used. If the appropriate notice was served by the leaseholder everything would eventually settle into place. It was also stressed that this was an "individual Act", it concerned one tenant and one landlord and was designed to work on that level. The Act would work if the forms were served, hence the Act was working. This argument was put more forcibly in the next meeting. The leaseholders had not in fact "tried" because they had not served the notice. If they did not do this they were not using the Act. The D.O.E. contended that C.D.P. had not shown that the failure was a result of the Act but rather the fault of the legal profession. The strategy now suggested was to form residents associations and use "test case" action. The Act would work if these added ingredients were present. The third meeting had a more political flavour in that the discussion was with the two politicians and less time was spent on whether the Act was working in Saltley. Dennis Howell pointed out that the Act worked when the parties were willing but it did not work when they were not. The solution put forward at this meeting was an official conference. Representatives from the D.O.E. would come to the Council House in Birmingham and talk about the Act and its operations to local solicitors. They would not address a public meeting of leaseholders or come to Saltley. Dennis Howell was against a public meeting. He would agree to address a representative meeting of leaseholders (delegates from any residents association or other body) but considered it much more appropriate to talk to professionals since the leaseholders did not understand technical discussions. In a letter to the New Statesman (1979) Dennis Howell confirms our views. This letter was a response to an article about urban renewal in Birmingham.

The D.O.E. did not keep statistics of the workings of the Act, although the D.O.E. does keep data on the number of houses occupied by long leaseholders in their unpublished National Dwelling and Housing Survey (1977). The contention which they put forward that it was working everywhere else, especially in the Rhondda, was based on talking to M.P.s, although only one was mentioned, and on reading the Estates Gazette, although at that time this journal had not dealt specifically with the working of the Act since 1969. The suggestion was that leaseholders would write to the D.O.E. if they had problems. Thus the evidence was based on the assumption that as they had not heard to the contrary, the Act was working. Saltley, they stressed, was atypical.

C.D.P.'s recommendation was for a change of method in obtaining an offer. Instead of requiring the leaseholder to shoulder the burden, the freeholder should be obliged to notify the leaseholder that after an appropriate period of residence (say five years) he was now eligible to buy the freehold. The Act should contain provisions for the actual determination of price based, perhaps, on the rateable value of the property concerned. Thus any leaseholder would know the price without resorting to an independent valuer. By combining these two changes much of the present cost and abuse could be avoided. Since the discussions tended to become centred on the operation of the Act little attention was paid to the reform proposals. On the first suggestion that there should be some system of automatic transfer, the D.O.E. said that it had not even been mooted in the 'compulsory purchase world'. The rights under the Leasehold Reform Act were already a unique case of private compulsory purchase and it would be unthinkable to introduce "such a revolutionary idea". The politicians agreed; one pointed out that the Labour Party was a "constitutional party" and freehold purchase by option did not concur with this fact. On the second suggestion that price be linked to gross rateable values, the D.O.E. stated that it would lead to arbitrary values and have repercussions throughout the whole land value system. It had been considered "up to cabinet level" at the time of the Act but it was thought to produce unjust results. It would become a lottery. Some freeholders would be undervalued, others overvalued. The politicians agreed that this was the fault in the rateable value system generally. C.D.P. suggested that if the multiple to be used with the rateable value were set low, it could always favour the leaseholder and there would be no problem over valuation. Kaufman did not think this feasible since the "law was not be be used to make economic adjustments".

Initially action at a national policy level was confined to C.D.P. alone, but as the leaseholders took on more action and understood more about the system their frustration with the difficulties increased and they started to demand changes in the Act to make it work. A public meeting was arranged by the Saltley ward Labour Party and C.D.P. to discuss leaseholders with Dennis Howell. Despite his earlier feelings, he agreed to address a meeting in April 1975 which was very well attended. While putting forward the D.O.E. brief that the Act was working everywhere else and that it was the failure to serve notices which was causing the problems in Saltley, he said that his officials had told him that there was "more difficulty in Saltley than the rest of the country put together". There was no need for automatic transfers and anyway it was not feasible. The solution to the problem was to form residents associations and fight test case actions. This was the added ingredient needed. The audience, many of whom had been in Norton Residents Association for five years, were not convinced. Mr. Howell did, however, suggest that "suitable" amendments might be considered when and if, the Labour Government introduced an amendment to the 1974 Housing Act to reinstate the rateable value limitations.

Leaseholders in the area were not satisfied by the meeting and decided to petition Parliament for amendments and to write a report with the aid of C.D.P. to show their difficulties and circulate it to M.P.s at the time of the petition. The petition made three demands, that:

1. The price of a freehold should be determined by a set formula to prevent freeholders asking extortionate prices.
2. Intermediary leaseholds should be abolished.
3. The legal procedure for buying the freeholds should be simplified and made less expensive.

The report would elaborate on the demands and explain the situation more fully. This strategy has resulted in "Leasehold Loopholes" (1979), which is a report on the operation of the Act, its context in Saltley and the reform demands.

The last major attempt to bring about change through rational argument at a national official level came in September 1975. I gave a paper at a colloquium on urban legal problems. The paper answered some of the objections which had been raised by the Department of the Environment officials. As "Leasehold Loopholes" points out:

> But any enthusiasm for leasehold reform which the conference might have given them [D.O.E. officials] had evaporated within a month. In a letter to Home Office officials they wrote "while the Department would naturally look carefully at any practical proposals from C.D.P. for amendment to the 1967 Act, they would not be in a position to do a lot of detailed work on them for some considerable time". (C.D.P., 1979, p. 12)

Law reform of any sort is never easy but in this case there is a stark and easy contrast between the ability of working-class leaseholders and their middle-class counterparts. One per cent of leaseholders were excluded from the provisions of the 1967 Act because of the rateable value limits. This minority wanted to be included in the Act. In 1974 they achieved their aim in the Housing Act. A considerable proportion of this one per cent of leaseholders live on the Calthorpe Estate in Edgbaston. The members of the residents association have strong connections with the D.O.E. and with politicians in prominent positions on both sides of the House. During the minority Labour Government their sponsors introduced the amendment into the Lords and it was passed into law.

Despite Dennis Howell's suggestions in 1975 that the Labour Government might introduce an amendment to cut out the high rateable value group, in December 1978 the D.O.E. announced that the Labour Housing Bill would permit this group to use the low rateable value assumptions when calculating the freehold price. This followed the outcry over the price fixed by the Lands Tribunal in the only case on high rateable value criteria *Norfolk* v. *Trinity College Cambridge* (1976). Saltley residents also demanded action on intermediary interests. They wanted to see these very minor interests extinguished without compensation when leaseholders bought their freeholds. Both recent Labour and present Tory Housing Bills suggest reform through a formula to fix a price. This scheme was advocated by a solicitor representing Calthorpe Estate. After initial rebuffs his suggestion has been adopted. If a problem is designated as a loophole then reform can be speedy. The Leasehold Reform Act 1979 was rushed through Parliament in a matter of weeks after the House of Lords decision in *Jones* v. *Wrotham Park Settled Estate* (1979) opened up a loophole in the 1967 Act. Subsequently residents in Saltley have combined with residents in South Wales and Shelter in an attempt to add their amendments to those already proposed in the 1979 Housing Bill. These called for a freehold formula and a reduction in the residential qualification period. The campaign was successful on the second demand which is now incorporated into the 1980 Housing Act.

Attempts to point out the problems were not limited to national officials. C.D.P. attempted to persuade the Birmingham City Council to intervene more directly by buying up local freeholds. Both local councillors and those councillors connected with departments which had direct relevance such as urban renewal and estates were approached. C.D.P. suggested three ways in which the local state could assist leaseholders. First, they could use corporate pressure to bring about a change in the Act. Secondly, they could provide active help for individuals and groups by pointing out to residents, with whom they were in contact, the importance of enfranchisement and by providing officials to assist with valuations. Thirdly, as the C.D.P. report suggests:

> Most short lease property is in proposed improvement areas. The Corporation could buy up the freehold interests now in order to create flexibility in designing and implementing the environment policies. Normally individual leaseholders could still enfranchise, but if the City was interventionist and positive, generating support from the local communities involved, then a joint management scheme might be what most residents would prefer. (C.D.P., 1974)

The leader of the Council agreed in principle to the purchase of freeholds but nothing happened for three years. The last attempt will be discussed in the next chapter.

In addition we sought pressure group support and articles appeared in the New Law Journal (1975) and New Society (1975). We sought press coverage at a local and national level and leasehold appeared in programmes on the T.V. The Labour Party mechanisms were sought independently from the C.D.P.'s special relationship so to quote ''Leasehold Loopholes'':

> So in the third phase of our campaign we managed to get the demand for a change in the Act adopted by the various local organisations of the Labour Party then in power, both in Birmingham and nationally. A resolution adopted by Saltley Ward Branch became the kernel of the resolution by the small Heath Constituency Labour Party to the Labour Party National Conference in 1976. Locally the Regional Labour Party adopted a similar position, and the leaders of the Labour Group on Birmingham District Council were persuaded of the shortcomings of the Act as one element in the problem of financing owner-occupation within inner city areas. (1979, p. 8)

The outcome of the entire struggle over two years was the agreement of the agent of L.C.&W. to settle ten cases and agreement in principle to proceed with others. The machinery for a more efficient processing of freehold purchase had been evolved. It had not gone into effective action.

We felt that despite these gains, weak owner-occupiers were beating their heads against a capitalist-supported company and an entrenched unassailable property system. We did not think that local owner-occupiers would be allowed to win. We were wrong. The next two years showed just how limited our static analysis was. Now we see that the owner-occupiers were compelled to 'win' eventually, that the Leasehold Reform Act was not an aberation to be explained away; that ultimately the property company was fighting a rearguard action. To assert that owner-occupiers would 'win' is strictly speaking incorrect: more precisely it is that the concept of owner-occupation would predominate, supported in chaotic manner by the state. The cost to individual residents of this right to be an owner-occupier is enormous and no victory.

Notes

1. Sections 121 and 124 of the 1974 Housing Act facilitate investigation. The first obliges a landlord to disclose his identity to a tenant and the second requires a landlord to inform a tenant of a change of ownership.
2. This depends on the calculated risk that the local authority will serve

notice to treat before the negotiations progress too far. Notice to treat prevents any further dealings with the property.

3. In 1980 the valuer retained by the various residents associations appeared in a Tribunal case brought by a tenant supported by the Saltley Action Centre and Leasehold Unit as the expert witness for the landlord. His evidence rested solely on negotiations conducted by himself whilst retained by the residents associations.

4. In order to offer free legal services, law centres have needed a waiver from the ordinary practice rules which make it professional misconduct to attract business by unfair means. Waivers from these rules are granted by the Law Society, and the waiver system has been treated by the Law Society as the means to control the establishment of Law Centres and what they should be permitted to do. (Zander, 1978, p. 89)

5. He had assured a client that it was possible to enfranchise after five years residence although the client had taken on a rental purchase agreement whereby he resided as a licensee, not as a tenant. In addition the lease would have expired by the time the total purchase price had been paid off.

6 The Saltley Struggle Transformed

In 1974 several developments occurred which led us to reconsider our analysis. First, in May we noticed that L.C. & W. had sold off ten houses into owner-occupation. These were not in a block but scattered over the estate. This was extremely puzzling because we had been aware of a concerted policy of buying in interests and consolidating the holding right up until this time. Secondly, after a long period of negotiation in November 1975 L.C. & W.'s weekly tenanted houses were transferred freehold to a housing association directed by the Council's land committee chairman. Although this transaction was a result of C.D.P. pressure on the Council throughout 1973 and 1974 to buy the whole L.C. & W. estates, L.C. & W. still refused to sell the rest of the land. Thirdly, after his acceptance of the ten test cases, in January 1974 L.C. & W.'s agent now expressed himself willing to sell off individual freeholds but at a high price. In 1975 C. & P. Estates announced that they too were willing to sell off their freeholds for a flat figure of £250 and in an interview with the manager of the Hutton Settled Estate I learnt that they were also willing to sell off. This was a very significant reversal of policy, baffling but encouraging although we soon realized that we had only cleared the first hurdle in the battle to enfranchise.

These developments were obviously not primarily a result of our campaign although the increased possibility of individual leasehold enfranchisement had made eventual control over the estates by the existing owners less likely. It was evident that the market was in flux and that the general restructuring of the property market was having a local impact. In addition these owners were being affected by the increasing dominance of a policy of renewal. We gained a greater awareness of the problems of owner-occupation for working-class leaseholders by shifting our focus to analysing the social relations involved in the consumption of

165

this type of housing commodity in the peculiar context of leasehold tenure. There is no doubt that the changes in strategy informed by this understanding had a significant effect on the struggle. This chapter sets out to analyse the new forces and to describe the action taken as a consequence.

It seemed to us that the dominant force in the market was not the presence of a large obstructive property company but the economic and ideological presence of owner-occupation. This form has developed as the primary housing tenure with the general economic and ideological support of the state which has spread the net of potential owner-occupiers by providing special concessions and incentives such as the option mortgage scheme for low-income buyers and through the local authority equity sharing and mortgage schemes. In 1977 the housing policy green paper suggested further incentives for first time buyers and the 1980 Housing Act widens the net still further by providing for compulsory council house sales. Ideologically owner-occupation has been pushed very hard indeed: to quote the former Labour Government's Green Paper on housing

> A preference for home ownership is sometimes explained on the grounds that potential home owners believe that it will bring them financial advantage. A far more likely reason is the sense of greater personal independence that it brings. For most people owning one's house is a basic and natural desire. (1977, p. 50)

But as a recent C.D.P. report (1980) argues

> the desire for owner-occupation has been manipulated by the failure to build enough council houses to decent standards, by cutting the council house building programme, by raising rents, and by the continued propaganda of construction companies, building societies, estate agents and solicitors who have a vested interest in maintaining a private housing market whether or not it provides better housing conditions. (C.D.P., 1980, pp. 13-14)

Owner-occupation as it exists today incorporates a number of assumptions. The most important of these is that the house has an investment value which will provide a hedge against inflation. The assumption of building society policy is that owner-occupiers will trade up: that lenders will buy (with a mortgage which depreciates in real cost) a house which appreciates in value and, within a short time, will buy another more expensive house using as a deposit the additional money provided by the sale of their existing house. The aim of Government and

Building Society policy is to allow people to place one foot on the first rung of the ladder. After that they are free to move inexorably up the ladder.

> House prices rise with wage rises. But an individual who refuses to sell her house and buy further up the owner-occupation ladder will gradually pay out a smaller and smaller proportion of her wages on mortgage repayments.
>
> Second, as important, old house prices have kept pace with new, have often indeed increased by a greater percentage so that they bear little relation to the historic cost of their construction. According to Nationwide Bulletin 135, new house prices rose by 813% between 1946 and 1975 whereas house over 40 years old increased by 875%. In Saltley houses built for £175 sold for around £600 in 1946 and around £5000 in 1975. Third, the owner-occupied market is structured so that an individual buyer borrows to the hilt just to meet the purchase price and is persuaded to ignore or minimise repairs as a significant part of total housing costs. (C.D.P., 1978, pp. 89-90)

A further related assumption is that the use value of the house will remain relatively constant since the market in houses takes little account of physical deterioration. There is some discount for a house in need of repair but at the bottom end of the market this discount becomes increasingly less significant.

This market structure creates problems for working-class owner-occupiers which (as Chapter 3 has described) become overwhelming when the state intervenes with a policy of slum clearance to eradicate physical decay. But the alternative state policies of improvement, which apparently protect an occupier's investment in a house, can be just as unworkable in poor working-class areas like Saltley for the following reasons. First, the houses are leasehold and as a result they are declining economic assets. Their investment value does not increase but declines rapidly towards the fag end of the lease. Secondly, leasehold tenure has not provided either landlords or owner-occupiers with the incentive to carry out repairs so the houses have deteriorated rapidly in the last 20 years. Thus the Leasehold Reform Act was essential to a policy which encouraged working-class owner-occupation in inner-city areas. Yet as will be shown later, the new market in freeholds actually inhibits improvement. Thirdly, the function of the market is to provide housing for a low wage area. House prices cannot rise too much beyond the limited means of the now largely unskilled Saltley residents. Therefore, the relatively low house prices in inner-city areas do reflect low incomes here and superficially reassert the connection between wages and housing costs. But this equation ignores repairs and also in leasehold areas, the cost of buying the freehold. What the buyer gets for his money in Saltley is a house which needs £6000-£8000 spent on it to clear the backlog of repairs and another £500-£1000 to obtain the freehold. The total cost of an ordinary terraced house is, therefore, around £14,000 at current prices, well beyond the reach of most people who live here. Taking as "reasonable", the ratio of wages to housing costs used by both the MoH 50 years ago and the National Housing Committee 30 years ago, wages in Saltley (even after taking account of tax relief and improvement grants) would need to average over £100 a week to meet mortgage repayments. They do not. (C.D.P., 1978, p. 90)

The use value of the house is declining as many houses physically deteriorate. Instead of the market generally discounting this, as building societies have done by individually refusing to lend by lowering prices, the reverse has happened. A clear example of the market is provided by a comparison between the purchase price paid by COPEC when they bought from L.C. & W. at an open market sale. COPEC paid £600 for each. An open market price for these houses would be between £4000 and £4500. The houses were tenanted but the difference is still large. So the proportion of wages reasonably set aside for housing costs is eaten into by the purchase price and the amount left over for repairs and maintenance is thereby reduced.

The dominance of owner-occupation in Saltley is a product of the broader social relations of property. Although these relations have evolved from those of the original building process, they have been transformed. Figure 13 sets out schematically the history of three building leases and the social relation of leasehold tenure. Ownership of the various interests change and is linked to developments in the local housing market. The pattern, as Chapter 3 showed, is a shift in the resident's tenure from one of weekly renting to owner-occupying on a long lease, usually via a transitional dealing relation. As the original land-lords, builders and financiers died, new owners bought blocks of houses with the aim of making a capital gain by selling them individually into owner-occupation. Sales were usually by underlease at an improved ground rent. The post-war period before 1975 is thus dominated by sale and exchange of leasehold houses as commodities fixed to a parcel of land which remains in separate ownership.

In 1980 only a tenth of Saltley's houses are owned by private rentiers,

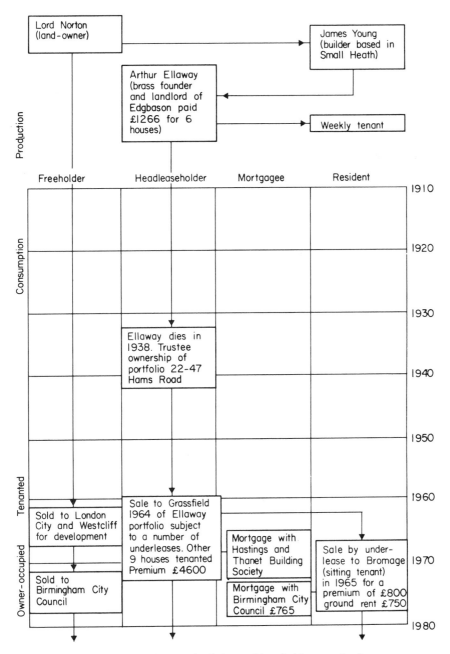

Fig. 13(a). The social relations of leasehold tenure in the
twentieth century — 28 Hams Road.

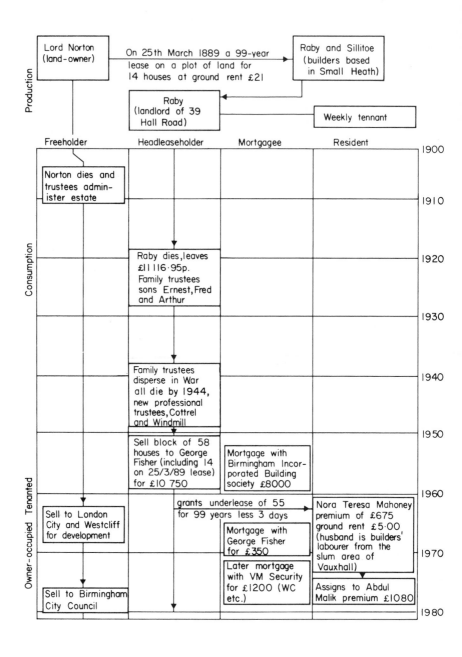

Fig. 13(b). The social relations of leasehold tenure in the
twentieth century — 55 St Saviours Road.

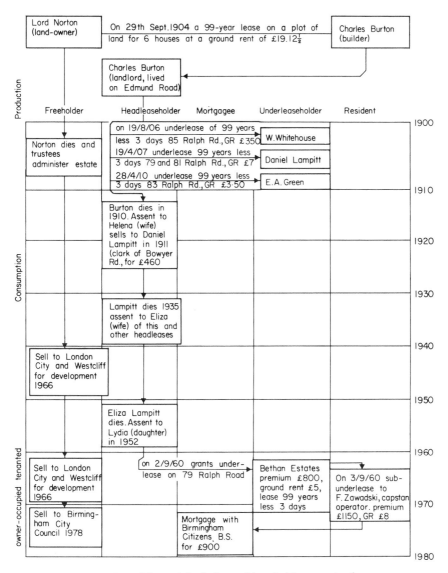

Fig. 13(c). The social relations of leasehold tenure in the
twentieth century — 79 Ralph Road.

about a third are owned either by the Council or by a housing
association.[1] Sales to either of these last two bodies in effect freezes any
further transactions (although councils do now sell off some council
houses). Money is made for the dealers in the housing market by

transactions 3 and 4 in Figure 14. This is achieved by the change of tenure and provision of finance. It is simple to enter the market because exchange values are low. Firms combine ownership with professional services like estate agency and brokerage. They start off as landlords but their aim is to sell into owner-occupation. During the initial period of renting they tend to disinvest in the physical fabric of the houses by neglecting repairs. This had little effect on the exchange value despite the decrease in use value. This provides a lump sum which can be reinvested in the new form of tenure or wherever is most profitable. One way of re-investing in the same property is to become a monopoly lender on the purchase of the property. This can be done by the original firm or by associates. Certainly in the crucial period 1972 to 1974 the alternative forms of mortgage finance were limited. The building societies, local authority, clearing banks and fringe banks were all potential lenders. However, building societies have not lent substantially in the inner ring of Birmingham for over ten years. They only lent to 8% of the new buyers in Saltley between 1972 and 1974 compared with around 50% 20

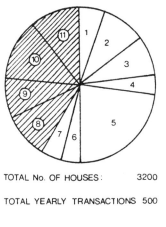

FIGURE 2   (Schematic)
YEARLY PROPERTY TRANSACTIONS
IN SALTLEY
HOUSES

1   Landlord → Council
2   Landlord → Housing Association
3   Landlord → Landlord
4   Landlord → Owner occupier
5   Owner occupier → Owner occupier
6   Owner occupier → Agent → Owner occupier
7   Owner occupier → Council

LAND
8   Non occupational freeholder →
       Occupational freeholder
9   Non occupational leaseholder →
       Occupational leaseholder
10   Non occupational freeholder →
       Non occupational freeholder
11   Non occupational leaseholder →
       Non occupational leaseholder

TOTAL No. OF HOUSES :   3200

TOTAL YEARLY TRANSACTIONS 500

The shaded part refers to transactions in land alone. The other refers to transactions in buildings (which incorporate a fixed relation to the land thay stand on, either a lease or freehold ownership)

Extracted from Green 1976

Fig. 14(schematic). Yearly property transactions in Saltley.

years earlier (C.D.P.; Karn, 1974).[2] Since 1974 attempts have been made to increase building society lending. When the Government announced the first cut back in council lending in June 1975, the building societies agreed to lend £100m to council nominees of which £2.5 was allocated to the West Midlands. By July 30th 1976 the three societies nominated to disperse the fund had only lent to 28 Council nominees in pre-1919 houses. Subsequently, to the annoyance of local authority housing officials, building societies would recommend a prospective buyer, who had just approached them, to go to the local authority first in order to be sent back to them as part of the scheme. Their policy does not seem to have changed since then. Economically their reluctance is perfectly justified since the houses in inner areas are hardly good investment assets.

The Council likewise has not been a major alternative source of finance because of cut-backs in public expenditure. The position is summarized in a leaflet distributed at the time:

> In the financial year 1974-1975, local Councils lent a total of £690m. Birmingham lent £13¼m for house purchase. In June 1975 the Government limited lending nationally to £250m and in Birmingham to £9m for the financial year 1975-76. But Birmingham had already committed this money when the order came so lending stopped until April 1976. In January 1976 the Government cut lending for 1976-77 to £220m or £276m (at 1976 prices) and Birmingham's share was £6.45m. Not more than 60% was to be allocated in the first six months. In August 1976 the Government cut the total money which could be lent during 1976-77 by 15% to £5.48m. As part of the big package of cuts in public expenditure announced by the Government in July 1976, local Councils can lend only about £100m on house purchase and improvement during 1977-78, Birmingham's share works out at £2.3m. (Birmingham C.D.P., September 1976)

During the credit boom from 1971 to 1973, dealers selling houses could also exclude the Council easily by raising the purchase price. The Council carried out careful and realistic market valuations and would not lend on over-priced houses. Though their policy is now more flexible and they obtain valuations independently from estate agents, they are still careful to check incomes and slow to process applications. Most borrowers still go to the banks. The clearing banks have dominated mortgage lending since the early 1970s and close connections between dealers and financiers have grown up. For example, Ghandee's firm of First Time Home Buyers, which acted both as estate agent and dealer, organized finance through Cedar Holdings or Julian Hodge; Melhuish, the estate agent who was a director of a number of dealing companies, persuaded buyers to use Constant Finance Company for mortgage finance.

A similar structure exists in the transactions between existing owner-occupiers. Here again financiers and professionals dominate. Houses in Saltley have had a low exchange value because of low incomes in the area and also because of the valuations of the traditional lenders. Both local authority and building societies, when they lend, make realistic market valuations and limit the ratio of income to mortgage outgoings. Estate agents operated in this conventional market until the late 1960s when alternative sources of finance became available. In 1971 the Conservative Government's Competition and Credit Control measures allowed clearing banks into the market and by 1974 they had obtained a half share of all new lending in Saltley, see Figure 15.

The new lenders paid less attention to valuation and income/outlay ratios but, in return, demanded substantial deposits and pushed up the price of houses far out of the local authority limits. The estate agents organized both buyer and seller, the financiers and the solicitors. Examples of arrangements with Fringe Banks are as follows. Gandhee would act as estate agent for a seller. He would first offer potential purchasers 100% mortgages and then suggest George Mitchell Colman as solicitors. Gandhee was a broker for Cedar Holdings who provided the mortgage. Money was made by creating unstable mortgages which lead to frequent buying and selling at higher and higher prices. Gandhee made money out of brokerage and estate agents' fees. George Mitchell Colman

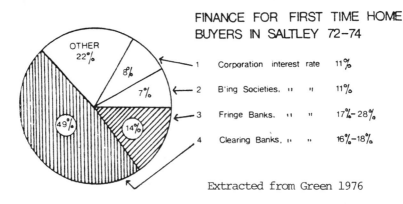

FINANCE FOR FIRST TIME HOME BUYERS IN SALTLEY 72-74

OTHER 22%

1 Corporation interest rate   11%

2 B'ing Societies, "   "   11%

3 Fringe Banks, "   "   17%-28%

4 Clearing Banks, "   "   16%-18%

Extracted from Green 1976

Fig. 15. Finance for first time home buyers 1972-1974.

made theirs by conveyancing fees in buying and selling, Cedar Holding made theirs by high fixed interest rates (from 17.25% to 25%) and large penalty claims (up to £150) from those who wanted to redeem their mortgage early. But these activities were not limited to fringe finance, Barclays Bank was also heavily involved.

Rental purchase also emerged in the early seventies. This scheme involves

> a contract for the sale of a dwelling, where payment is to be made in instalments while the purchaser is in possession, completion normally taking place, if at all, when all the instalments have been paid. (Hoggett, 1972, p. 325)

It is, in fact, hire purchase of real property. It involves no mortgage and is not to be confused with the mortgage back system in which a sale takes place at the outset and the dwelling is then mortgaged to the vendor. To quote the Francis Committee Report

> rental purchase ... is used chiefly for the sale of the sort of house that would be unlikely to qualify for a mortgage to the sort of purchaser of whom the same is true. (1971, p. 112)

In Saltley it was operated by one Birmingham based company with highly dubious methods. Weekly payments were far in excess of a registered weekly rent yet the time period for the payments was fixed so that when the occupier is entitled to transfer of the legal estate the lease has almost expired. An example would be a rental purchase agreement in which the licensee occupier pays instalments for 15 years to purchase a leasehold house with 18 years left to run. The occupier becomes a long leaseholder only three years before the lease expires and therefore has no opportunity to purchase the freehold since he could not before the reduction in qualifying period introduced by the 1980 Housing Act satisfy the residence qualification. The occupants were encouraged to use a solicitor favoured by the company and they often were unaware of the consequences of the agreement. The system also defeats any programme of renewal.

> Every application for an improvement grant by a resident who has an instalment mortgage has to be refused by the City Council because they do not fall within section 57 (3) of the 1974 Housing Act. This section states that ''a local authority shall not entertain an application for a grant unless they are satisfied that the occupant has, in every parcel of land on which the improvement works are to be carried out, an interest which is either an estate in fee simple absolute in possession, or a term of years absolute of which not less than 5 years remain unexpired.

At the date of application the licensee purchaser fulfils neither criteria. The only method of obtaining an improvement grant on such a property would be for the vendor mortgagee to apply. But this would defeat the object of operating such a system, as section 60 of the Act stipulates that a certificate of future occupation must be granted. In the present circumstances the vendor would be obliged to obtain a certificate of availability for letting under subsection (5). If this were obtained, the occupants of the house would definitely become tenants covered by the terms of the Rent Acts.

Birmingham City Council had recognised the necessity of preventing this takeover (by exploitative agencies) and had been operating, prior to the Government cutbacks, a mortgage conversion scheme. The mortgagors in such situations were permitted to transfer to a more secure mortgage with the local authority. Unfortunately, licensees with an instalment mortgage are not eligible for this scheme. Section 37 of the 1974 Local Government Act states that a transfer can be obtained to enable applicants to retain an interest on their home, and to enable improvement works to be carried out. But the City Council interpret this section of the Act strictly, arguing that a transfer is impossible because residents affected have no interest to retain in the first place. (Shutt and Stewart, 1976, p. 217)

In 1974 the property market collapsed and, with the aftermath, a number of changes appeared in the local market. The clearing banks left for a time and valuations became more realistic. Fringe banks collapsed and, because of bad publicity, the survivors, like Julian Hodge, became more careful. Overall the conditions are broadly as they were before the financial crisis. Building societies are still not lending significantly and local authority lending is still controlled by the levels of public expenditure. In 1980 the clearing banks again dominate the market lending at interest rates of over 20% which are similar to those of the now discredited secondary banks. Some of this finance facilitates the sale of the remaining tenanted houses into owner-occupation. More usually it facilitates the purchase of already owner-occupied houses. When the next property boom arises the same or similar excesses will occur. In the meantime the trend remains. New owners of intermediary interests are not rentier landlords but small companies interested in selling owner-occupation to sitting tenants or Asian newcomers.

The collapse of the property market had its effect on all property relations including freeholders. In Saltley the major freeholders, who had bought in order to develop, found by 1973 the forces weighted heavily against them. In addition to the inhibiting policies of owner-occupation and renewal they were faced with an acute financial crisis which was wiping out asset values. They suffered substantial losses. To quote a financial report for London City & Westcliff.

> After interest of £411,274 on the centre Nord office building and other interest of £1.37m compared with £1.87m, L.C. & W. properties incurred a loss of £724,535 for the half year to March 31, 1976, against £358, 845 for the corresponding period and £499,060 for the last full year. (Financial Times, 9th September 1976)

The sales noticed earlier were explicable: consolidation was no longer possible. The freeholders' policies changed first to sell off individual freeholds but, very soon after, to move out of the market altogether. In 1977 C. & P. Estates offered the freeholds to individual residents but sold off a number of blocks of freeholds to small property companies (often holding as landlords the leasehold interest of a number of houses in the block) before selling out altogether to another, smaller company based in Jersey. After some individual sales in the Hutton Settled Estate area, the interests have been sold off to a number of small companies. Notorious are Frederick Yorke Brookes, Dennis Fell and his companies, and Arthur Wood and Company. The position with L.C. & W. was slightly different. By 1976 they needed financial assistance. Lonrho bought in shares during 1976 and finally took them over for £13 million later in the year. We judged that Lonrho would not be interested in freeholds in Saltley and that they too would sell off this part of the L.C. & W. portfolio. We proved to be correct.

Thus the pattern became clearer. The large companies were not interested in individual sales, so they sold to those who were. Some of the buyers were dealers who already held the lease on a block of houses pending their sale into owner-occupation. They recognized that by the time they gained vacant possession of each house, the lease would be so short as to make selling difficult. The best course was to marry the existing lease to the newly bought freehold and sell the house freehold or create a new long lease. Similarly intermediary interests were traded in their own right, through exchange with those of other property companies. Their aim is to maximize capital gains through eventual purchase by occupiers. Examples of sales between dealers in intermediary interests are as follows: in 1961 Congreve Investments, owners of a number of such interests in Saltley, packaged them with 101 others all over Birmingham and sold them to Asho Property Co. for £6687.1.11. The total ground rent was £475. In 1975 Pereira Estates Ltd sold the intermediary leasehold of 26 of these properties in Ralph Road, Saltley to Villagate Properties for £690. In a similar deal in 1962 S.J.J. Ltd sold five houses to Blossomfield investments for £1750. In 1966 Blossomfield sold just one of these five for £1575 by underlease, raising the ground rent from £2.04 to £8.00. Less than half a mile down the road there was a similar pattern of dealing by the Fell group of companies. In 1964 a variety of Fell property companies — mainly Blossomfield Investments and Grassfield Investment bought the headleasehold interest in consecutive numbers 22 to 47 Hams Road which is shown in Fig. 9, together with the nine houses in the block which had not been sold off to owner-occupiers by the original landlord, George Ellaway, brassfounder and Conservative councillor. They paid £4600 and got a mortgage from the Thanet & Hastings Building Society. When the tenants died, left or were pressured into buying, the Fell Group sold off each of the remaining houses by way of underlease for an average profit of more than £1000. Each time the ground rent has increased, in some cases up to £15 a year. And in one case an extra underlease was created by Blossomfield Investments selling to Grassfield Investments before they sold it to the resident.

When residents wanted to buy their freeholds in 1976, the headlease-holder at first asked tenants for 30 times the difference between the new ground rent paid by the tenant, and the rent in respect of each house passed on by the headleaseholder to the freeholder. Mr Sassons from 39 Hams Road, who paid £15 ground rent of which only £2.20 was passed on to the freeholder, would have had to pay £384 for the headleasehold on top of the £215 for his freehold. These examples of intermediary prices can be multiplied many times over in Saltley. These are the companies which were involved in Membury Road in 1974. Their existence is now explicable whereas, as Chapter 5 showed, their significance between 1972 and 1975 was lost to us.

Thus the nature of the social relations of property have changed in the early 1970s. The dominant force in the market is the creation of freehold owner-occupation. Only the resident is concerned at a successful outcome, the other parties are interested in the processes of either selling rented property into owner-occupation or selling freehold and leasehold interests to the new owner-occupiers. The owners are, in the main, specialized dealers who are eager for sales. Obviously price is of central importance. The higher the better. The new freeholders rely on the leaseholders' inability to determine a reasonable price and their eagerness or necessity to purchase in order to carry out the obligatory programme of renewal. Many examples can be given. Mallett, acting on behalf of L.C. & W. demanded totally unreasonable prices by Lands Tribunal standards for the ten test cases as did Trimidon Investments. See Table IX.

TABLE IX

Prices offered and accepted by L.C. & W. and Trimidon Investments

L.C. & W.			Trimidon Investments		
Road	Asking price	Fair price	Road	Asking price	Fair price
83 Ralph	300	190	52 Ellesmere	400	270
103 Ellesmere	360	190	92 Ellesmere	400	270
65 Hams	250	153	80 Highfield	450	310
183 St Saviours	350	301	104 College	450	310
101 Ralph	325	173	13 Hartopp	450	260
5 Ellesmere	425	231	4A Bowyer	400	240
149 St Saviours	400	287	21 Bowyer	500	360
103 Reginald	530	312	70 Bowyer	450	360
61 St Saviours	400	310	107 Bowyer	500	360
17 Hall	700	300	192 St Saviours	450	320

The local Birmingham firms are eager often to claim even higher profits because their holdings are smaller. Examples from various local owners are given in Table X.

The opportunities for capital gain are increased where tenants who qualify to enfranchise do not follow the legislative procedure. That small proportion who do follow the procedure formally often find that any decrease in capital gain for the freeholder is compensated for by the increase in professional costs. In Saltley these costs are very closely linked to the price since the same groups are involved in ownership and professional servicing. An example is provided by the agent for the freeholders of 174 Havelock Road.

We are also advised our client [sic] has sold similar ground rents at the figures suggested and we are sure that he will be reluctant to

TABLE X

Prices offered by local owners

Owners	Road	Details	Asking price	Fair price
Fell	120 College	16 yrs unexpired term £5 g.r.	750	*380
Fell	86 Bowyer	58 yrs unexpired term £15 g.r.	500	265
Larkcroft	54 Herrick	15 yrs unexpired term £5 g.r.	1250	*450
Larkcroft	22 Herrick	15 yrs unexpired term £8 g.r.	1500	*450
G. Fisher	119 College	21 yrs unexpired term £5 g.r.	595	260

*Each owner asked for agency fees in addition to the legal costs. Fell asked for £35, Larkcroft for £40.

accept a lower offer, although in order not to enter into protracted negotiations which will, of course, increase our costs, we are prepared to submit to our client a recommendation for acceptance an offer of £700 plus legal costs and our surveyors costs of £75 plus value added tax.

The local market which developed in the early seventies has created a particular relationship between owners and professional servicers. First, in their capacity as merchant professionals, dealers acting also as estate agents service the exchange of other people's property and take a percentage of the transaction. Over 50% of houses now circulate

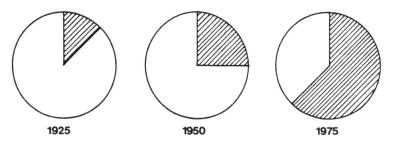

1925　　　　1950　　　　1975

▨ Change of resident involving change of ownership

Extracted from Green 1976 : 51

Fig. 16. Yearly turnover of households — 100% = 360°.

between owner-occupiers where every change of occupant is a change of owner. See Fig. 16. This arrangement is the most profitable for the professionals, particularly as owner-occupied property changes hands more frequently than rented accommodation. As blocks of houses are split up into individual ownership the cost of professional services increases as a percentage of exchange value. For example an estate agent would not have charged much more for selling the block of 26 houses in Hams Road already referred to, than he would have for arranging the sale, at a quarter of the price, of an individual house in the block.

But the owner-occupied market in Saltley can be professionally more remunerative than the usual arrangement of building society, estate agent and two solicitors. Owner-occupation has been particularly unstable because of the organization of the market with fringe finance, high exchange values and low wages and leasehold tenure. Not only is the turnover high but the exchange process itself is managed by the groups of owners, financiers and professionals who specialize in the market. But secondly this relationship is often much closer since the professionals

Taken from G. Green (1976). Fig. 17.

often act as merchant capitalists rather than merchant professionals. They insert themselves into the transactions as middlemen buying and reselling at a profit rather than merely servicing an exchange of property.

The Leasehold Reform Act facilitates a close relationship between owners and servicers and thereby allows them to reap a high return. Section 8 of the Act requires the enfranchising leaseholder to pay all the reasonable costs of enfranchisement. This process is shown in diagrammatic form in Fig. 17. The prices and fees have doubled since the leaflet (from which this was extracted) was produced by C.D.P. in 1975.

The leaseholder pays all the parties. An example of solicitors' costs are given below.

> With reference to your letter of the 16th instant we have now obtained the title deeds from our clients and it would appear that our Clients only hold an underleasehold interest on 183 and 185. They pay £6 on the two houses and collect £3 from your client. Accordingly there is no improvement.
> Our clients are therefore prepared to assign their interest in the property at a nominal figure of £5 subject, of course, to the Head Lessee reducing the ground rent by £3 per annum.
> In addition your Clients would be responsible for the Surveyor's fees amounting to £2.50 plus VAT and our fees of £50 plus VAT.

When the owners are also professionals they reap both benefits. The example of Hams Road was given on page 178. For each of the intermediary interests, Dennis Fell asked for £20 of valuation fees. The valuation was done by themselves. It is extremely difficult to see any justification for demanding valuation fees for intermediary interests, since the process of valuation seems to amount to demanding as much as the resident can pay. It bears little relation to the nominal value of the interests. Valuers presumably cannot claim fees for the art of deducing residents ability to pay. Yet the Act allows them to charge valuation fees for assessing the value of these interests.

It is more common for freehold interests to be held by estate agents rather than by solicitors, although some firms of solicitors do have strong links with companies holding these interests. For instance, Reginald Eyre, solicitor, is a director in a company holding freehold and leasehold interests. Neville Bosworth, of Bosworth Bailey & Cox, is associated with the Dennis Fell group of companies. But as "Leasehold Loopholes" points out:

> The financial advantage to solicitors of intermediary leasehold

interests is not so clear cut. They have been technically responsible for the great proliferation of underleases as owner-occupation has expanded in the inner areas of Birmingham. And they must be aware that this convenient legal device has to be unravelled when the intermediary lease is finally bought by the resident. This means more work for them. Conveniently the Leasehold Reform Act, by putting the burden of legal costs on the resident effectively manages the potential conflict between the headleaseholder and his expensive legal advisor. If the headleaseholder had to pay his own legal costs he would naturally minimise them. Since he does not have to pay it does not matter to him how much the solicitor charges. (C.D.P., 1978, p. 26)

The market for costs, which has been created by the Act, is profitable if it is conducted by a few specialist concerns. This is the state of the Saltley market. One-off arrangements would be of no significance to professionals. An arrangement whereby a few firms control the local market can transform the profitability level. The leaseholder is powerless against the range of owners and linked servicers. He can only attempt to minimize his own costs. A very modest example of the outcome for a leaseholder is given in Fig. 18. The problem of costs must, however, be

To agreed figure for freehold interest	£280.00
Freeholder's solicitors' costs (estimated)	30.00
Freeholder's Agents' charges (estimated)	30.00
Our costs	25.00
VAT on the above	6.80
To agreed purchase price of headleaseholder interest	20.00
Solicitors' costs (estimated)	30.00
Agents' charges (estimated)	15.00
Our costs	25.00
VAT on the above	5.60
To agreed purchase price of head underleasehold interest	20.00
Solicitors' charges	30.00
Agents' charges	10.00
Our costs	25.00
VAT on the above	5.20
Disbursements including Land Registry fees and Search fees (estimated)	7.50
	£565.10

Fig. 18. Unavoidable costs of freehold purchase 1979.

seen in conjunction with the other elements in the market. The problem can be overwhelming for a leaseholder who is burdened with a fringe bank mortgage for an over priced house and who is buying the freehold mainly to facilitate improvement. All the elements come together over the renewal issue. This has superceded the obstruction of the freeholders, to become the central problem which confronts residents.

The crisis is most evident in the Housing Action Area. The full ramifications of this renewal policy are discussed in "From Failure to Facelift" published by Birmingham C.D.P. (1980). As we have seen in Chapter 3, the Housing Act 1974 provides for grants to cover the cost of obligatory improvement. The grants level seem high: 75% of the cost up to a ceiling figure, but some people, primarily old age pensioners, can qualify for a grant of 90%. Despite this seemingly generous aid, the problems are manifest. Successive ceiling figures only briefly catch up with actual improvement costs. The increase to £5000 in August 1977 was soon outstripped by rising building costs. At the beginning of 1980 it fell short of the average cost of improving a house in Saltley by over £3000. A resident receiving the maximum grant of £3750 (75% of £5000) would have to contribute an average of over £4250.

The problem for owner-occupiers at the bottom end of the market lies in market prices which do not effectively discount enfranchisement and, more importantly, improvement costs. George Arthur Road provides an example. In 1977 the houses had a market value leasehold of between £2000 and £3000. Despite the shortening of the leases the prices had continued to rise with wage inflation. As they had been the first to be built in the area, the leases were shortest and the houses were of relatively mean quality, opening on to the street unlike most of the other houses in the area. Residents were usually paying off mortgages obtained to purchase the house but they also needed loans from the local authority to finance their contribution to the improvement cost. The problem was that despite the inflated market price of the house, the equity or security did not cover the total borrowing requirement. The Birmingham city solicitor has recognized the problem of providing potentially unsecured loans. By 1976 he had interpreted the provisions of the Housing Act 1974 in a restrictive manner. First, as the grant might be repayable if the owner-occupier sold his house within five years of receiving it then the amount of the grant received also had to be deducted from the market valuation before deciding the size of the loan to be given. Secondly, the improvement loan could not be given without knowing the amount of the loan which would be required for the acquisition of the freehold. If it was appropriate both of the factors had to be considered at the same time. The second stipulation is important. The longest lease in this road was 16 years in 1977, George Arthur Road was in the old L.C. & W. area. After the test cases George Arthur was one of the first streets to attempt to negotiate prices *en bloc* with Mallett, the agent for L.C. & W. Negotiations took place between November 1975 and March 1976. Prices for 34 properties were agreed upon. These varied between £302 and £812 depending on the length of lease, the ground rent paid and the size of the plot of land to be sold. These prices were only for those who had lived in their houses for over five years. Those who had not and were not therefore eligible to purchase under the L.R.A. had to pay more.

TABLE XI

Freehold Prices negotiated 1975-1977 in George Arthur Road

Length of lease 1975	Eligible		Not eligible	
	Cost £	No.	Cost £	No.
18 months	670-812	3		
12 years	337	1		
13½ "	317-401	9	470-600	4
14 "	380	2		
15 "	310-366	5	515-689	2
17½ "	320-410	3	512-639	2
18½ "	302-371	2	711	1

Figures provided by Birmingham C.D.P.

Most leaseholders in the road had one or two intermediary interests to buy out as well as the freehold interest. On average these interests cost £25. When the legal costs of about £150 are added to the bill, the final costs for residents were between £500 and £1000 depending on the length of lease. This expenditure had to be incurred before improvements could start. Leaseholders with leases of less than five years unexpired term are not eligible for improvement grants while loans from the Council are not available to people with leases of less than ten years. All loans must be paid back before this ten year deadline, so leaseholders with a 13½ year lease would be obliged to pay back any loan within 3½ years. Most owner-occupiers in the road needed loans to help them pay their share of the grant and to purchase the freehold. Only eight residents out of the 34 did not require a loan to purchase the freehold. Twenty-five of these required loans from the city council. The city solicitor's ruling required that the loan requirements for both freehold purchase and improvement had to be considered together.

> The mechanics were impossible. It meant that residents had to begin the improvement process, brief architects, draw plans and get schedules estimated long before they were actually going to improve. Invariably the estimates would have to be revised later. However, since estimates were by mid 1976, coming in at well over £6,000, when the leasehold loan requirement was added there was nearly always an equity problem and the application would be turned down. (C.D.P., 1980, p. 26)

The outcome is shown in Table XII. By May 1978 of the 41 residents who finally negotiated collectively for a price, 35 needed mortgages and could not obtain them and only a handful of owner-occupied houses had been improved in the four years since the declaration of the Housing Action Area (H.A.A.).

Obviously renewal was unworkable and since 1978 the local state has intervened more directly in the process using a "facelift" scheme. This involves improving the external parts of each house free. Three streets in the H.A.A. had £1 million spent on roofs, doors, walls and other necessary repairs. Using this level of expenditure it would cost £54 million to improve the rest of Saltley in the same manner.

TABLE XII

George Arthur Road — Position May 1978

Ownership	Improved or in hand	Unimproved	Total
Owner-Occupied (7 freehold)	13	46	59
Private Landlord	0	2	2
COPEC Housing Trust (33 freehold)	33	0	33
Council owned	2	0	2
Other (void commercial)	0	4	4

Figures provided by Birmingham C.D.P.

Thus the consequences for housing held under the leasehold system of disinvestment and devaluation have conflicted with the dominant force of owner-occupation. The Leasehold Reform Act was an attempt to stem these consequences and provide freehold owner occupation. It however seems to have relied on the existence of the original social relations of leasehold tenure: a landed estate, a rentier landlord or, in more recent times, a family successor holding a headleasehold interest in a now owner-occupied house. Where this relation exists or one closely moulded on it, the costs and prices can be low and enfranchisement relatively simple. In Ellesmere Road, one of the best roads in Saltley with many owner-occupiers from the time it was built, the headleaseholder was often a neighbour who had, by chance, purchased the interest when he took on his own house. Here the arrangement was easy, both parties had a common purpose to purchase the freeholds. The headleasehold interest was simply surrendered in exchange for the legal costs which were minimal since the same solicitor acted for both after obtaining permission from the local law society.

The freeholder was assumed by the 1967 Act to be interested in the reversionary value of the individual plot. But the dominant social relations of leasehold tenure had already changed by the time the Act was passed. Specialist dealers had displaced rentiers both as holders of mere improved ground rents (in the form of leasehold or underleasehold interests) and as landlords of houses let to weekly tenants. Bigger property companies had displaced traditional land-owners, and were interested in the reversionary value of the land for redevelopment of large areas. And by the mid 1970s they were in turn displaced by property dealers, buying land not for its redevelopment potential or rental income, but in order to sell it for a profit to owner-occupier leaseholders. Land was traded as a commodity. The Act allowed dealers to create a commodity market. Before 1967 leasehold and freehold interests had very little commodity value; now they have a specialized one to a certain type of dealer. The Act has created the new market and it seals the arrangement by insisting on professional services which are provided by the dominant groups in the market. The freehold commodities are not landed they are merely tributes transferred to finance capital because of ownership.

But conflicts exist. These finance capital groups divert a high proportion of wages to an unproductive sector. The Act was passed to facilitate improvement, which would be provided by builders in the industrial productive sector. Yet it has created a submarket which undermines this aim. Thus in order to eliminate the leasehold system, money has to be spent on enfranchisement which is desperately needed for physical improvement. Enfranchisement adds nothing tangible to the use value. New roofs, windows and wiring are crucial. Enfranchisement merely upholds the exchange market system by supposedly adding to the price of the house. Yet still the equity will not support the improvement costs. The whole pyramid based on the social relations of leasehold tenure involves a massive conflict of aims which exacerbate the contradictions of working-class owner-occupation in areas like Saltley.

We no longer saw ourselves fighting for a legal right which was denied by a powerful protagonist. Nor did we see professional servicers as economically independent from the market but colluders with an ideology of property rights in the abstract. Now we saw them as specialists operating in a particular local market created by the leasehold system.

The action strategies were aimed at reducing prices and fees to offset the problem of total housing cost. An attack was launched on the particular finance capital stranglehold. First, in 1974 C.D.P. in conjunction with the Centre for Urban and Region Studies carried out the survey already mentioned to find out precisely the nature of the mortgage market. The results showed clearly that the local authority was not an important stabilizing element in Saltley since only 8% of incoming residents had council mortgages and most of the other new owners had fringe or clearing bank arrangements. C.D.P. attempted to bring pressure on the local authority to make their mortgage facilities more widely known and to increase their efficiency by writing a report which described the inefficiencies such as delay in processing applications and lack of publicity and which spelt out the consequences of the state failure. Leaflets outlining the results of the research and its consequences were circulated locally along with information on council mortgages. C.D.P. also arranged a scheme whereby local residents with intolerable mortgage arrangements could transfer to a council mortgage using section 37 of the Housing Act 1974. In June 1975, when the scheme was only starting to work, public expenditure cuts stopped all local authority lending. Although a few residents used the scheme when it became available again in May 1976, the market had changed. The clearing banks had moved out and the fringe banks had moderated their practices. Since 1976 local authority mortgages should have been available and should have been used. Despite their availability, a number of cases have appeared where mortgages have been granted by the Bank of Ireland.[3]

To counteract the effect of the professionals C.D.P. put out a black list of estate agents who had been operating the dubious schemes already described. The solicitors who had been involved in malpractice were also attached. The Law Society eventually fined one company and struck off another. We attacked the system of rental purchase and those who operated it first by publishing an article in a national journal to publicize the nature of the scheme and secondly, by writing articles in local newspapers (see further Hoggett, 1972, 1976). The campaign was two-pronged: to offset the exploitative operation of the present system but to attempt to outlaw it altogether by legislation. On the first point the West Midlands Consumer Protection Department was asked to use the provisions of the Consumer Credit Act to prevent trading by estate agents cum property companies. The Act stipulates that operators, before they can provide finance, will need a licence which the Director of Fair Trading has power to withhold if evidence shows that

> either in the past or present a firm has engaged in business practices appearing to be deceitful, oppressive or otherwise unfair or improper (whether unlawful or not). (S25(2) d Consumer Credit Act 1974)

But, although this provision was helpful, it was not immediately relevant in 1975 and 1976 when only two sections of the Act were in force. Licensing did not begin until April 1976 and it was estimated that it might take over three years to complete.

As well as the report to the Consumer Protection Department we attempted to take court action against the particular arrangement in Saltley. We obtained a council's opinion for one case which was not particularly encouraging.

> I am driven to the conclusion that there would be virtually no prospect of success if an attempt were made to persuade the Courts that rental purchase is a device which is capable of being struck down as being repugnant to legal principles or public policy ... I have also considered whether the Moneylenders Act might be involved, but I am unable to discern a sufficient basis for arguing that the vendor is lending money to the purchaser.

He was, however, of the opinion that the solicitors were guilty of negligence in the handling of the purchase. But the solicitors had already acted:

> By arranging for a replacement of the instalment purchase by an ordinary purchase on mortgage [the solicitors] will have mitigated the damage to a point where little will be required by way of compensation.

Counsel's opinion on lodging a complaint with the Law Society was not encouraging:

> I should add that the outcome . . . is not likely to be of any practical consequence. The Law Society usually avoids action or even decision, by indicating that any remedy for negligence lies in the courts and it is unlikely to find unprofessional the conduct of a solicitor who claims to have had a client introduced by an estate agent (albeit the latter is well known to him) and to whom he wrote for confirmations of instructions. To get some positive response on this aspect it would be necessary to go further and show that there was something in the nature of a conspiracy between the agents and the solicitors. At present there is nothing to support such an accusation.

He was correct, we heard no more from the Law Society although the solicitor involved was obliged to explain and a copy of the explanation was sent to the residents by the Law Society. Outlawing the system by legislation also proved to be abortive. A Prevention of Slum Landlords Bill (1974) which attempted to abolish the rental purchase system was introduced independently by Ken Weetch in the House of Commons. It was not, however, successful.

We developed two ways of reducing the overall cost of freehold purchase: the private negotiation system described in the last chapter and a strategy of local state intervention. The first method was used on the Old Norton Estate. Although we knew that the Norton Estate had been split up and that L.C. & W. had bought in 1962, the identity of other purchasers was not clear. However, we discovered the extent of the holding through two means. First, Michael Pinney, one of the philanthropic beneficiaries of the Norton Trust, gave us a map of land blocks and leases and secondly a resident supplied us with a letter which referred to County & Provincial Estates. We also learned that the free-holders' solicitors were Reginald Eyre & Co. When we carried out a company search on C & P Estates we found that there was a substantial mortgage on an estate of 750 houses in favour of Sterling Industrial Securities. We thought it probable that they would be willing to sell off since they were unlikely to be mortgaged because they were in financial difficulty rather because the company was highly geared.[4]

When C.D.P. contacted the agents it was clear that the company would be willing to sell for £250 plus costs. Various tasks had to be completed. First, the residents organized themselves into C & P Estates freehold fighters and by June 1975 they had 70 residents who were interested in purchasng. Secondly, the organization had to appoint a solicitor. They decided to tender applications to five firms. The firm chosen was the cheapest and had experience of Saltley since they were solicitors for Norton Residents. Twenty-seven cases, chosen because it was thought that there were no intermediary interests, were sent to the solicitors in July for processing. Thirdly, the freeholders' agents and valuers' costs were reduced. The valuers agreed to reduce their fees from £25 to £18 and the solicitors agreed to reduce their fees from £37.50 to £32.50, the latter fee also included the purchase of any intermediary interest. However, because C & P Estates were mortgaged, residents had to pay an extra £8 to the mortgager's solicitors.

Difficulties soon appeared. First, the initial 27 was reduced to 24 because three freeholders were not owned by C & P Estates. Secondly, it was discovered that they did have intermediary interests which had not been evident because the same agent had acted for both freeholder and underlessee. Thirdly, local authority lending for freehold purchase ceased in June 1975 and did not start again until May 1976. Fourthly, the residents had problems with their solicitor. So these cases were not completed until May 1976. The next batch of sales stopped in March 1977 when it became obvious that the freeholders were considering a deal. Eventually in November 1977 the agents revealed that the estate had been sold and that the new agent was Leeson, Son and Hacket. In February 1978 we learned the name of the new solicitors and through them we discovered that the new freeholder was Trimidon Investments, a Jersey based property company. It was obvious that they had bought the estate in order to reap a capital gain on sale. We do not know how much they paid for the estate but circumstantial evidence points to less than £250 per house. In April 1978 the agents sent out a letter to lease-holders offering the freeholds for between £400 and £500 plus costs, £20 of which were for their surveyors. The residents renamed themselves Saltley Freehold Fighters, expanded and started negotiations. They also adopted a policy of serving notice of Leaseholders' Claim Forms to prevent another setback by further sales. The organization continued to grow until the summer of 1978 when there were 101 residents involved. In September the agents agreed to meet a representative from Saltley

Leasehold Unit, the organization which now supported the residents' group. After two meetings the prices dropped to an acceptable level. The figures are shown in Table XIII.

TABLE XIII

Prices negotiated with Trimidon Investments

	1st asking price May 1978	2nd asking price Oct. 1978	Final price Dec. 1978
52 Ellesmere Road	400	325	310
92 " "	400	325	310
80 Highfield Road	450	400	365
104 Clodeshall Road	450	325	300
104 College Road		425	350
13 Hartopp Road	450	350	325
4A Bowyer Road	400	300	300
21 " "	500	450	385
70 " "	450	425	375
107 " "	500	450	385
192 St Saviours Road	450	400	365

These 11 which formed the basis for the rest were a product of hard negotiating. We did not employ a valuer for two reasons: first we felt we had sufficient expertise and secondly, because the negotiators had no professional loyalties or conflict, we were able to fight all the way to obtain the lowest price.

The same machinery was designed for the London City and Westcliff area. But it was in the area owned by L.C. & W. that our new analysis was put to the strategic test. As the first section showed we knew that by 1974 the material context had shifted against L.C. & W. interests. First, we broke the blockade with the test cases, then we attempted to manage the individual sales. But crucially we recognized that the next step would be for Loncho to sell the entire estate to a smaller dealer. Our aim was to persuade the local authority to be the purchaser. Then residents would be able to have a larger control over the process through the political apparatus and also purchase at bulk prices. Further we realized that there was a conflict of interest between the freeholds and their agent. If sales were to take place then his interest lay in the commission to be made on individual purchases not in a transaction which took away his fees. The rest of the chapter will be taken up in describing the action we took to carry out this strategy.

It should be made clear that N.R.A. which is the oldest strongest resident's association in Saltley is not autonomous in the sense that it internally controls its activities. C.D.P. resurrected the association in 1973 and has, through its workers, always acted as a dominant force. One worker from C.D.P. has been secretary of N.R.A. since 1973. He remains so now despite the demise of C.D.P. in August 1977. He also now runs, voluntarily, Saltley Leasehold Unit which is situated in Saltley Action Centre and services residents associations in their attempts to enfranchise. Thus in the description that follows the presence of state professional workers is highly significant. It will also be obvious from the following description that N.R.A. with a membership of over 200 and an active committee of residents is not merely a tool through which professional workers act out their own strategies.

The test cases were settled in December 1974. The settlement figures, set out in Table XIV represent a success for N.R.A. Two final figures are less than the N.R.A. initial bargaining offer; four are within £20 and of the remaining four, three are within £50 and one within £60. In contrast L.C. & W. were obliged to reduce their figures considerably; only two were within £100, five within £100 and £125, the difference on the remaining three were £145, £230 and £350. As already suggested external circumstances tended to assist the N.R.A.'s bargaining position. As a result of the dramatic fall in value of stock exchange securities L.C. & W. incurred substantial losses. These amounted to £1.49 million in the half year to 31st March 1974. Not included in this figure was a further £2.7 million which was tied up with the collapse of the Anglo Israeli Bank. In addition L.C. & W. were experiencing liquidity problems.

When the prices were settled N.R.A. were elated. Prematurely as it turned out since it took until mid December 1976 to complete nine out of the ten conveyances. Thus it took more than three years to complete the entire transaction and two after the agreement of the prices. The last case was not completed until mid 1978. There were three linked but distinct difficulties. First, and most crucial, the presence of intermediary interests; secondly, the activities of professionals and thirdly the availability of credit facilities.

It is no accident that the first two completed transactions involved no intermediary interests and no need for credit. Some of the intermediary

TABLE XIV — Norton Residents Test Cases

Address	Name	Interest	Unexpired Term Years	g.r. £	RV £	Date of Service of notice	Capital value used £	N.R.A. value £	L.C. & W. value £	Final value £
83 Ralph	Hughes	Under-leasehold	30½	3.50	56	28.11.73	4000	190	300	200
103 Ellesmere	Gibbons	Subunder-leasehold	28	5.00	60	28.11.73	4000	190	360	250
65 Hams	Hobbs	Subunder-leasehold	30¾	2.50	36	28.11.73	3600	153	250	175
183 St Saviours	Gibson	Subunder-leasehold	20¾	3.00	44	28.11.73	4000	301	350	250
101 Ralph	Mitchell	Under-leasehold	31	3.50	69	28.11.73	4000	173	325	225
5 Ellesmere	Griffiths	Subunder-leasehold	26½	5.00	62	28.11.73	3600	231	425	280
149 St Saviours	Kelleher	Under-leasehold	20½	3.00	40	28.11.73	3800	287	400	275
103 Reginald	Wright	Under-leasehold	18¾	5.00	30	28.11.73	3300	312	530	300
61 St Saviours	Gaynor	Under-leasehold	14½	5.00	35	28.11.73	2800	310	400	320
17 Hall	Raheim	Under-leasehold	14½	4.00	53	4.12.73	3000	300	700	350

interests were difficult to trace, others simply did not reply to requests for prices. Even if the parties were identifiable the complexity of the arrangement took time and money to unravel. Perhaps the best example of this is the case of 101 Ralph Road which was the last to be completed.

In 1975 London City & Westcliff held the freehold interest, having bought it from the Norton Estate. A lease was created on 3rd July 1905 of a piece of land containing 2818 square yards which included the property numbers 87-101 Ralph Road and some other land on which there are about 30 garages. The lessee was obliged to pay a rent of £25 per annum. In 1975 this lease was held by P.P. Day, whose agents were J.S. Godsall and Company and whose solicitors were Morgan Lugsdin and Huskins. Out of this lease an underlease of an area of 1920 square yards comprising the sites of numbers 87 to 101 was created on 15th August 1906 for 99 years less 3 days, from 29th September 1904. The underlessee was obliged to pay a rent of £25 per annum. In 1975, when there were 28 years unexpired, the underlessees were Dad and Lal both of whom were resident at 89 Ralph Road. Dad and Lal lived in this house and held the seven remaining properties on five subunderleases. One such subunderlease was created on 1st September 1919 for a term of 99 years less six days from the 29th September 1904. It covered numbers 99 and 101 Ralph Road and reserved a ground rent of £7.00 per annum; the original subunderlessee of 101 was the present occupier's father. On the same day a further sub subunderlease was created on 99 Ralph Road which reserved a ground rent of £3.50 per annum. The structure can be laid out as in Fig. 19.

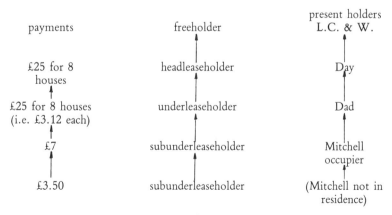

Fig. 19. Structure of a Ralph Road lease.

Mitchell wished to purchase the two superior interests from Dad and Day. The total amount of improvement involved is 38p payable by Mitchell to Dad. The complication does not stop at the structure. Dad and Lal had mortgaged their intermediary interest in the eight houses in 1966 to General and Housing Finance Ltd, a finance company which was represented by London solicitors. As the mortgage covered all eight properties the consent of the mortgages was required before Dad and Lal could act at all. In addition Dad was, at the time of negotiations, away in Pakistan but had left a power of attorney.[5] As the solicitors for Dad and Lal pointed out

> our clients cannot really be expected to understand the operation of the Leasehold Reform Act 1967, as, so far as they are concerned, they are occupying 89 Ralph Road as owner-occupiers, paying a ground rent themselves, and never looked upon themselves as landlords.

At first the underlessees wanted £25 for their 38p interest and their legal costs were estimated by the solicitors to be roughly £40. They were not charging any valuation costs. The headlessees wrote to say that they had put the matter in the hands of a valuer, presumably to value their nil profit rental. Eventually both sets of interests agreed to £10 plus costs although the problem with the underleaseholder still existed in January 1976. The dispute was with their mortgagees who would not supply the necessary deeds.

The price of the intermediaries' interests also caused considerable delays and problems. Figures of up to £100 each were not uncommon. With the complexity of the intermediary structure and the number of professionals involved for whom the leaseholder is obliged by the Act to pay, costs were another serious problem. Even if each party were moderate in their demands the sum would be substantial. Others were not so moderate. Although the Act requires a leaseholder to pay for an expert valuation it is not a requirement that such an exercise should take place. It seemed unnecessary to engage an expert to estimate the price of a three day interest which gives no profit rent yet valuation costs were asked for on, for instance, 101 Ralph Road property, 5 Ellesmere Road, 65 Hams and 183 St Saviours Road. The first two required £10 and the city council required £7.87 per house for the last two.

Another major issue for two of the ten cases was the lack of credit facilities. The third problem which affected the progress of the majority of the cases was the activities of the professionals involved in the transaction. L.C. & W.'s solicitors were dilatory and often did not communicate for months at a time. Only five freeholds had been completed by the end of February 1976. Another four were settled by December. The last was completed in 1978; not unpredictably it was the Ralph Road property.

N.R.A. attempted to standardize the costs of valuers and solicitors. The rate negotiated for freehold valuations was £8 rising to £10 in 1976. The Association solicitor charged £25 per freehold and £20 per intermediary interest. The freeholder's solicitor was reasonable and charged £30 per transaction. The agent for L.C. & W. required £30 for his valuation fee plus £10 extra where he had served a dilapidation order in 1966. He finally agreed to drop the £10 and to reduce his valuation fee to £20 per calculation. Despite all this effort the bills were still high. The two lowest bills for residents, who had no intermediaries or other legal problems, were £287.60 and £446.30. The freehold prices were £275 and £350. Thus the costs came to £112.60 or 29% of the total bill and £96.30 or 22% of the total bill. These were considered to be reasonable. One resident with two intermediary interests had a bill of £565.10 for a freehold costing £280. The price of the intermediary interests were £20 each so the interests amounted to £320 in total. The costs were therefore £245.10 or 43% of the total bill. N.R.A. was powerless to prevent the escalation of costs where intermediary interests were involved since the same negotiation and standardizing the costs could not take place with individual intermediary landlords and their professional advisers.

From the summer of 1975 until the Spring of 1977 the rest of N.R.A. attempted to purchase their freeholds by collective negotiation. The aim was to apply this process to all the streets on the L.C. & W. estate. As it turned out only four streets benefited and the last of these, George Arthur Road, involved the purchase of just seven freeholds. The problems revolved primarily around the intermediaries, rights of way, prices of finance. It is perhaps most appropriate to describe the intermediary test case here. The occupiers of 29 and 31 Ellesmere Road, the first street to follow the test cases, wanted to purchase their freeholds in 1975. They also needed to buy out their intermediary interests from Hussain who owned a considerable number of interests in the area. In June Hameed received an offer from Hussain of £50 plus costs for the interest in number 31. This was totally unacceptable. By October we had determined the structure of the lease to be as in Fig. 20. There was a £1.50 improvement for Hussain but it was on 29 Ellesmere not 31

Ellesmere. Thus Hussain was asking £50 plus costs for a two days interest with a nil improvement ground rental.

It was decided by N.R.A. and Hameed to fight this as a test case as N.R.A.'s valuer gave the interest a deficit value. No intermediary interest had ever been reported at the Lands Tribunal. In fact it took us until 23rd March 1977 to reach the date of a hearing at the Lands Tribunal. It was a bizarre scene, a huge room with the member of the Lands Tribunal and his clerk, and the N.R.A. entourage. This involved a London barrister, the head of the firm of N.R.A.'s solicitors, another member of the firm, the valuer, three members of C.D.P. and three residents besides Mr. Hameed. Hussain did not appear. All went smoothly, the valuation which we submitted was accepted by the Tribunal, although this was not known until May 5th when the decision was read out in Chancery Lane. The problem was that the Tribunal member refused to report and formally approve the method we used because there was no ground rent improvement and no Hussain.

As far as Hameed was concerned it was a success. For N.R.A. it was a dismal failure. After two years they needed a precedent. They did not obtain one and it cost £366 for N.R.A. alone. These costs were awarded to N.R.A. Hussain who was obliged to pay asked for this bill to be taxed and it was reduced to £294 because the court felt that N.R.A. should have used a local barrister.

The next year another intermediary case was brought, this time from Warren Road leaseholders. The resident was represented by the lawyer from Saltley Action Centre and it seemed that there was more chance of

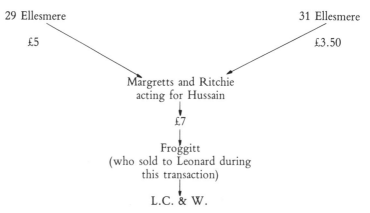

Fig. 20. Structure of an Ellesmore Road intermediary interest.

success. There was a profit rental and the other side, George Fisher &
Co., were going to attend. The night before the hearing George Fisher
& Co. phoned the Action Centre lawyer to say that they now agreed to
the figure asked. This involved a drop from £50 to £23. There was no
alternative but to accept although the lawyer did persuade Fishers to
appear the next day and explain. The member listened to the argument;
that it would help over 150 people in the Saltley area if he could place his
seal of approval on the valuation method used. He refused. There was no
dispute, therefore he considered that the Tribunal had no function.
Another individual success had been achieved but it was still a collective
failure. The intermediary landlords can always win by conceding the
individual case to maintain their overall market freedom.

Numerous difficulties were encountered in private negotiation during
the 18 months which followed this test case. Problems arose over grossly
inflated intermediary prices, delays to the test case legal formalities,
acrimonious exchanges with L.C. & W.'s agent, which resulted from his
failure to provide promptly schedules of prices for the designated roads.
The Association also had its own problems. First it was very difficult to
limit the activities of the valuer and prevent professional camaraderie
taking over. Messages and warning over lack of progress from the L.C.
& W. agent were relayed consistently through N.R.A.'s valuer. Whilst
this was understandable, since the two men met regularly, it did mean
that the N.R.A. felt uneasy about the status and loyalty of their professional. There was very little that the Association could do to change
the position. Secondly a complaint was made against N.R.A.'s solicitors
to the Birmingham Law Society that they had been touting for work
through the Association. Another firm, who had lost clients to them,
claimed that residents were obliged to use this firm if they were members
and that the firm had, through C.D.P., advertized their existence. This
was potentially very serious for the firm and much time was spent in the
Spring of 1976 explaining the position and overcoming the allegations.
The complaint was eventually dropped and the blame fixed on C.D.P.,
not the solicitors. The outcome, though, was that more attention had to
be paid to the documentation sent to residents explaining their right to
choose other solicitors.

Despite all the difficulties some freeholds were bought. Twenty-one in
Ellesmere, 23 in Ralph, 11 in Hams and seven in George Arthur. In
March 1977 all negotiations stopped and the Association told its
members to stick together and not buy individually. The degree of

solidarity proved to be astonishing. Private negotiation broke down because it was clear that Lonrho, who were now in control, were not interested in individual sales and that the agent was stalling for time whilst, we believed, the company arranged a bulk sale. If successful, such a deal might have had disastrous consequences: fragmented freehold ownership, high prices, delay and new professionals who were perhaps more involved with sales and less amenable to negotiating reduced costs. We were determined to provide Lonrho with a suitable purchaser, so we set about persuading the local authority to intervene. The immense difficulties facing the urban renewal officers in implementing the renewal programme had opened their eyes to the leasehold problem. The lack of sufficient equity in the houses was giving senior officers in a number of departments a headache. Politically the awareness that the whole renewal system might break down had produced a desire to force it to work at all cost. Although the idea of bulk purchase was not new in 1977 (there had been two major and two minor attempts to persuade the local authority to intervene), the time was right.

The last major initiative began in earnest in January 1977. It was conducted by N.R.A. and in particular by the secretary of the N.R.A. who was also at that time director of C.D.P. The aim was to persuade L.C. & W. to sell off and to arrange for the Council to buy in that order. The city were not asked to intervene only to respond once the initiative had been taken. A further aim was to avoid the obstruction which N.R.A., from experience, knew existed on both sides, notably with the officials in the estates department and the agent at L.C. & W. (The latter had obstructed a deal in 1976 which would have transferred the freeholds to the housing association which had originally bought the L.C. & W. tenanted properties, by asking an inflated price of £110 000 compared to the offer price of £55 000.) Both seemed professionally to be opposed to the bulk nature of the deal. Mallett had a material interest in maintaining an individual basis since his fees depended on this despite his agency for L.C. & W. The estates department seemed unwilling and antagonistic to the notion. One can speculate that this was because of a professional bias as valuers and surveyors and perhaps also an ideological opposition to the idea of cheap purchase. Thus we attempted to negotiate direct with the company assuming that they would wish to dispose of their interest and at the same time to obtain the co-operation and support of those sections of the council most keenly affected by the leasehold problems: housing and urban renewal. Lonrho had bought out L.C. & W. in 1976. They now had a 93.7% share. It was even more obvious that now was the time to persuade them to pressurize L.C. & W. into selling.

The secretary of N.R.A. wrote at the end of January 1977 to Lonrho stressing the decline of the area and the low wages which prevailed and the leasehold systems part in the problems. He received a sympathetic letter from a director of Lonrho and later a letter in February from a director of L.C. & W. which stated as follows:

> this company would be interested in considering a reasonable reduction in the quoted price provided that some form of collective sale of our estate can be negotiated rather than to deal with the matter on the present individual basis. (Hicks, February 1977)

During March the dealings turned to the city. Officers in the housing department were sympathetic to the aims of N.R.A. and were willing to help. A report for the city and for the Housing Corporation were prepared on the proposed bulk purchase. It was distributed to relevant bodies, local urban renewal officers, to the housing department manager to estates department officers and the politicians. In March the chairwoman of the City Housing Committee came to Saltley to see the area. She met leaseholders and interested parties. She became convinced of the need to purchase the freeholds. Thus the lobby was strengthened. It now had the support of housing department officers and an important politician. The secretary felt able to write on 23rd March 1977 to L.C. & W.:

> The chairman [sic] of Birmingham Council's Housing Committee has agreed in principle to the purchase of the Norton Estate from your company (so long as the price is right), for resale to occupational leaseholders where this can be arranged. (Green, March 1977)

Despite this early success the next stages were more difficult. First, the secretary received a letter from Lonrho stating that a meeting has taken place with Mallett to communicate the position to him. The secretary immediately wrote to a director at Lonrho asking for the agent not to be directly involved.

> From our experience over the last five years such an arrangement has not been very productive and it seems at this stage that it may be in Mr. Mallett's own interest to push for individual sales in the estate. (Green, April 1977)

On the 15th April the agent wrote as follows:

It is not proposed to offer to dispose of the whole of the company's interest in the Norton estate but rather to proceed on the basis of valuation and offer in respect of each individual freehold reversion. (Mallet, April 1977)

Yet Lonrho had written on 6th April:

I do hope that your fears are unfounded. An agent's job is to act on behalf of his Principal. If there is a firm offer to purchase the bulk of the estate then it is the agent's obligation to put it forward. (Tarsh, April 1977)

He lated added that he had asked L.C. & W. to advise the agent that an offer to purchase the estate on a bulk basis would be considered. On the 25th April the secretary received a discouraging letter from N.R.A.'s valuer:

regrettably following a meeting between Mr. Mallett and the board, they have decided not to offer this for sale en bloc.
This I gather reverses an earlier letter by the company direct but before a meeting with their professional adviser. (Lloyd, April 1977)

Therefore by June all seemed to be in confusion with a struggle going on to prevent Mallett obtaining the controlling influence. Equally the attempts to gain approval from the City were in trouble. Between July and September N.R.A. lobbied the relevant politicians and arranged a highly successful public meeting. The secretary wrote an open letter on 5th October to the Chairman of the Land Committee describing the meeting and demanding some concrete information. Three days later a report appeared in the Evening Mail newspaper. The council had received "the go ahead from the district valuer to try to agree a price for the free-holds of the homes on the Norton Estate". Conservative leader Neville Bosworth said:

We want these properties to assist the residents, and to uplift the standards and conditions of the area. We see it was part of our drive to improve the inner city areas. (Evening Mail, 8th October 1977)

On the same day Lonrho wrote:

I am sure that if the offer from Birmingham Council is reasonable then discussions should not get 'bogged down'. (Tarsh, October 1977)

The formal resolution came at the land subcommittee on December 16th:

> That in the circumstances now reported the City Estates Officer be instructed to hold exploratory talks with the property company concerned regarding the possible purchase of the remaining freehold interests in the Norton Estate Saltley and that the Housing Committee be informed accordingly.

It should have been a high spot for N.R.A. but it was not. They had almost despaired of any progress. It had taken nine months to obtain agreement in principle. How long was it to take before the freeholds would be transferred? Until June 1978 during which time N.R.A. increasingly found themselves to be outsiders to the operation rather than initiators. Their struggle was to keep the pressure on the city to negotiate. They lobbied, enlisted city-wide support and tried to extract information. Despite all their experience and knowledge of the portfolio they were consistently refused access not only to the discussions but even to information. Ironically they found Lonrho their best source of information.

Despite all the delays, difficulties and secrecy the chairman of the Environmental Services Committee wrote to N.R.A. on the 1st June 1978 that:

> [the land committee chairman] tells me that he will be making a public statement tomorrow [Friday] concerning this purchase but I am led to believe that negotiations with the owners have been successfully completed. (Hales, June 1978)

The report appeared in the local newspaper Evening Mail of June 3rd. It was suggested that residents would pay about £225 each which in turn suggested that the city paid £100 000 for the estate.

N.R.A. were once again happy at this progress but a further stage was necessary. The details of the resale had to be worked out. During June and July N.R.A. argued for a flat rate of £225 or £250 for each resident. They drew up a list of 117 ready to purchase immediately. They also asked for a meeting and were turned down.

Difficulties again developed. First, the estates department were opposed to flat rate sales "because of the need to illustrate market value in each transaction". Secondly, although the lack of concrete information continued, unofficial sources showed that another new issue had arisen in October. The department considered that if it were to resell at £225 which was below a market price they would first have to obtain permission from the D.O.E. and secondly they would want to attach conditions. There was little clarity on the precise terms of the conditions but gradually it became clear that it would involve an obligation to renew the house before the resale of the freehold. These improvements would have to be to the standard set by the Urban Renewal Department. In November 1978 a mere 12 houses in Saltley had been renewed to that standard. Eventually in the Summer of 1979 the Council started to sell off freeholds. The conditions were less arduous than the original proposal. This was probably a result of a meeting held between N.R.A. and the D.O.E. in which N.R.A. explained their position and the D.O.E. intimated that Birmingham's standard of improvement was unacceptably high. The conditions attached to the sales permitted those residents with standard amenities to buy at a fixed price generally between £175 and £400, depending on the length of lease unexpired. Those without were obliged to either renew or pay a price for the freehold far above the unacceptable L.C. & W. offers in 1975. There were a number of houses left out of the portfolio despite the time it took to prepare. N.R.A. had had the knowledge to prevent this chaos but they had not been allowed to use it.

Ten years after they started N.R.A. have achieved considerable success. Hardly any residents broke ranks in the long hard years between Spring 1977 and Autumn 1979. See Table XV.

The great majority of leaseholders who had wanted to buy have now done so at a reasonable price.[6] In the end the conveyancing transactions

TABLE XV

Freeholds Purchased 1973 — June 1978[a]

Type of purchaser	Number	Percentage
Individual	79	49
N.R.A.	68[b]	
non N.R.A.	11	
Housing association	73	46
Dealers	7	4

[a]These are the latest figures available. They are taken from the office copy supplied by the Land Registry.
[b]N.R.A. Sales amount to 86% of the total sales to individuals.

have been handled efficiently and cheaply. At a national level we campaigned for reforms to be made through the medium of the Housing Act 1980. The time for our campaign seemed propitious. "Leasehold Loopholes", the N.R.A. and C.D.P. report advocating reform was available; South Wales had a strong campaigning group; Shelter was giving national pressure group backing and the Conservative party was heavily committed to owner-occupation. We did not achieve our main demand, a freehold formula but we did achieve a reduction in qualifying period to three years residence and a formula for intermediary interests. (Further changes are contained in sections 141 and 142 and schedule 21 of the Housing Act 1980.)

Notes

1. The following description of Saltley's property transactions is based on Green (1979).
2. The building society policy of withdrawing from vulnerable areas is called 'red lining' because they informally draw a red line around these areas on their maps: see Weir (1976) and Boddy (1976).
3. The Centre for Urban and Regional Studies is carrying out a back-up survey in 1980 to plot changes which have occurred in the market. The results are not yet available.
4. Gearing: the ratio of borrowing to assets, a highly geared company is one that borrows heavily to buy real property in the belief that asset values will rise to more than cover loan interest repayments.
5. The power of attorney is a general power given to somebody to act on behalf of the original party.
6. In the autumn of 1980 we tried once again to obtain a Lands Tribunal decision to fix the price for those leaseholders outstanding. The case was brought on behalf of the leaseholder jointly by Saltley Action Centre and Saltley Leasehold Unit and, this time, the case came to the Tribunal and obtained a full hearing. The freeholders, using N.R.A.'s former valuer as an expert witness, argued totally on the basis of the market in freehold sales created by the Act, in other words that the market should define the price paid, not any figure arrived at by adopting valuation mechanisms which reflected the original assumptions in the Act. We argued for a more formal approach based on a review of the procedure adopted by the Tribunal, and we used a 25% figure for calculating site value and an adverse differential of 2%. We await the reserved decision.

Conclusion

Saltley enters the 1980s with the decline of both its economic base and physical environment accelerating. The rationalization of British Leyland, Saltley's biggest employer, will further limit the jobs available to local residents. Unemployment levels, which are already high, will increase disproportionately and damage further an already poor area. The current income levels amongst both whites and Asians are low enough for the overwhelming majority "to qualify" for the "exceptional hardship grant" which is available in Housing Action Areas.

Limited state environmental works have failed to stem the physical decay. Half of the industrial wasteland which was mapped by C.D.P. five years ago is used only by flytippers. The other half has been developed into small warehouse estates which replace few of the ten thousand jobs lost in the last ten years. The heavy traffic they generate penetrates the residential core of Saltley and huge lorries use roads built for the horse and cart. They are not only noisy and dangerous for pedestrians but also damage the physical fabric of 90 year-old houses.

But what of the houses? Is it not possible to feel a glimmer of well-founded optimism? The aim of the residents, and C.D.P., was to change the dominant form of tenure from leasehold to freehold. After a decade of struggle against obdurate opposition, working-class leaseholders have been successful. Not only have a substantial number of leaseholders bought their freeholds but a high proportion of these have done so at relatively cheap prices. An even larger number have paid reasonable professional costs and have also obtained a good service. Leaseholders might eventually have managed to buy their freeholds individually without the campaign but the method would have led to far higher payments to finance capital.

The campaign's first success was breaking the blockade by L.C. & W. through the test case strategy. The cases never reached the Lands

Tribunal because L.C. & W. realized that there were no more obstacles available to them except time and that eventually the Lands Tribunal would establish a method of fixing the prices for the entire estate. They preferred to negotiate. The second success was the creation of an efficient system for the negotiation and purchase of the freeholds. The third, and most significant success, was persuading the local authority to purchase Lonrho's portfolio. Without the campaign, the picture described in Chapter 6, of small local dealers buying out the large freeholders and selling on to residents would have developed on the Lonrho estate. This would have had disastrous consequences, fragmented ownership, vast numbers of different professionals, a pattern of chaos in which any residents' association would have had difficulty surviving. The bulk purchase by the local authority involved the transfer of unified ownership and was the basis of success. Despite the long wait and numerous frustrations, very few broke ranks and bought individually. The group maintained its solidarity throughout and was also able to ensure the Council's resale prices were modest.

It is pleasing to point to the change in the attitude of the Conservative group on the Council. This can be done by comparing the local evening newspaper reports of May 25th 1962 and October 8th 1977. Alderman H.E. Tyler was quoted in 1962 as saying:

> It is a Socialist land grab and nothing more. This is not a "twilight area" and there are some very good properties. The occupiers should be given the opportunity to buy their own freehold.

In 1977 Councillor Bosworth said:

> We want these properties to assist the residents, and to uplift the standards and conditions of the area. We see it as part of our drive to improve the inner city areas.

This about face can have political implications but Saltley residents have not changed Tory ideology or policy. Their aims remains the same, to encourage owner-occupation, but the material changes in the area have modified the means of achieving that goal. The political consequence is that a Conservative dominated local authority has been obliged to interfere more directly in the newly defined 'inner city'.

Although residents won a battle, the freeholders also stopped fighting. The era of redevelopment was over by the early 1970s. The linked policy of extended working-class owner-occupation and privatized rehabilitation had taken over by 1967 although we did not realize it at the start of our campaign. The new configuration of forces was not clear in Saltley because of the presence of L.C. & W. fighting a rearguard action. Freeholders, unable to redevelop under the new conditions, became willing to sell to occupants although they preferred to sell to dealers. The local market changed to encourage freehold owner-occupation.

As Chapter 3 points out the twentieth century has seen a shift from private renting to owner-occupation. The battles won by the working class to achieve rent control to reduce the proportion of wages spent on housing has led to both state provision of housing but also owner-occupation. Private landlordism has received very little subsidy or encouragement and is seen as a politically unacceptable method of providing mass housing for the working classes. Owner-occupation provides a more suitable alternative politically to that of council housing. The conflict between wages and housing costs remains. Saltley has experienced this shift in tenure. The exchange professionals and owners have operated for some years in the area transforming residents into lease-holding owner-occupiers. Now, under the new conditions, they have extended their operation to include the transformation to freeholding.

Residents, one might argue, can take comfort in this shift in conditions which increases their ability to become freeholders and so achieve the security which freehold status brings. They can also renovate their homes through the grant-aided improvement schemes. They no longer have to face the process of clearance with all the delays and problems involved in displacement and rehousing. The shift to renewal, however, did not occur merely because the outcome of clearance was socially unacceptable. Renewal is a cheaper alternative and supports the dominant ideology of owner-occupation with its privatized system of physical improvement. But the property-owning democracy is not going to work in Saltley. Neither the policy of enfranchisement nor renewal has brought the desired results.

First, all types of freehold owners, but particularly the new breed of dealers, have obtained high tributes from residents in the process of freehold purchase. Some of the surplus remaining after residents have paid for the necessaries of subsistence has been transferred to finance capitalists rather than put into physical repair and improvement, and pro-fessional services have obtained a further share. Thus the necessary prerequisite to renewal, freeholder status, has hindered its achievement. Secondly, the renewal process, even without the additional burden of enfranchisement, is in crisis. Working-class residents in Saltley and elsewhere are not carrying out the policy. The 1976 English House Condition Survey (1979) provides further evidence to our local experience shown in the Housing Action Area report (1980).

> In 70 pages, the fundamental principle behind [the government's] housing policy is demolished. Home ownership, by itself, does not maintain the housing stock. Proportionately, in fact, far more unfit houses are in the hands of owner-occupiers than any other form of ownership . . . .
> Only 3 per cent of the owner-occupied properties built before 1919 were rehabilitated in the year of the survey. An estimated 34 per cent was a static figure, the problem would not be so serious. Over a period of 10 years, the programme could be completed. But this overlooks two inconvenient facts; in the next 10 years many more houses will be added to the rehabilitation list. (About 70,000 houses a year become unfit.) Worse still, if work on some of the houses already on the list is delayed, their deterioration could become so serious that rehabilitation is no longer worthwhile. (Guardian, 16th January 1980)

Chapter 6 showed why. Residents cannot afford to pay out the amount required to improve. Years of disinvestment in the houses prior to owner-occupation has removed much of the use value from them. Exchange value is affected far more by the level of wages than by disrepair. House prices rise in Saltley, as elsewhere, but rise slowly, because wages are low. The total housing cost is far in excess of the available wages. The contradiction remains for a substantial proportion of the working classes that wages do not cover housing costs. So, as the report suggests, some houses in Saltley, although in General Improvement Areas, are now structurally unsound. They need to be demolished and rebuilt. The problems caused by the impossibility of the present renewal programme have provoked intervention by the local authority in the leasehold problem and in the facelift scheme in which Birmingham City Council gave away free roofs and curtilage works to all houses in the Housing Action Area in an attempt to stimulate individual improvement. The latter action highlighted the vulnerability of owner-occupation. The system, which was carried out by reputable contractors in an efficient collective manner unhindered by privatized form of ownership, was a great success.

In Saltley, then, freehold status brings its own insecurity. If the houses are not repaired soon they will have no use value left. Residents will then be faced with two potential options: a return to state provision of housing after clearance or owner-occupation of houses with more use value. The first seems politically unviable at the moment, the second could not be financed from wages but would require massive state subsidy. Any compensation payable for the existing houses would hardly cover a deposit on a better quality house.

Thus even for those residents who seem to have beaten freeholders through collective action, the outcome is not a significant improvement in housing conditions. And not everybody in Saltley is a freeholder. In the areas apart from the old L.C.&W. estate, the dealers are entrenched. The particular set of social relations created by leasehold tenure and described in Chapter 6 allows dealers to make a substantial profit. They dominate the local market. The Leasehold Reform Act, which was based on an assumed market arrangement, has in practice created one. Dealers either buy up freehold interests to sell to occupiers or they sell intermediary leasehold interests held over from their earlier tenurial transactions. Not only has the Act made a business out of leasehold enfranchisement but it obliges the leaseholder to pay all the costs. Residents can only exert influence, if at all, over their own professionals to keep costs down. They have no control over the other parties' professionals and when, as we have seen, the professional and owner elements are not distinct, the Act creates a stranglehold through which finance capital can extract high tributes.

Chapter 3 and 4 described how the Act came into being and the way it operates to create these social relations. A policy of working-class owner-occupation lay behind the Act and caused no dissension on party political grounds. The compensation payable by the leaseholder to the freeholder did. Not only was the Act badly drafted, due to hostility and lack of understanding, but it incorporated this notion of a market process with a non-market price. The parties were to negotiate over a fair price. Consequently the market process has dominated and residents in Saltley, without assistance from partisan experts and group solidarity, would not have achieved a fair price as determined by the Act.

The Act had at its core a flaw as far as residents were concerned, it did not define the price to be paid it just provided a set of assumptions upon which a price could be negotiated. We have sought reform to section 9 of the Act and our total lack of success at social democratic reform is described in Chapter 5. Five years ago we were called cranks by government ministers. But we tried again. The conditions had changed: the renewal crisis was worse, the politics of the property owning democracy was stronger, the pressure from residents in other parts of the country, in particular South Wales, and national pressure groups was greater and the vehicle, the Housing Bill, which already possessed certain clauses dealing with the enfranchisement process was available. We remained extremely sceptical, not only because of our previous lack of success, but because of our analysis of legal form. Our scepticism was well founded.

Working-class housing is provided, because of the internal contradictions of capital, in owner-occupied form. This type of provision, more direct than any other, is based on the capitalist notion of the private ownership of property. The State through law protects this notion vigorously so that if the right of ownership is lost compensation must be paid. A further corollary at the present time is that ownership of property will yield profit, it has investment value. Normally owner-occupied housing is presented in the legal form of freehold. In Saltley, historically it has not been so. The Leasehold Reform Act aimed to provide that form to residents. But the Act is in an ambiguous position. It involves, in capitalist terms, private compulsory purchase. It therefore must provide compensation. Freehold status is set in a context to private ownership of property. The individual right to the freehold is presented in the legal form of a duty to compensate.

Many residents reject this assumption. Long established residents see no reason to pay further for something they feel they have paid for over and over again through their ground rents. They also know that their present problem is a result of monopoly land-ownership in the nineteenth century. They recognize further that, as Chapter 4 suggested, they are compensating freeholders for their loss of betterment. In 1967 the State intervened to control the massively increased rents for prime urban land demanded by capitalist land-owners. At the same time the Leasehold Reform Act required working-class leaseholders to pay representatives of the same sector for their potential loss of rent from development. Throughout the debate on compensation the ideological limits were narrowly defined. The question remained a choice between market and fair price. At a political level there was no challenge to the ideology of compensation.

Residents' reform would be a right to a freehold without compensation. In capitalist terms, expropriation. Yet even this demand would assume a framework of housing provision in its present form. Politically such a demand is unacceptable. Reform has to be confined within the existing framework of legal rights, in this case an individual right to purchase a freehold on the basis of compensation. Our proposal is to provide a formula to calculate the freehold purchase price. It looks highly complex and technical. In fact it is based on the proposed formula for intermediary interests which is included in the 1980 Act (and is described in Chapter 4) and the existing Lands Tribunal practices. But we did consider carefully our analysis of the relationship between substance and procedure before proposing this approach. We feel that this reform challenges the framework of the Act by cutting across the market procedure. If adopted some of the present procedural problems with the Act would be overcome. The cost of valuers would be unnecessary. Solicitors and advisers generally would have less freedom to exert independent control over the process. Fixing the price would change the present market in freeholds. Dealers would not be able to rely on resale at prices unrelated to a fair price and unrelated to their own purchase price. Their margin of freedom and profit would be substantially narrowed and this might make the whole business unviable. We attempt in a limited way to shift the balance of relations created by the Act and thereby loosen the local market arrangements in which the dealers operate.

But any right under the Act is an individual right to become a full member of the property-owning democracy. Like all legal rights it has a privatizing force. Most campaigners around housing law have experienced the difficulties of fostering and maintaining political action around rights. Eventually the procedures, professional advisers, courts and the legal form destroy collective solidarity if the basis of the campaign rests on the struggle over a legal right. We consciously built our struggle away from legal enforcement. Instead, we built a strong residents group which gained knowledge and confidence of the legal issues but which did not collapse if we lost the test cases. We extended our analysis to the nature of the local market, to find out who owned Saltley, who was dealing with whom, and why. We tried to understand the housing market rather than confine ourselves to the reasons for the failure of a piece of legislation. As Chapter 5 shows it took us time to fully develop our analysis. It is also not to deny the importance of a rigorous analysis of the legislation and its implementation, only to suggest the need to extend that analysis into the social relations of property. Our earlier analysis created in us the determination to control the professional servicing and to become our own experts. But if we had seen the enforcement of the right as the goal of the campaign we would have missed the significance of the shifts in forces in 1975. We might have seen the selling of individual freeholds as a success if we had not incorporated this into a fuller understanding of the consequences of the sales. We would not have persuaded Lonrho to sell to the Council and the market now would be more chaotic and more exploitative.

So we concentrated on local housing action not on national rights campaigns. We aimed to intervene in the social relations of leasehold tenure. We impeded the local stranglehold through the intervention of the local state, we organized the leaseholders' professional costs, by acting as our own valuers and by retaining a solicitor, we negotiated with freehold and intermediary interest holders to reduce their costs by bulk dealings, and generally managed the process to cut out the worst excesses. The real success lies here. Costs, prices and efficiency have been greatly affected. By concentrating on the form of the provision of housing we hope to avoid the traps of social democratic reform. We may not have changed the privatized basis of the legal right nor have we transformed the contradiction of housing provision, but leaseholders in Saltley have undoubtedly used the analysis to reduce the exploitation caused by the particular market forces.

In addition the use of leasehold tenure in Saltley has provided a concrete form through which to analyse the nature of law. Ball argues that,

> Tenures represent the legal recognition of the separate sets of social relations which intervene between the production of housing and its consumption as a use value. (1978, p. 85)

This statement seems to make a number of assumptions that must be challenged. Clarke's statement, although made in a different context, is apt.

> The "relations of production" seem to be conceptualised as technical or economic rather than social. Class relations are rooted in them but actually *constituted* as distributional relations, in a sphere of 'civil society' which is inserted *between* the essentially 'economic' sphere of production and the State. (Clarke, 1977, as quoted in Picciotto 1979, p. 168)

Furthermore,

> Legal relations are seen as *external* to the relations of production. There is no way in which their contradictory development can be grasped as part of the actual historical development of the capitalist mode of production. (Picciotto, 1979, p. 168)

The study of Saltley shows clearly that law is not constituted in the sphere of civil society. It is not neutral, an empty vessel that can be filled with whatever content society chooses (Picciotto, 1979, p. 168). Leasehold tenure has been integral to the entire process of production. By the end of the nineteenth century the building lease had become a relatively sophisticated mechanism which facilitated the building process. It was used to organize the elements of production. Norton was able to exploit his land and yet retain an interest in it. He was able potentially to reap a high reversionary value by setting a high standard of building, providing a sound infrastructure and strict management of the site. He was also able to collect a steady income by this management since he could sustain building in a falling market and organize the release of the commodities to prevent swamping. Builders were attracted to the site because they were not obliged to finance the purchase of the plot nor its infrastructure. They were further assisted by the concession on the first year's ground rent. Finance for building was not abundant. Rates seem to have been higher for leasehold finance than for freehold so the less need the better. Builders were interested in building houses which a landlord could let at a profit rent. He was not necessarily interested in small houses although he would be more interested in density. The Norton estate was spaciously laid out but there is no evidence of lack of take-up by landlords. The financiers were persons with limited capital rather than the large institutions which existed but were not predominate. Landlords wanted houses they could rent profitably. They would not be concerned that the houses were leasehold since the leases were new. The houses provided one type of tenant with reasonable shelter free of the squalid unhealthy conditions existing in the inner core areas.

Although it seems a way of minimizing the difficulties of production there were clear signs of contradictions. It was argued strongly at the time that the market could not bear the standards set by the monopolistic land-owners. Land-owners laid down such strict covenants and stipulations for building that builders were obliged to build houses which landlords could not rent out profitably. Evidence from Cardiff, London and Birmingham, although not particularly in Saltley, shows the result to be house sharing, overcrowding and, in more suburban areas, empty houses. The houses built at this time were primarily to provide shelter for the relatively higher industrial wage earners not for the poor who remained crammed into the central slum areas. The latter were seen as a social and political problem to be tackled by the intervention of the State.

Although ideologically the problem was seen as a land question, it was a housing problem created by the structure of nineteenth century wages. Leasehold tenure could exacerbate that problem since land forms a part of housing costs and landlords, in monopoly positions, no doubt extracted high transfer payments or, in Marxist economic terms, possibly absolute rent. But it did not cause the housing problem nor is there evidence in Saltley to suggest that development on leasehold tenure produced houses which cost more than freehold equivalents. The outcome politically was an attack on leasehold tenure. Leasehold reform even in the form of enfranchisement was a major demand in the 1880s and 1890s. The land-owners who developed estates on leasehold were singled out for attack because their position in the production relation was exposed unlike a freeholder who obtained as much rent yet was hidden in the economic equation.

In the twentieth century the social relations of Saltley have been transformed with the unfolding of the contradictions and underlying tendencies of the dominant mode of production. Owner-occupation has spread bringing with it a set of relations dominated by finance capital. But the legal form of leasehold has created a specific configuration of dealers and exchange professionals. The Leasehold Reform Act 1967 designed to further the dominant mode of housing production has created the further set of social relations described in Chapter 6. Lease-hold tenure no longer facilitates a landed relation but one of finance capital. It has ceased also to facilitate the dominant form of housing provision although it has contributed to its spread. The extractions by finance capital through the leasehold market structure impede physical renewal. But as in the nineteenth century the legal form does not cause the contradiction in the provision of working-class housing. It does, however, expose the problem by clearly defining the role of finance capital. Although it does not cause the basic problem this legal form is part of the relations of production in Saltley. It has shaped the area and will continue to do so even when every leaseholder has become a free-holder—but of houses unfit for human habitation.

This grim reality has arrived in the autumn of 1980. The local authority, faced with a total central government freeze on improvement grants, is carrying out a complete review of the 6000 privately owned houses in Saltley. Informal estimates suggest that they will redefine at least half this number as in need of clearance. There is no prospect of new council house building with the present huge cuts in public expenditure.

This strategy can only be seen as a way of limiting the number of houses which will be eligible for grant aid once the funds are available. Those in need of substantial improvement will presumably be left to rot.

Bibliography

Adderley, C.B. (Lord Norton) (1814-1905). *Norton Papers*. Birmingham Collection Local Studies Department.' Birmingham Central Reference Library.

Adderley, J. (1910). *Sixty Years of Saltley Parish, 1850-1910*. Allday, Birmingham.

Aspinall, P.J. (1978). *Building Applications and the Building Industry in 19th Century Towns: The Scope for Statistical Analysis*. Centre for Urban and Regional Studies, Memo. 68, University of Birmingham.

Aspinall, P.J. (1978). *The Evolution of Urban Tenure Systems in 19th Century Cities*. Centre for Urban and Regional Studies, Memo. 63, University of Birmingham.

Ball, M. (1976). *Marx's Theory of Rent and the Role of Landed Property*. Birkbeck College Discussion, Paper 48. University of London.

Ball, M. (1978). British Housing Policy and the House Building Industry. In *Capital and Class 4*, pp. 78-99. Bulletin of the Conference of Socialist Economists, London.

Beirne, P. (1977). *Fair Rent and Legal Fiction*. Macmillan, London.

Bellman, H. (1927). *The Building Society Movement*. London.

Boddy, M. (1976). Building Societies and Owner-Occupation. In *Housing and Class in Britain*, pp. 30-43. Conference of Socialist Economists Housing Workshop, London.

Bournville Village Trust (1956). Birmingham Collection. Local Studies Department, Birmingham Central Reference Library.

Bridges, L. *et al.* (1975). *Legal Services in Birmingham*. Institute of Judicial Administration. University of Birmingham.

Briggs, A. (1952). *History of Birmingham Vol.2 : Borough and City 1865-1938*. Oxford University Press, Oxford.

Broadhurst, H. (1884). The Enfranchisement of the Urban Leaseholder. *Fortnightly Review*, XXVII (March).

Broadhurst, H. (1885). Leasehold Enfranchisement. *Nineteenth Century* (June).

Bruegel, I. (1975). The Marxist Theory of Rent and the Contemporary City. In *Political Economy and the Housing Question*, pp. 34-46. Conference of Socialist Economists Housing Workshop, London.

Burke, J. (1976). *Osborn's Concise Law Dictionary*. Sixth Edition. Sweet and Maxwell, London.

Chapman, S.D. and Bartlett, J.N. (1971). In *The History of Working-Class Housing : A Symposium* (S.D. Chapman, ed.), pp. 240-256 David and Charles, Newton Abbot.

Clarke, S. (1977). Marxism, Sociology and Poulantzas's theory of the State. In *Capital and Class 2*, pp. 1-31. Bulletin of the Conference of Socialist Economists, London.

Community Development Project (1973). *Household Survey*. Conducted by Social Evaluation Unit, Department of Social Administration, Oxford University. (Unpublished).

Community Development Project (1974). *Possible Corporation Action over the Leasehold Problem*. Report to Birmingham City Council, August 22. (Unpublished).

Community Development Project (1974). *A Mortgage Survey*. Conducted in conjunction with the Centre for Urban and Regional Studies by V. Karn, University of Birmingham. (Unpublished).

Community Development Project (1977a). *Workers on the Scrapheap*. Final Report 2. Birmingham.

Community Development Project (1979). *Leasehold Loopholes*. Final Report 5 : The Problems of Owner Occupation in Inner Birmingham. Birmingham.

Community Development Project (1980). *From Failure to Facelift*. Final Report 6. Urban Renewal. Birmingham.

Community Development Project (Benwell) (1978). *Private Housing and the Working Class*. Final Report 4. Benwell.

Community Development Project (National) (1977b). *Costs of Industrial Change*. Home Office, London.

Community Development Project (National) (1977c). *Gilding the Ghetto*. Home Office, London.

Crabb, L. (1975). Leasehold Covenants, Merger and the Leasehold Reform Act 1967. *Journal of Planning and Environmental Law*, 509-522.

Crossman, R. (1975). *The Diaries of a Cabinet Minister, Vol. 1, Minister of Housing, 1964-1965*. Hamish Hamilton and Jonathan Cape, London.

Daunton, M.J. (1977). *Coal Metropolis, Cardiff 1870-1914*. Leicester University Press, Leicester.

Daunton, M.J. (1979). Review of P.J. Aspinall. The Evolution of Urban Tenure Systems in 19th Century Cities. In *Urban History Year Book*, pp. 162-163.

Department of the Environment (1977). *National Dwelling and Household Survey*. (Unpublished).

Dyos, H.J. (1961). *Victorian Suburb : A Study of the Growth of Camberwell*. Leicester University Press, Leicester.

Engels, F. (1935). *The Housing Question*. Martin Lawrence. Three Articles on Proudhon. First published in the Leipzig Volkstaat, 1872.

Fabian Society (1891). *The Truth about Leasehold Enfranchisement*. Tract 22. The Society.

Fallows, J.A. (1899). *Housing the Poor*. Birmingham Collection, Local Studies Department, Birmingham Central Reference Library.

Fallows, J.A. and Hughes, F. (1905). *The Housing Question in Birmingham*. Birmingham Collection, Local Studies Department, Birmingham Central Reference Library.

Green, G. and Stewart, A. (1975). Why the Leasehold Reform Act is not Working. *New Law Journal* (April) **24** 400-402.

Green, G. and Stewart, A. (1975). Leasehold Loopholes. *New Society* (April) **3**, 19-20.

Green, G. (1976). Property Exchange in Saltley. In *Housing and Class in Britian*, pp. 50-63. Conference of Socialist Economists Housing Workshop, London.

Hall, S. *et al.* (1978). *Policing the Crisis : Mugging, the State, and Law and Order*. Macmillan, London.

Hay, D. *et al.* (1977). *Albion's Fatal Tree*. Penguin (Peregrine Books), Harmondsworth.

Hennock, E.P. (1969). *Fit and Proper Persons : Ideal and Reality in the 19th Century Urban Government* (Studies in Urban History, 2). Edward Arnold, London.

H.M.S.O. (1908). Board of Trade Report into Working Class Rents, Housing and Retail Prices, 3864. H.M.S.O., London.

H.M.S.O. (1919). Report of Departmental Committee on Increase of Rent and Mortgage Interests (War Restrictions) Act, Cmd 658. H.M.S.O., London.

H.M.S.O. (1946). Second Interim Report of Reith Committee on New Towns, Cmd 6794. H.M.S.O., London.

H.M.S.O. (1950). Uthwatt Jenkins Committee on Leasehold, Cmd 7892. H.M.S.O., London.

H.M.S.O. (1953). Government Policy on Leasehold Property in England and Wales, Cmd 8713. H.M.S.O., London.

H.M.S.O. (1953). Houses — The Next Step. White Paper, Cmd 8996. H.M.S.O., London.

H.M.S.O. (1962). Residential Leasehold Property Summary of Reports By Professional Bodies, Cmnd 1789. H.M.S.O., London.

H.M.S.O. (1965). Housing in Greater London. Report of the Milne Holland Committee, Cmnd 2605, H.M.S.O., London.

H.M.S.O. (1966). Leasehold Reform in England and Wales. White Paper, Cmnd 2916. H.M.S.O., London.

H.M.S.O. (1971). Report of the Francis Committee on the Rents Acts, Cmnd 4609. H.M.S.O., London.

H.M.S.O. (1974). Land. White Paper, Cmnd 5730. H.M.S.O., London.

Hoggett, B.M. (1972). Houses on the Never-Never : Some Legal Aspects of Rental Purchase. In *36 Conveyancer (NS) 325*.

Hoggett, B.M. (1976). Houses on the Never-Never. In *39 Conveyancer (NS) 343*.

Howell, D. (1979). Letter to *New Statesman*, 7th September 1979.

Inns of Court Conservative and Unionist Society (1965). *Report of Committee on Leasehold Enfranchisement*. The Society.

Jenkins, S. (1975). *Landlords to London : The Story of a Capital and its Growth*.

Constable, London.
Johnson, T.J. (1972). *Professions and Power.* Macmillan, London.
Jones, G. Stedman (1976). *Outcast London : A Study in the Relationship Between Classes in Victorian Society.* Penguin (Peregrine Books), Harmondsworth.
Kellett, J.R. (1969). *The Impact of Railways on Victorian Cities.* Routledge and Kegan Paul, London.
Kidd, H. (1979). Even Freeholders May Have Human Rights. *Estates Gazette,* January 6th, 31-33.
Labour Party (1967). *Leasehold Reform.* Talking Points 2. Labour Party.
Law Commission (1975). Transfer of Land. *Report on Rent Charges 68.* House of Commons Official Report 602 Session 74/55.
Lenin, V.I. (1970). Imperialism. *The Highest Stage of Capitalism.* Foreign Language Press, Peking.
Liberal Party (1914). *The Land.* The Report of the Land Enquiry Committee. Vol. 2. Urban. London.
Marriott, O. (1967). *The Property Boom.* Hamilton, London.
Marx, K. (1970-1972). *Capital* (Moore and Aveling Translation). Lawrence and Wishart, London.
Marx, K. (1973). *Grundrisse.* Pelican Marx Library. Penguin, Harmondsworth, and New Left Review, London.
Massey, D. and Catalano, A. (1978). *Capital and Land : Landownership by Capital in Great Britain.* Edward Arnold, London.
Mayhew, L. and Reiss, A.J. 1969. The Social Organisation of Legal Contacts. *American Sociological Review.* 34 No. 3, June, 309-318.
McAuslan, J.P.W.B.M. (1975). *Land, Law and Planning.* Weidenfeld and Nicolson, London.
McPherson, C.B. (1975). Capitalism and the Changing Concept of Property. In *Feudalism, Capitalism and Beyond* (E. Kamenka and R.S. Neale, eds), pp. 105-124. Edward Arnold, London.
Mearns, A. (1883). *The Bitter Cry of Outcast London : An Inquiry into Conditions of the Abject Poor.* Reproduced 1970 by Victorian Library, Leicester.
Mergarry, R. and Wade, H.W.R. (1966). *Modern Law of Real Property,* 3rd Edition. Stevens, London.
Monday Club (1967). *Housing Study Group report on Leasehold Enfranchisement.* The Club.
Morris, D.S. and Newton, K. (1970). Profile of a Local Political Elite : Businessmen as City Decision Makers in Birmingham 1838-1966. *New Atlantis* 2, Winter, 111-123.
National Federation of Property Owners (1967). *Leasehold — Reform or Confiscation?* The Federation.
Nevitt, A.A. (1966). *Housing, Taxation and Subsidies : A Study of Housing in the United Kingdom.* Nelson and Sons, London.
Partington, M. (1980) (2nd edn). *Landlord and Tenant.* Weidenfeld and Nicolson, London.
Pashukanis, E.B. (1978). *Law and Marxism* (C. Arthur ed.) Ink Links, London.
Pashukanis, E.B. (1980). *Pashukanis : Selected Writings on Marxism and Law*

(P. Bierne and R. Sharlet, eds). Academic Press, London and New York.

Pemberton, W.S. Childe (1909). *Life of Lord Norton, 1814-1905 : Statesman and Philanthropist.* John Murray, London.

Picciotto, S. (1979). The Theory of the State, Class Struggle and the Rule of Law. In *Capitalism and the Rule of Law*, pp. 164-177. Hutchinson, London.

Pollock, F. (1885). *The Land Laws*: The English Citizen, His Rights and Responsibilities. Macmillan, London.

Poulantzas, N. (1973). *Political Power and Social Classes* N.L.B. and Secker and Warburg, London.

Ratcliffe, J. (1976). *Land Policy : An Exploration of the Nature of Land in Society.* Hutchinson, London.

Reeder, D.A. (1961). The Politics of Urban Leaseholds in Late Victorian England. *International Review of Social History* 6, Pt III, 18.

Renner, K. (1949). *The Institutions of Private Law and their Social Functions.* Routledge and Kegan Paul, London.

Rowlands, T. (1971). *Second Report of Select Committee on Procedure 1970-71.* Process of Legislation, July 28, pp. 334-344.

Rubin, I.I. (1972). *Essays on Marx's Theory of Value.* Translated by M. Samardzija, and F. Perlman, From 3rd Edition. Black and Red, Detriot.

Saunders, P. (1979). *Urban Politics : A Sociological Interpretation.* Hutchinson University Library, London.

Society of Labour Lawyers (1953). Subcommittee Report on *Leasehold Enfranchisement.*

Shutt, J. and Stewart, A. (1976). Rental Purchase : A Way of Avoiding The Rent Acts? *New Law Journal*, February 26th, 217-219.

Skeffington, A. (1963). *Leasehold Enfranchisement.* Fabian Research Series 180. First Published 1956.

Sutherland, D. (1968). *The Land Owners.* Anthony Blond, London.

Taylor, V. William (1977). 25 Years of Landlord and Tenant. In *Estates Gazette*, June 4th, p. 795.

Thompson, E.P. (1976). The Grid of Inheritance: A Comment. In *Family and Inheritance: Rural Society in Western Europe, 1200-1800* (J. Goody, J. Thirsk and E.P. Thompson, eds), pp. 328-360. Cambridge University Press, Cambridge.

Thompson, E.P. (1977). Whigs and Hunters. Penguin (Peregrine Books), Harmondsworth.

Town and Country Planning Association (1966). *A Note on the Leasehold White Paper.* By Eccles, J., for Executive Meeting, March 15th. The Association.

Town Holdings. (1888). *Report, Proceedings, Evidence, Appendix and Index.* 1886, XII, 367. 1887, XIII, 41. 1888, XXII, 1.

Vance, J.E. (1967). Housing the Worker: Determinative and Contingent Ties in 19th Century Birmingham. In *Economic Geography* 43, No. 2, 95-127

Walters, J.C. (1901). *Scenes in Slumland: Pen Pictures of Black Spots in Birmingham.* Birmingham Collection, Local Studies Depart., Birmingham Central Reference Library.

Watchman, P. (1979). The Origin of the 1915 Rent Act. In *Law and State* 5, 20-50.
Weir, S. (1976). Red Line Districts. In *Roof*, Vol. 1, No. 4. pp. 109-114. Shelter, London.
Willey, F. (1967). *Second Reading of Leasehold Reform Bill.* 742 House of Commons Official Report 1277.
Wise, M.J. and Thorpe, P.O.N. (1970). The Growth of Birmingham, 1800-1950. In *Birmingham and Its Regional Setting: A Scientific Survey.* S.R. Publishers, London.
Zander, M (1978). *Legal Services for the Community.* Temple Smith, London.

Unpublished Letters

Glover, D., private secretary, Department of the Environment (D.O.E.) to D. Henson, Calthorpe Estate Residents' Association. June 1977.
Green, G., secretary, Norton Residents' Association (N.R.A.) to P. Tarsh, director, Lonrho. March 1977.
Green, G., N.R.A. to P. Tarsh, Lonrho. April 1977.
Hales, R., chairman, Environmental Services Committee, Birmingham City Council to G. Green, N.R.A. June 1978.
Hicks, D.C., director, London City & Westcliff (L.C. & W.) to G. Green, N.R.A. February 1977.
Howell, D., Minister of State, D.O.E. to J. Kelleher, N.R.A. May 1975.
Lloyd, P.J., valuer to G. Green, N.R.A. April 1977.
Mallet, A.E., agent, L.C. & W. to G. Green, N.R.A. April 1977.
Sharp, R., civil servant, D.O.E. to J. Wintour, Shelter. November 1979.
Tarsh, P., director, Lonrho to G. Green, N.R.A. April 1977.
Tarsh, P., director, Lonrho to G. Green, N.R.A. October 1977.

Cases

Carthew v. *Estate Governors* (1974) 231 E.G. 809
General Estates (Belgravia) Ltd v. *Woolgar* } (1972) I Q.B. 48
Liverpool Corporation v. *Husan* }
Custins v. *Hearts of Oak Benefit Society* (1969) 209 E.G. 239
Delaforce v. *Evans* (1970) 215 E.G. 315
Embling v. *Wills and Lampdon Charitable Trustees* (1978) 247 E.G. 909
Finkel v. *Simon* (1974) 231 E.G. 329
Gallagher v. *Walker* (1974) 230 E.G. 359
Hameed v. *Hussain* (1977) 242 E.G. 1063
Haresign v. *St John the Baptist's College, Oxford* (1980) 255 E.G. 711
Jones v. *Wrotham Park Settled Estate* (1979) 1 All E.R. 386
Miller v. *St John Baptist Oxford* (1977) 243 E.G. 535
Mimmack v. *Solent Land Investments Ltd* (1972) 226 E.G. 1771
Norfolk v. *Trinity College Cambridge* (1976) 238 E.G. 421
Official Custodians of Charities v. *Goldridge* (1973) 227 E.G. 1467
Ugrinic v. *Shipway Estates* (1977) 244 E.G. 893

Index

Explanation of terms used in the index

Ch. = chapter
Fig. = figure
q.v. = ''which see'', i.e. there are related references under this heading
N = subject is referred to in notes on page concerned.